Joseph Smith's Quorum of the Anointed, 1842–1845

JOSEPH SMITH'S

QUORUM
of the
ANOINTED
1842–1845

A DOCUMENTARY HISTORY

Edited by
DEVERY S. ANDERSON
GARY JAMES BERGERA
Foreword by
TODD COMPTON

Signature Books • Salt Lake City • 2005
A Smith-Pettit Foundation Book

Jacket design by JSK Design

www.signaturebooks.com

*Joseph Smith's Quorum of the Anointed, 1842-1845: A Documentary
History* was printed on acid-free paper and was composed, printed,
and bound in the United States of America.

2016   2015   2014   2013   2012   8   7   6   5   4   3

LIBRARY OF CONGRESS CATALOGING-IN-PUBLICATION DATA
Joseph Smith's Quorum of the Anointed, 1842-1845 : a documentary
    history / edited by Devery S. Anderson and Gary James Bergera.
        p. cm.
    "A Smith-Pettit Foundation book."
    Includes bibliographical references and index.
    ISBN 1-56085-186-4
        1. Quorum of the Anointed. 2. Church of Jesus Christ of
    Latter-day Saints—Illinois—Nauvoo—History—19th century.
    I. Anderson, Devery S. II. Bergera, Gary James.

BX8659.J67 2005
289.3'77343—dc22
                                              2005042884

For Amanda, Tyler, and Jordan
and
In memory of Lorena Eugenia Washburn Larsen

CONTENTS

FOREWORD

Todd Compton

THIS IS AN IMPORTANT BOOK, DOCUMENTING A KEY CHAPTER IN Latter-day Saint history that few Mormons know about. The Quorum of Anointed (also known as the Holy Order) was the secret, elite group which founding prophet Joseph Smith organized and to which he revealed for the first time the ordinances of washing and anointing, the endowment, and the "fullness of the priesthood"—the foundation of modern LDS temple ritual. This is the first full-length record of the quorum to appear in print and will be a key source for studying the development of LDS history and ritual. It sheds light on many aspects of Mormonism. For example, it provides background for an important chapter in the history of Mormon polygamy. The documents are also an important source for Mormon feminist writers, as Joseph Smith allowed women to enter this quorum and thus to participate in temple ritual, which in Old Testament times defined the essence of priesthood. The documents provide a striking first-hand picture of the contrast between the late Joseph Smith and early Brigham Young administrations, the first such succession in LDS history. This history also adds valuable biographical information for any number of important Nauvoo Mormons, from Joseph and Brigham to many less prominent but equally intriguing figures such as Emma Smith, Hyrum Smith, William Law, William Marks, Cornelius Lott, and Newel K. Whitney.

Nauvoo, Illinois, will always be fascinating, and elusive, for Mormon researchers and readers because so much was going on behind the scenes. Joseph Smith undoubtedly stood at the center of things; around him revolved a number of social circles, many of them secret, that only occasionally intersected. There was the extremely secret inner circle of those who had been introduced to, and were beginning to practice, plural marriage; there was the Council of Fifty, the *sub rosa* political kingdom of the church, which would privately crown Joseph Smith king of the theocratic kingdom of God. Then there were the circles of the official church, publicly united, but behind the scenes divided deeply over Joseph's practice of plural marriage: the First Presidency, including two counselors, Sidney Rigdon and William Law, in the process of rejecting polygamy; the Nauvoo stake presidency and high council, again including many members who would never accept polygamy such as stake president William Marks and high councilor Austin Cowles; the Quorum of Twelve Apostles, led by Brigham Young and Heber C. Kimball, who accepted polygamy as a revelation from God while others, John Taylor and Orson Pratt, had initial difficulties with it; the women's Relief Society, led by Emma Smith, who was generally an opponent of polygamy and did not know of many of her husband's plural marriages; and her counselors, Elizabeth Whitney, the mother of one of Joseph's wives, and Sarah Cleveland, herself a wife of Joseph. Finally, there was the circle documented in this book, the Holy Order, the Quorum of the Anointed, sometimes simply called the priesthood, intersecting with all these groups. Joseph Smith remains a controversial figure—viewed by believing Mormons, then and now, as receiving revelations directly from God; viewed by many non-Mormons, then and now, as a gifted, even inspired myth-maker who perhaps sincerely believed his own revelations. Nauvoo Mormonism was enormously complex; but to have one of those esoteric circles documented so thoroughly brings us that much closer to a full understanding of that moment in history.

Anyone interested in Mormon history, believer or skeptic, non-Mormon or Mormon, should find this record of immense value. Those devoted to temple work (one of the major emphases of contemporary Mormonism) will find here the beginnings of the washings and anointings and endowment ordinances still practiced by the church today. This marks the beginning of temple work in what Mormons believe is "the dispensation of the fullness of times."

Primary documents often present illuminating behind-the-scenes records of public events. In this book, we participate in the excitement of attending these Quorum of the Anointed meetings, vicariously through the
medium of historical documents, as we imagine what it felt like for the select few early Saints to attend, to fellowship with other elite Saints, to receive these new doctrines and ordinances from their prophet. As in all history, the documents solve many puzzles and raise new questions.

As an example of how this record dovetails with my own research
into Nauvoo polygamy, when I examined the dates for all of Joseph
Smith's plural marriages, I found that there was a gap between August
1842 and February 1843. I speculated that the apostasy and departure of
John C. Bennett may have accounted for this temporary cessation of plural marriages in Nauvoo.[1] From June 28, 1842, the last certain meeting of
the quorum that year, until May 26, 1843, there was a simultaneous cessation in meetings of the Anointed Quorum, caused, we now know, by
Bennett's apostasy (see the entry for June 28 and notes). This break cor-
responds neatly with the break in plural marriages, strengthening the in-
terpretations of past researchers and historians. The editors of this volume suggest that the Quorum of the Anointed, to which Joseph Smith
introduced the LDS temple rites, was closely connected to his introduction of plural marriage to his most trusted disciples. The Quorum of the
Anointed facilitated the teaching of secrecy; and Joseph's polygamy,
which could have had disastrous legal implications and caused adverse
publicity if it became public knowledge, was one of the main reasons secrecy was needed. In addition, sometimes the reward of entering the
quorum gave Mormons motivation for accepting polygamy.

Perhaps the most important aspect of this history for contemporary
readers will be its relation to the development of Mormon feminism. In
contemporary "mainstream" Mormonism, women are generally viewed
as separated from priesthood. Yet in the Anointed Quorum meetings, we
find, under the jurisdiction of the prophet, women admitted into an important priesthood quorum, one of its names being in fact "priesthood."
The history of the quorum impacted Margaret Toscano's article, "The
Missing Rib: The Forgotten Place of Queens and Priestesses in the Es-
tablishment of Zion."[2] D. Michael Quinn's "Mormon Women Have Had

1. *In Sacred Loneliness: The Plural Wives of Joseph Smith* (Salt Lake City: Signature
Books, 1997), 2.
2. *Sunstone,* July 1985. See also Margaret Toscano's article, "Put on Your

the Priesthood Since 1843" also made use of the Holy Order's history.[3] Evidence from the Holy Quorum and elsewhere has never connected women with the totality of ecclesiastical priesthood experience; for instance, no woman was ever brought into the Quorum of the Twelve Apostles.[4] Nevertheless, scholars such as Margaret and Paul Toscano and Michael Quinn have shown that many aspects of priesthood, such as attendance in a priesthood quorum, were shared with women through their membership in the Holy Order. *Joseph Smith's Quorum of the Anointed* will continue to publicize this, one of the most significant events in Nauvoo Mormonism. Heber C. Kimball's rough prose preserves a striking example: "My self and wife Vilate was announted [anointed] Preast and Preastest [Priestess] unto our god under the Hands of B. Young and by the voys [vows] of the Holy Order" (Jan. 20, 1844). Brigham wrote in his diary on November 1, 1843, "Mary A. young admited in to the p[r]iest orderer Priesthood."

Before I read the present volume, the Quorum of the Anointed was known to me only through a few limited or unpublished secondary treatments. Bringing all of these primary sources together and making them available to the general readership of Utah and Mormon history is a landmark publishing event.

Strength, O Daughters of Zion: Claiming Priesthood and Knowing the Mother," in Maxine Hanks, ed., *Women and Authority: Re-emerging Mormon Feminism* (Salt Lake City: Signature Books, 1992), and Margaret and Paul Toscano, *Strangers in Paradox: Explorations in Mormon Theology* (Salt Lake City: Signature Books, 1990), chaps. 16 and 17.

3. Quinn's article appeared in Hanks, *Women and Authority.*

4. See Gregory A. Prince, *Power from on High: The Development of Mormon Priesthood* (Salt Lake City: Signature Books, 1995), 201-10.

EDITORS' INTRODUCTION

AFTER JOSEPH SMITH (1805-44) ORGANIZED THE CHURCH OF Christ in April 1830, the new denomination was both embraced and ridiculed for its claims of new scripture and modern revelation. For some, such concepts fell outside traditional Christianity; for others, they were signals that God once again had a living church on the earth over which Joseph Smith presided as prophet. Yet observers across the spectrum found little unusual in the church's first ordinances: baptism by immersion and the laying on of hands. Additionally, believers partook of bread and wine as emblems of Christ's flesh and blood, as did other Christians.

In time, however, Joseph Smith added rites and ceremonies unlike those of contemporary Christianity, although he proclaimed them to be restorations of ancient ordinances of salvation. In 1833, he began to introduce these innovations piecemeal as, according to his own explanation, he slowly came to understand them. In 1840, he introduced baptism for the dead. The next year, he began to marry couples for eternity. By 1842, this progression of doctrine and ordinance resulted in the endowment ceremony, including washing and anointing. In 1843, he inaugurated the last of his temple-related ordinances: the second anointing or "fullness of priesthood."

The concept of "endowment of power" had been taught soon after the organization of the church, although its meaning and significance developed over time. In December 1830, Joseph received a revelation announcing that "it is expedient in me that they [the church]" should leave western New York and "assemble together at the Ohio" (D&C 37:3). The next month, the Saints learned why: "that ye might escape the power of the enemy, and be gathered unto me a righteous people, without spot and blameless— ... Wherefore, for this cause I gave unto you the commandment that ye should go to the Ohio; and there I will give you my law; and there you shall be endowed with power from on High" (D&C 37:3; 38:31-32).

Joseph's followers understood that they had begun to attract enemies, and God's warning to leave New York was clear. Less clear was the meaning of the promised gift of power. Weeks later, this idea received additional attention in another revelation: "Ye are to be taught from on high. Sanctify yourselves and ye shall be endowed with power, that ye may give [instruction in the glories and mysteries of the kingdom] even as I have spoken" (D&C 43:16, 12-13). The promised endowment was fulfilled, at this early stage, in Kirtland, Ohio, on June 3, 1831. On this occasion, male members of the church received what was called the higher priesthood, an event accompanied by a spiritual outpouring in preparation for their callings as missionaries.

The next year, new ordinances were introduced which, in time, would become associated with an expanded endowment. On December 27, 1832, Joseph received this revelation: "Organize yourselves; prepare every needful thing; and establish a house, even a house of prayer, a house of fasting, a house of faith, and a house of learning, a house of glory, a house of order, a house of God" (D&C 88:119). He was also told to establish a "school of the prophets" where those called to the ministry would receive "instruction in all things that are expedient for them." In this school would be introduced a new ordinance: "Ye shall not receive any among you into this school save he is clean from the blood of this generation; ... and he shall be received by the ordinance of the washing of feet, for unto this end was the ordinance of the washing of feet instituted. And again, the ordinance of washing feet is to be administered by the president, or presiding elder of the church" (vv. 127, 138-40).

On January 23, 1833, Joseph washed the feet of the members of the School of the Prophets, re-enacting the New Testament scene where Jesus washed the feet of his disciples in an act of humility (John 13). The 1833 event took place in a room above Newel K. Whitney's general store. The minutes imply eternal blessings to those taking part:

Opened with Prayer by the President [Joseph Smith] and after much

speaking praying and singing, all done in Tongues proceded to washing hands faces feet in the name of the Lord ... each one washing his
own after which the president girded himself with a towel and again
washed the feet of all the Elders wiping them with the towel. ... The
President said after he had washed the feet of the Elders, as I have done
so[,] do ye[;] wash ye therefore one anothers feet pronouncing at the
same time through the power of the Holy Ghost that the Elders were
all clean from the blood of this generation but that those among them
who should sin wilfully after they were thus cleansed and sealed up
unto eternal life should be given over unto the buffettings of Satan until the day of redemption. Having continued all day in fasting & prayer
before the Lord at the close they partook of the Lords supper.[1]

This School of the Prophets consisted of eighteen founding members,
all men, who met from January to April 1833.[2] As new members joined,
they too participated in the washing of feet. The rite not only served to el-
evate the status of this group of priesthood holders, it had the spiritual significance of "cleans[ing] and seal[ing] up unto eternal life." The ordinance
served to unify the men, setting them apart as a cohesive group with a
strong spirit of brotherhood. It also functioned as precedent for other ordinances that would develop in Kirtland and later in Nauvoo, Illinois.

The notion of "sealing"—whereby priesthood ordinances performed
on Earth are recognized in Heaven—surfaced in the Book of Mormon.
At its publication in March 1830, the Book of Mormon referred to
"power, that whatsoever ye shall seal on earth shall be sealed in heaven"
(Hel. 10:7). The next year Joseph elaborated that "the order of the
High-priesthood is that they have power given them to seal up the Saints
unto eternal life."[3] This sealing power fulfilled the prophecy Book of
Mormon prophet Moroni made to Joseph in 1823: "Behold, I will reveal
unto you the Priesthood, by the hand of Elijah the prophet, before the

---

1. Qtd. in Lyndon W. Cook, *The Revelations of the Prophet Joseph Smith* (Salt
Lake City: Deseret Book, 1985), 186.

2. Known members included Zebedee Coltrin, Levi Hancock, Martin Harris,
Solomon Humphrey, Orson Hyde, Lyman Johnson, John Murdock, Orson Pratt,
Sidney Rigdon, Hyrum Smith, Joseph Smith, Joseph Smith Sr., Samuel H. Smith,
Sylvester Smith, William Smith, Ezra Thayer, Newel K. Whitney, and Frederick G.
Williams (see Cook, *Revelations of the Prophet,* 186-87).

3. Donald Q. Cannon and Lyndon W. Cook, eds., *Far West Record: Minutes of
the Church of Jesus Christ of Latter-day Saints, 1830-1844* (Salt Lake City: Deseret
Book, 1983), 20-21. See also D&C 68:2, 12.

coming of the great and dreadful day of the Lord. And he shall plant in the hearts of the children the promises made to the fathers; and the hearts of the children shall turn to their fathers. If it were not so, the whole earth would be utterly wasted at his coming" (D&C 2:1-3). Thirteen years later, Old Testament prophet Elijah conveyed this authority to Joseph, announcing: "The keys of this dispensation are committed into your hands; and by this ye may know that the great and dreadful day of the Lord is near, even at the doors" (D&C 110:16).

Four months after the first meeting of the School of the Prophets, construction began on the Kirtland House of the Lord or Kirtland temple. As the building neared completion three years later in early 1836, Joseph was ready to introduce a new endowment to the highest leaders, now organized as a Quorum of the Twelve Apostles and various presidencies and councils. The previous fall, Joseph had announced that "the house of the Lord must be prepared, and the solemn assembly called and organized in it, according to the order of the house of God; and in it we must attend to the ordinance of washing of feet."[4] Although this solemn assembly would be held in conjunction with the temple dedication in March 1836, the washing of feet had been renewed two months earlier. This ritual—now a part of the anticipated "endowment"—included and went beyond the washings of 1833 and was accompanied by ceremonial anointings with oil. Apostles and other church leaders became the focus of these ordinances beginning on January 21, 1836. In receiving the ordinance, participants were washed and perfumed in the attic above the church's printing office. That evening, they moved to the unfinished temple where their washings were "sealed" with an anointing. These ceremonies continued through early February.[5]

The Kirtland washings and anointings were followed by the temple dedication and solemn assembly. Apparently, these ceremonies were initially to be performed only on this occasion, as one participant recorded: "Brother Joseph Smith ses [says] whoever is Her[e] at the endowment wil always regois [rejoice] and whoever is not will away [always] be Sor-

---

4. Joseph Smith Jr. et al., *History of the Church of Jesus Christ of Latter-day Saints. Period I. History of Joseph Smith, the Prophet, by Himself*, 6 vols., ed. B. H. Roberts (Salt Lake City: Published by the Church/Deseret Book, 1902-12), 2:309; a seventh volume was published in 1932 (hereafter *History of the Church*).

5. See David John Buerger, *The Mysteries of Godliness: A History of Mormon Temple Worship* (San Francisco: Smith Research Associates, 1994), 11-20.

ry[. T]his thi[n]g will not take place a gain whil[e] time last[s]."[6] The idea of restricting the endowment soon changed, however, as the ordinances were repeated the next year, according to Wilford Woodruff, "for those that were not endowed in Kirtland the strong hold of the daught[ers] of Zion in the spring of 1836 & as I was absent at that time my day is now come & my time at hand for those blessings." The next day, Woodruff recorded a format similar to that followed the previous year: after being washed earlier in the day, the company retired to "the upper part of the Lords house at early candle light to receive our anointing."[7]

The importance of this endowment was illustrated again the next year. John Taylor, who had not joined the church by 1836, was ordained an apostle two years later. As he and others were en route to serve proselyting missions in England in late 1839, they stopped in Kirtland where he now received his endowment at a time when the majority of Saints had left town.[8] As before, the group cohesiveness achieved among the Twelve as a result, in part, of the ritualized empowerment remained even as the various elements and eternal significance of the endowment continued to evolve.

After the Saints left Ohio, they moved briefly to established Mormon communities in Missouri before conflicts with non-Mormon settlers resulted in their expulsion from the state. They were next welcomed as refugees in Illinois and soon began to establish themselves in Commerce, Hancock County, which they renamed Nauvoo. As they built a city to rival Chicago in size, new doctrines would bring both peace and conflict for Joseph and his successor, Brigham Young.

As he had in Ohio and Missouri, Joseph unveiled plans for a temple—a building three times the size of its Kirtland predecessor. In the fall of 1840, he purchased four acres for the edifice, and construction began shortly thereafter.[9] In a revelation on January 19, 1841, the temple re-

---

6. Roger Orton, Letter to "Deer Father," Jan. 1836, qtd. in Gregory A. Prince, *Power from on High: The Development of Mormon Priesthood* (Salt Lake City: Signature Books, 1995), 130.

7. Scott G. Kenney, ed., *Wilford Woodruff's Journal,* 9 Vols. (Midvale, UT: Signature Books, 1984), 1:128-29.

8 Buerger, *Mysteries of Godliness,* 34. For the Mormon removal from Kirtland, Ohio, see Davis Bitton, "The Waning of Mormon Kirtland," *BYU Studies* 12 (Summer 1972): 455-64, and Milton V. Backman Jr., *The Heavens Resound: A History of the Latter-day Saints in Ohio, 1830-1838* (Salt Lake City: Deseret Book, 1983), 342-67.

9. See Glen M. Leonard, *Nauvoo: A Place of Peace, A People of Promise* (Salt Lake City: Deseret Book, 2002), 235-43.

ceived attention as a holy place where the new ordinance of proxy baptisms for the dead, initially performed in the Mississippi River,[10] could be undertaken:

> Verily I say unto you, how shall your washings be acceptable unto me, except ye perform them in a house which you have built to my name? For, for this cause I commanded Moses that he should build a tabernacle, that they should bear it with them in the wilderness, and to build a house in the land of promise, that those ordinances might be revealed which had been hid from before the world was. Therefore, verily I say unto you, that your anointings, and your washings, and your baptisms for the dead, and your solemn assemblies, and your memorials for your sacrifices by the sons of Levi, and for your oracles in your most holy places wherein you receive conversations, and your statutes and judgments, for the beginning of the revelations and foundation of Zion, and for the glory, honor, and endowment of all her municipals, are ordained by the ordinance of my holy house, which my people are always commanded to build unto my holy name. And verily I say unto you, let this house be built unto my name, that I may reveal mine ordinances therein unto my people; For I deign to reveal unto my church things which have been kept hid from before the foundation of the world, things that pertain to the dispensation of the fullness of times. (D&C 124:37-41)

In addition to the familiar references to washings and anointings, the revelation hinted at greater ordinances to be revealed in connection with the temple. This understanding was reinforced by the physical layout of the temple wherein ordinances would be revealed in stages, the first being an expansion of the earlier rituals of Kirtland.

Events in Nauvoo, at first unrelated to the future ordinances alluded to, played a role in shaping them by the time Joseph was ready to reveal them. As construction on the temple progressed, the church sought to establish, within the new city, a lodge of Freemasons. Masonry had flourished in America before falling into disfavor in the 1820s and 1830s due to William Morgan's exposé and his mysterious disappearance.[11] Yet by

---

10. For a study of this ordinance, see M. Guy Bishop, "'What Has Become of Our Fathers?' Baptism for the Dead at Nauvoo," *Dialogue: A Journal of Mormon Thought* 23 (Summer 1990): 85-97. See also Susan Easton Black and Harvey Bischoff Black, eds., *Annotated Record of Baptisms for the Dead, 1840-1845, Nauvoo, Hancock County, Illinois,* 7 vols. (Provo, Utah: Center for Family History and Genealogy, 2002).

11. See William Morgan, *Illustrations of Freemasonry* (Baltavia, NY: author, 1826).

1840, it was already enjoying a revitalization, and a new Grand Lodge had been organized in Quincy, Illinois, with LDS convert James Adams as Deputy Grand Master. Over the previous two centuries, Masonry had developed from a network of crafts guilds into a fraternity that emphasized personal study, self-improvement, and service. One of the organization's important benefits from a Mormon standpoint was the pledge of protection that members swore to each other.[12]

Joseph supported the idea of a Nauvoo lodge for the prestige it would bring to the city and church. Initially, requests to the Grand Lodge in June 1841 were denied, yet four months later Abraham Jonas of the Columbus Lodge approved the Saints' application. In December 1841, eighteen Masons met to organize the lodge at the home of Joseph's older brother, Hyrum Smith. Jonas officially installed the lodge and its officers on March 15, 1842. Joseph Smith and Sidney Rigdon, Joseph's counselor in the First Presidency, were both initiated on this occasion in a room above Joseph's Red Brick Store. Mormons took such an interest in Masonry that more than 500 joined or were elevated within the first five months, causing Nauvoo's Masons to outnumber all others in the state.[13]

Two months after becoming a Mason, Joseph began to reveal his expanded endowment to a few trusted individuals. As in Kirtland, he revealed the ritual before the temple was finished, a move which proved to

---

12. There are many studies dealing with Freemasonry, both generally and in connection with Mormonism. See, e.g., Robert F. Gould, *Gould's History of Freemasonry throughout the World,* 6 vols. (New York: Charles Scribner and Sons, 1936); Douglas Knoop and G. P. Jones, *The Genesis of Freemasonry: An Account of the Rise and Development of Freemasonry in Its Operative, Accepted, and Early Speculative Phases* (Manchester, Eng.: University of Manchester Press, 1947); John Hamill, *The Craft: A History of English Freemasonry* (Wellingborough, Eng.: Crucible, 1986); Roy A Wells, *The Rise and Development of Organized Freemasonry* (London: Lewis Masonic, 1986); and Kent Logan Walgren, *Freemasonry, Anti-Masonry, and Illuminism in the United States, 1734-1850: A Bibliography,* 2 vols. (New Castle, Delaware: Oak Knoll Press). For studies on Mormonism and Masonry, see Kenneth W. Godfrey, "Joseph Smith and the Masons," *Journal of the Illinois State Historical Society* 64 (Spring 1971): 79-90; Reed C. Durham Jr., "Is There No Help for the Widow's Son?" typescript 1974, privately circulated; Mervin B. Hogan, *Mormonism and Freemasonry: The Illinois Episode,* in *Little Masonic Library,* 2:267-327 (Richmond, VA: Macoy Publishing & Masonic Supply Co., 1977); Robin L. Carr, *Freemasonry in Nauvoo, 1839-1846* (Bloomington, IL: Masonic Book Club and the Illinois Lodge of Research, 1989); and especially Michael W. Homer, "'Similarity of Priesthood in Masonry': The Relationship between Freemasonry and Mormonism," *Dialogue: A Journal of Mormon Thought* 27 (Fall 1994): 1-113.

13. Homer, "Similarity of Priesthood," 185.

be farsighted as he was killed prior to the temple's completion.[14] He chose the room above his store—the same room in which he had been initiated into Masonry—as the stage for the endowment ceremony. It consisted of rituals and instructions regarding man's relationship to God and his eternal destiny. Joseph asked a few friends, all Masons, to prepare the room for presentation of the endowment, a task they carried out on May 3, 1842. Lucius Scovil said Joseph "told us that the object he had was for us to go to work and fit up that room preparatory to giving endowments to a few Elders that he might give unto them all the keys of power pertaining to the Aaronic and Melchisedec Priesthoods."[15] The scenery used to help visualize the stages of man's progression through life was similar to that used later after the temple was completed, with potted plants and shrubbery representing the Garden of Eden. Mormon historian Andrew F. Ehat, who has studied the Nauvoo endowment, explains: "What they brought in as additional furnishings to organize the other subrooms (representing the Creation, the World, the Terrestrial and the Celestial orders of progression) we are not informed; we do know that they worked under the Prophet's detailed and total supervision, finishing by midday. They were then dismissed." According to archaeologist Robert T. Bray, the northwest corner of the room featured a painted mural of a pastoral scene.[16] Joseph dedicated the room for administering the ordinances before performing them.[17]

The next day, May 4, Joseph and nine other men assembled in the room to take part in the ceremony for the first time. Eight of those gath-

14. According to Orson Hyde, Joseph Smith said prior to December 1843 that "there is something going to happen; I don't know what it is, but the Lord bids me to hasten and give you your endowment before the temple is finished" (*Times and Seasons* 5:651).

15. In the *Deseret News Semi-Weekly*, Feb. 15, 1884, 2.

16. Robert T. Bray, *Archeological Investigations at the Joseph Smith Red Brick Store* (Columbia: University of Missouri, 1973), 73-74, qtd. in Roger D. Launius and F. Mark McKiernan, *Joseph Smith, Jr.'s Red Brick Store* (Macomb: Western Illinois University, 1985), 28.

17. Andrew F. Ehat, "Joseph Smith's Introduction of Temple Ordinances and the 1844 Succession Question," M.A. thesis, Brigham Young University, 1982, 27. Ehat's study is essential reading for anyone interested in the Nauvoo endowment. Also insightful are Lisle G. Brown, "Temple Ordinances as Administered in Nauvoo, Illinois, 1840-1846," *The Research Report* 1 (Mar./Apr. 1990): 1-21; and Lisle G. Brown, "The Ordinances of Godliness: A Paradigm of Mormon Sacerdotal Ceremonies," *The Research Report* 1 (Nov./Dec. 1989): 1-15.

ered were to receive the endowment from Joseph and Hyrum Smith: James Adams, Heber C. Kimball, William Law, William Marks, George Miller, Willard Richards, Newel K. Whitney, and Brigham Young. Joseph and Hyrum themselves would receive it from the others the next day.

As Joseph's scribe later recorded, this first endowment consisted of Joseph's

> instructing them in the principles and order of the Priesthood, attending to washings, anointings, endowments, and the communications of keys pertaining to the Aaronic Priesthood, and so on to the highest order of the Melchisedek Priesthood, setting forth the order pertaining to the Ancient of Days [Adam], and all those plans and principles by which any one is enabled to secure the fullness of those blessings which have been prepared for the Church of the First Born, and come up and abide in the presence of the Eloheim [God] in the eternal worlds.[18]

According to LDS historian Glen M. Leonard, the men's washings and anointings were

> followed by instructions and covenants setting forth a pattern or figurative model for life. The teachings began with a recital of the creation of the earth and its preparation to host life. The story carried the familiar ring of the Genesis account, echoed as well in Joseph Smith's revealed book of Moses and book of Abraham. The disobedience and expulsion of Adam and Eve from the Garden of Eden set the stage for an explanation of Christ's atonement for that original transgression and for the sins of the entire human family. Also included was a recital of mankind's tendency to stray from the truth through apostasy and the need for apostolic authority to administer authoritative ordinances and teach true gospel principles. Participants were reminded that in addition to the Savior's redemptive gift they must be obedient to God's commandments to obtain a celestial glory. Within the context of these gospel instructions, the initiates made covenants of personal virtue and benevolence and of commitment to the church. They agreed to devote their talents and means to spread the gospel, to strengthen the church, and to prepare the earth for the return of Jesus Christ.[19]

Brigham Young explained that the group first assembled in "a little side room" to be washed, anointed to become kings and priests, and re-

---

18. *History of the Church,* 5:2.
19. Leonard, *Nauvoo: A Place of Peace,* 258-59.

ceive a new name and ceremonial clothing, including a specially marked undergarment to be worn thereafter. Next, the men moved into the larger room where a veil had been hung. There they received "our instructions as we passed along from one department to another, giving us signs, tokens, penalties with the Key words."[20] These words were intended to enable one to "gain your eternal exaltation in spite of earth and hell."[21] The instructions related to man's journey on the plan of salvation, along with tests of that knowledge and a method of praying. In fact, one of the primary purposes of the endowment was to teach initiates the "true order of prayer," thereby endowing them with power to ask questions of God with confidence that their prayers would be answered.

The men who gathered above Joseph's store that day were all members of Nauvoo's Masonic lodge. Some had been Masons before the local lodge was formed or before they became Latter-day Saints.[22] Joseph's explanation of the similarities between the two ceremonies, according to Heber C. Kimball, was that "masonary was taken from presthood but has become degenerated."[23] Nineteenth-century accounts of the two rituals show that they contain a handful of nearly identical words and gestures.[24] For those believing in the restoration of all that had ever been revealed to man, such parallels pointed to the ancient origins of Free Masonry.[25] "Lit-

20. L. John Nuttall, Diary, Feb. 7, 1877, L. Tom Perry Special Collections, Harold B. Lee Library, Brigham Young University, Provo, Utah.

21. Brigham Young, in *Journal of Discourses,* 26 vols. (Liverpool, Eng.: Latter-day Saints' Book Depot, 1855-86), 2:31.

22. Ehat, "Introduction of Temple Ordinances," 42-43.

23. Heber C. Kimball, Letter to Parley and Mary Ann Pratt, June 17, 1842, Archives, Historical Department, Church of Jesus Christ of Latter-day Saints, Salt Lake City, Utah (hereafter LDS Archives). An additional possible Masonic connection is the manner in which the ordinances were conferred. "It may not be coincidental that the Holy Order consisted of nine men," writes Michael Homer in his study of Mormonism and Masonry. "A Royal Arch Chapter, also known as the Holy Order of the Royal Arch, consists of at least nine Master Masons, and was the next logical step on Freemasonry for those who had advanced to the third degree" ("Similarity of Priesthood," 38).

24. See Buerger, *Mysteries of Godliness,* 53-55.

25. The view that Masonry originated during the construction of King Solomon's temple has been largely abandoned by modern scholars, and most Mormons today do not believe that the divinity of the endowment depends on the ancient origins of Masonry. As LDS sociologist Armand L. Mauss notes: "That the Masonic ceremony itself changed and evolved even in recent centuries does not necessarily invalidate Joseph Smith's claim that he was restoring, by revelation, an even more

tle room for doubt can exist in the mind of an informed objective analyst," concluded Mervin Hogan, himself both a Mason and a Mormon, "that the Mormon Temple Endowment and the rituals of ancient Craft Masonry are seeming intimately and definitely involved."[26] In noting such similarities, however, historian D. Michael Quinn has cautioned: "The Mormon endowment or Holy Order had the specific purpose of preparing the initiate for 'an ascent into heaven,' whereas Freemasonry did not."[27] "Smith drew upon Masonic rites in shaping the temple endowment," added David John Buerger; "still, the temple ceremony cannot be explained as wholesale borrowing, neither can it be dismissed as completely unrelated."[28] As Leonard pointed out, another clear contribution to the endowment narrative was Joseph's study of the Bible and the Book of Abraham.

On May 5, the leading men of Nauvoo met again, this time to endow Joseph and Hyrum.[29] All together, this elite group consisted of some of the highest ranking and most trusted leaders of the LDS church. Hyrum was assistant church president; William Law a member of the First Presi-

ancient temple ceremony to which the Masonic one bore certain resemblances. On the other hand, neither does that claim constitute a declaration of the total independence of the Mormon temple ceremony from any external cultural influences, including Masonry. ... Since prophets and religions always arise and are nurtured within a given cultural context, itself evolving, it should not be difficult to understand why even the most original revelations have to be expressed in the idioms of the culture and biography of the revelator" ("Culture, Charisma, and Change: Reflections on Mormon Temple Worship," *Dialogue: A Journal of Mormon Thought* 20 [Winter 1987]: 79-80).

26. Mervin B. Hogan, *Freemasonry and Mormon Ritual* (Salt Lake City: Author, 1991), 22.

27. D. Michael Quinn, *The Mormon Hierarchy: Origins of Power* (Salt Lake City: Signature Books in association with Smith Research Associates, 1994), 115.

28. Buerger, *Mysteries of Godliness,* 56. See also Matthew B. Brown, *The Gate of Heaven: Insights on the Doctrines and Symbols of the Temple* (American Fork, UT: Covenant, 1999), 299-311, "Appendix: The LDS Temple and Freemasonry."

29. Ehat notes the fact that this order of receiving the endowment had precedent in previously revealed ordinances: "This procedure for first conferring priesthood power is reminiscent of 1829 when Joseph Smith received the Aaronic and then the Melchizedek Priesthood. After he and Oliver Cowdery, his assistant in the Book of Mormon translation, had received these two different ordinations from heavenly messengers, ... Joseph Smith was instructed to administer the ordinances to Oliver Cowdery, and then Oliver Cowdery was in turn instructed to administer the ordinances to Joseph Smith. These experiences established in Mormon theology a rule for the only exception to the general rule that one cannot administer an ordinance one has not received" ("Introduction of Temple Ordinances," 25-26).

dency; Brigham Young, Heber C. Kimball, and Willard Richards apostles; William Marks the Nauvoo stake president; and Newel K. Whitney the Presiding Bishop. James Adams and George Miller held important positions of local leadership. By participating in these ordinances those two days in early May, the men set themselves apart from the rest of the church and formed the beginnings of the Holy Order, the men (and later women) whose initiation and special status within the church gave them access to special power.

The Anointed Quorum met on at least two subsequent occasions (and perhaps as many as four) before the end of 1842. Apparently only one other individual, Vinson Knight, was initiated that year, although this is not certain.[30] Those who left accounts of the gatherings recorded that they often received instruction, discussed items of business and current interest, and engaged in prayer. For example, on June 26 and 28, 1842, their talk focused on "the situation of the pine country & Lumbering business" in Wisconsin where lumber was being cut for construction of the temple. On each occasion, quorum members "united in solemn prayer," asking, for example, for aid in dealing with legal matters that faced the church and for protection of a quorum member who was to leave the next day to bring his family to Nauvoo.[31]

After a few more gatherings in July and possibly September 1842, the Anointed Quorum did not meet again until May 1843. This gap may be credited to certain events that effectively placed much of church affairs, including construction of the temple, on hold. John C. Bennett, who had moved to Nauvoo in September 1840, had quickly risen to prominence in the community. Within five months he was mayor of Nauvoo, chancellor of the University of Nauvoo, and major general of the Nauvoo Legion. Two months later, he was sustained as acting counselor to Joseph

30. The source for Vinson Knight's initiation is John C. Bennett. In his exposé of Mormonism, Bennett cited a letter he received from George W. Robinson on August 8, 1842, with the claim. Knight died days earlier on July 31, 1842, so his initiation would have occurred sometime between May 6 and his death. Although not mentioned in any descriptions of quorum meetings, Knight is included in the list of members in this book. His status as bishop of Nauvoo's Lower Ward, as well as his being an early polygamist, make him a probable candidate. For Bennett's reference to Knight, see Bennett, *A History of the Saints; or, An Exposé of Joe Smith and Mormonism* (Boston: Leland & Whiting, 1842), 247-48.

31. See Joseph Smith, Diary (kept by William Clayton), in "Book of the Law of the Lord," June 26 and 28, 1842, in *The Papers of Joseph Smith, Volume 2: Journal, 1832-1842,* ed. Dean C. Jessee (Salt Lake City: Deseret Book, 1992).

Smith. But church leaders soon learned that Bennett had secretly appro-priated Joseph's new doctrine of plural marriage to his own ends. Joseph had begun revealing his plural wife doctrine to other church leaders, in-cluding members of the Quorum of the Twelve Apostles, in mid- to late 1841. Joseph branded Bennett's activities as adultery, and Bennett left the church shortly after the organization of the Anointed Quorum in May 1842.

During the fall of 1842, Bennett published a book-length exposé of Nauvoo plural marriage, the church's political ambitions, and the Anointed Quorum. Although many of his claims were based on hearsay, others re-flected first-hand knowledge. This situation posed a dilemma for Joseph Smith, who wanted to keep knowledge of plural marriage and the Anointed Quorum private. Public discussion over Bennett's charges of "spiritual wifery" forced Joseph to denounce Bennett's allegations while remaining committed to the doctrines he had been teaching.[32]

The situation intensified as Anointed Quorum members Hyrum Smith, William Law, and William Marks, who apparently were unaware of Joseph's polygamy, attempted to rid the church of such teachings. Joseph's private secretary, William Clayton, recorded on May 23, 1843: "Con-versed with H[eber] C. K[imball] concerning a plot that is being laid to entrap the brethren of the secret priesthood by Brother H[yrum] and oth-ers."[33] Apparently in the next day or two, Hyrum approached Brigham Young with suspicions: "I have a question to ask you," he began. "[Y]ou and the twelve know some things that I do not know. I can understand this by the motions, and talk, and doings of Joseph, and I know there is something or other, which I do not understand, that is revealed to the Twelve. Is this so?" Young responded: "I do not know any thing about what you know, but I know what I know." Hyrum continued: "I have

32. For a study of plural marriage during Joseph Smith's lifetime, see George D. Smith, "Nauvoo Roots of Polygamy, 1841-1846: A Preliminary Demographic Re-port," *Dialogue: A Journal of Mormon Thought* 27 (Spring 1994): 1-72. Other histori-cal studies through the Utah period are Richard S. Van Wagoner, *Mormon Polygamy: A History* (Salt Lake City: Signature Books, 1986), and Kathryn M. Daynes, *More Wives than One: Transformation of the Mormon Marriage System, 1840-1910* (Urbana: University of Illinois Press, 2002). For Joseph's plural marriages, see Todd M. Compton, *In Sacred Loneliness: The Plural Wives of Joseph Smith* (Salt Lake City: Sig-nature Books, 1997).

33. George D. Smith, ed., *An Intimate Chronicle: The Journals of William Clayton* (Salt Lake City: Signature Books in association with Smith Research Associates, 1991), 105.

mistrusted for a long time that Joseph has received a revelation that a man should have more than one wife, and he has hinted as much to me, but I would not bear it. ... I am convinced that there is something that has not been told me." Brigham then responded:

> [B]rother Hyrum, I will tell you about this thing which you do not know if you will sware with an uplifted hand, before God, that you will never say another word against Joseph and his doings, and the doctrines he is preaching to the people. He replied, "I will do it with all my heart;" and he stood upon his feet, saying, "I want to know the truth, and to be saved." And he made a covenant there, never again to bring forward one argument or use any influence against Joseph's doings. Joseph had many wives sealed to him. I told Hyrum the whole story, and he bowed to it and wept like a child, and said, "God be praised." He went to Joseph and told him what he had learned, and renewed his covenant with Joseph, and they went heart and hand together while they lived, and they were together when they died, and they are together now defending Israel.[34]

Hyrum's conversion to plural marriage may have prompted the resurgence of the Anointed Quorum, which met for the first time in at least eight months on May 26, 1843. The interval between Clayton's diary entry, Hyrum's conversation with Young, and the quorum's reunion was only three days. Clayton recorded that day (May 26) that "Hyrum received the doctrine of priesthood," meaning that he accepted plural marriage.[35]

Andrew Ehat suspects that discussion of Hyrum's conversion to plural marriage occurred outside the Anointed Quorum because William Law, who never accepted plural marriage, was present at the quorum meeting. Ehat writes: "According to his testimony, William Law never knew from Joseph Smith that plural marriage was a practice of the Church until D&C 132 was recorded. This was seven weeks *after* the 26 May meeting."[36] Joseph may have broached the topic indirectly. Michael Quinn, another historian of the Anointed Quorum, believes that Hyrum's conversion prompted Joseph to re-endow everyone who had been endowed the previous year with the exception of William Marks and George Miller who were absent. Whether or not Joseph instructed quo-

---

34. Brigham Young, qtd. in Ehat, "Introduction of Temple Ordinances," 57-59.
35. Smith, *Intimate Chronicle,* 106.
36. Ehat, "Introduction of Temple Ordinances," 62.

rum members in plural marriage at this time, Hyrum's acceptance of it served to revitalize the quorum and Joseph's plans for it. According to Quinn, Hyrum's change of heart resulted two months later in Joseph's decision to designate his brother as his successor. Quinn sees this May 26, 1843, meeting as a turning point for the quorum: "Hereafter events in the Quorum of Anointed and other groups associated with the secret practices of Nauvoo were often more crucial than events occurring within open, public forums."[37]

On this occasion, the quorum renewed the practice of praying together in a circle, a ritual which would become a prominent part of quorum meetings and which was considered the pinnacle of the endowment ritual—the means by which the "endowment of power" was manifested.[38] Some of the diary entries referring to gatherings of the Holy Order become simply, as an example, "prayer meeting at J[oseph's]."[39]

Two days after May 26, another ceremony was introduced to the Anointed Quorum: marriage sealings for eternity.[40] On May 28, Joseph Smith and James Adams were sealed to their spouses, Emma Hale Smith and Harriet Denton Adams. This was an important moment, as Emma Smith, much like Hyrum, had opposed her husband's teachings on plural marriage; yet prior to her sealing, she would have had to reconcile herself to the doctrine, a requirement for all hoping to receive the ordinance.[41] Unlike Hyrum's change of heart, Emma's was temporary.[42] The

---

37. Quinn, *Origins,* 54-55.

38. See D. Michael Quinn, "Latter-day Saint Prayer Circles," *BYU Studies* 19 (Fall 1978): 79-105.

39. Willard Richards, Diary, Nov. 12, 1843, LDS Archives.

40. Joseph Smith had actually begun marriage sealings for eternity in April 1841 when he married his first documented plural wife, Louisa Beaman. See Gary James Bergera, "The Earliest Eternal Sealings for Civilly Married Couples Living and Dead," *Dialogue: A Journal of Mormon Thought* 35 (Fall 2002): 41-66.

41. See Ehat, "Introduction of Temple Ordinances," 74-75.

42. Emma Smith accepted plural marriage after being told she could select her husband's wives. Shortly before her sealing to Joseph, she had chosen sisters Emily and Eliza Partridge and Sarah and Maria Lawrence as Joseph's wives. Emma was not aware that Joseph had already married at least sixteen women, including the Partridge sisters, two months earlier. By the time Joseph dictated the revelation sanctioning polygamy (D&C 132) in July 1843, Emma had a change of heart. Ironically, it was Hyrum Smith who read the revelation to her, after which he reported to Joseph: "I have never received a more severe talking to in my life. Emma is very bitter and full of resentment and anger" (qtd. in Linda King Newell and Valeen Tippetts Avery, *Mormon Enigma: Emma Hale Smith* [Garden City, NY: Doubleday, 1984], 142-52).

next day, Hyrum, Brigham Young, and Willard Richards were sealed to their spouses.[43]

Four months later, on September 28, the demographics of the quorum began to change. For the first time, women were initiated as regular members, beginning with Emma, who received her endowment on or just before that date. The previous year, Joseph had organized the all-female Relief Society; using Masonic terminology, he had instructed the women in his vision of their organization to let their presidency serve as "a *constitution*," proposing that "the society go into a close *examination* of every *candidate* ... that the Society should grow up by *degrees*." He added that God would "make of this Society a *kingdom of priests* as in *Enoch's day*."[44]

At the Anointed Quorum's September 28, 1843, meeting, Joseph "was by common consent and unanimous voice chosen President of the quorum and anointed and ord[ained] to the highest and holiest order of the priesthood (and companion [Emma])."[45] This ordinance, called the second anointing or "fullness of the priesthood," fulfilled the promise of the first anointing.[46] According to Glen Leonard, this "crowning ordinance" was "a promise of kingly powers and of endless lives. It was the confirmation of promises that worthy men could become kings and priests and that women could become queens and priestesses in the eternal worlds."[47] "For any person to have the fullness of that priesthood," Brigham Young explained, "he must be a king and priest. A person may have a portion of that priesthood, the same as governors or judges of England have power from the king to transact business; but that does not make them kings of England. A person may be anointed king and priest long before he receives his kingdom."[48] Such members, wrote twentieth-cen-

---

43. Scott H. Faulring, ed., *An American Prophet's Record: The Diaries and Journals of Joseph Smith* (Salt Lake City: Signature Books in association with Smith Research Associates, 1986), 381.

44. Nauvoo Female Relief Society, Minutes, Mar. 17, 1842, qtd. in Buerger, *Mysteries of Godliness*, 51 (Buerger's emphasis). These allusions to Masonry prompted Bennett to accuse Joseph of establishing a lodge of female Masonry. See the reference in Quinn, "Latter-day Saint Prayer Circles," 85-86.

45. See Faulring, *American Prophet's Record*, 416.

46. For more, see David John Buerger, "'The Fulness of the Priesthood': The Second Anointing in Latter-day Saint Theology and Practice," *Dialogue: A Journal of Mormon Thought* 16 (Spring 1983): 10-44.

47. Leonard, *Nauvoo: A Place of Peace*, 260-61.

48. *History of the Church*, 5:527.

tury apostle Bruce R. McConkie, "receive the more sure word of prophecy, which means that the Lord seals their exaltation upon them while they are yet in this life. ... [T]heir exaltation is assured."[49] During the ordinance, explains historian Lyndon W. Cook, a husband is "ordained a priest and anointed a king unto God," while wives are "anointed priestesses and queens unto their husband."[50] "These ordinances," Ehat adds,

> depending on the person's ecclesiastical position, made the recipient a "king and priest," "in," "in and over," or (as only in Joseph Smith's case) "over" the Church. Moreover, the recipient had sealed upon him the power to bind and loose on earth as Joseph explained in his definition of the fulness of the priesthood. Another blessing growing out of the promise of the sealing power was the specific blessing that whatever thing was desired, it would not be withheld when sought for in diligent prayer.[51]

"There is no exaltation in the kingdom of God," concluded Church Historian and later church president Joseph Fielding Smith, "without the fulness of priesthood."[52]

Throughout the remainder of 1843, the Anointed Quorum continued to expand the number of eternal sealings and second anointings. The quorum also continued to address the most important issues confronting the church. For example, on November 12, after Alpheus and Lois Cutler received their second anointing: "I [Joseph Smith] spoke of a petition to Congress, my letter to [James A.] Bennett, and intention to write a proclamation to the kings of the earth." On December 3, with "all present except Hyrum and his wife," William W. Phelps read Joseph's appeal to the Green Mountain Boys of Vermont, who Joseph hoped would help bring the State of Missouri to justice for the wrongs it had committed against the Saints. Joseph's written appeal "was dedicated by prayer after *all* had spoken upon it."[53] As Quinn points out, for the first time in LDS history, men and

49. Bruce R. McConkie, *Mormon Doctrine,* 2nd. ed. (Salt Lake City: Bookcraft, 1966), 109-10.

50. Lyndon W. Cook, *Joseph C. Kingsbury: A Biography* (Provo: Grandin Book Co., 1985), 94.

51. Ehat, "Introduction of Temple Ordinances," 95-96.

52. In Bruce R. McConkie, comp., *Doctrines of Salvation: Sermons and Writings of Joseph Fielding Smith* (Salt Lake City: Bookcraft, 1956), 3:132.

53. Faulring, *American Prophet's Record,* 429-30, emphasis added.

women together took part in theocratic issues during these meetings of November and December 1843. This precedent would continue.[54]

This is not to suggest that the Anointed Quorum had administrative or legislative authority. It is important to note that the quorum, composed of men and women, possessed authority by virtue of their anointing and endowment that was seen as spiritual in nature. For instance, the appeal to the Green Mountain Boys was made a matter of prayer. The quorum did vote on matters affecting the group, however. When William Law rejected plural marriage, he stopped attending quorum meetings. As a result, he was expelled in early 1844. Bathsheba Smith, a member of the quorum, remembered: "I was present when William Law, Joseph Smith's counselor, was dropped from that quorum by each one present voting yes or no in his [or her] turn."[55] In summarizing the activities of the quorum, Quinn wrote: "All available evidence shows that the Holy Order's only administrative function pertained to the conduct of the endowment ordinances from 1843 to 1845," and he stressed that "even when male members of the Anointed Quorum conducted administrative business, they sometimes made a distinct separation between meeting in their church capacity to discuss administrative matters and meeting as the Quorum of Anointed to have a prayer circle about the matters discussed."[56]

By the end of 1843, the quorum counted more than thirty-eight individuals and had met on at least thirty-two occasions, mostly to endow new members, advance others in the ordinances, and attend to the true order of prayer. Eighteen women had been initiated into the quorum and had received their endowments. Fifteen members had received the second anointing, while as many as seventeen couples had been sealed for eternity.

An important aspect of the quorum, which became more noticeable as it grew, was family relatedness (see Table 1). The quorum not only included a number of Joseph's blood relatives and others who had married into his family, but also relatives through plural unions, which broadened Joseph's family connections. Eventually, some thirty-nine initiates (44 percent of all quorum members) shared ties to Joseph through birth or marriage. This helped to strengthen existing bonds of loyalty and increased the trust Joseph hoped to foster and maintain within the group.

54. Quinn, *Origins,* 116.

55. Bathsheba W. Smith, "Recollections of Joseph Smith," *Juvenile Instructor* 27 (June 1, 1892): 345.

56. Quinn, "Latter-day Saint Prayer Circles," 90-91.

TABLE 1. Joseph Smith's relationship to other quorum members, 1842-45

Quorum member	Family connection
Louisa Beaman	plural wife
Agnes M. Coolbrith	plural wife
Elizabeth Davis Durfee	plural wife
Hannah G. Fielding	sister-in-law (wife of Joseph Fielding)
Joseph Fielding	brother-in-law (brother of Mary and Mercy Smith)
Olive Grey Frost	plural wife
Marinda Nancy Johnson Hyde	plural wife
Orson Hyde	co-husband (husband of Marinda Nancy Johnson)
Zina D. H. Jacobs	plural wife
Heber C. Kimball	father-in-law (father of Helen Mar Kimball; stepfather of Fanny Young)
Helen Mar Kimball	plural wife
Vilate Murray Kimball	mother-in-law (mother of Helen Mar Kimball; step-mother of Fanny Young)
Joseph C. Kingsbury	co-husband (husband of Sarah Ann Whitney;) brother-in-law (husband of Caroline Whitney, deceased)
Mary E. Rollins Lightner	plural wife
Joseph Bates Noble	brother-in-law (husband of Mary Beaman)
Mary Adeline Beaman Noble	sister-in-law (sister of Louisa Beaman)
Mary Ann Frost Stearns Pratt	sister-in-law (sister of Olive Frost); possible plural wife
Parley P. Pratt	brother-in-law (husband of Mary Ann Frost); possible co-husband
Jennetta Richards Richards	sister-in-law (wife of Willard Richards)
Levi Richards	brother-in-law (brother of Rhoda Richards)
Rhoda Richards	plural wife
Willard Richards	brother-in-law (brother of Rhoda Richards)
Sylvia Porter Sessions	plural wife
Bathsheba Bigler Smith	cousin-in-law (wife of George A. Smith)
Clarissa Lyman Smith	aunt (wife of John Smith)
Emma Hale Smith	first wife
George A. Smith	first cousin (son of John and Clarissa Smith)
Hyrum Smith	brother
John Smith	uncle (brother of Joseph Smith Sr.)
Lucy Mack Smith	mother
Mary Fielding Smith	sister-in-law (wife of Hyrum Smith)
Samuel H. Smith	brother
William Smith	brother
Eliza Roxcy Snow	plural wife
Mercy Fielding Thompson	sister-in-law (sister of Mary Smith; plural wife of Hyrum Smith)
Elizabeth Ann Whitney	mother-in-law (mother of Sarah Ann Whitney)

TABLE 1. *(continued)*

Quorum member	Family connection
Newel K. Whitney	father-in-law (father of Sarah Ann Whitney); stepfather-in-law (stepfather of Fanny Young)
Sarah Ann Whitney	plural wife
Fanny Murray Young	plural wife

The year 1844 was a prosperous if difficult period for the quorum. Members were expelled by vote, as in the case of William Law on January 7, noted above, and new members were added in much the same way. For example, William Clayton recorded two weeks later that "Brother [Reynolds] Cahoon came to my house to say that a vote had been taken on my being admitted into the quorum and I was accepted."[57] It is unknown if recommendations for admission came solely from Joseph or from other quorum members. What is clear is that each member had a say in the matter and that admissions were based on a unanimous vote. In her reminiscence of the decision to drop Law, Bathsheba Smith recalled: "One member hesitated to vote, which called forth earnest remarks from the Prophet Joseph. He showed clearly that it would be doing a serious wrong to retain him longer. After his explanation the vote was unanimous."[58]

Although the quorum met primarily for prayer and ordinance work, meetings also included more generalized instruction on scripture and doctrine. For example, on January 28, 1844, in addition to the usual prayer circle, Joseph spoke on the coming of Elijah as recorded in the fourth chapter of Malachi. The next week, he expounded on the scriptural teaching of the 144,000 in the Book of Revelation. Days earlier, John Taylor had addressed the quorum and "made some appropriate remarks unto edifycation."[59]

During the months following his expulsion, William Law became further alienated from his colleagues and from the church in general and was finally excommunicated on April 18, 1844, along with his wife and brother. Three days later, he helped found the Reformed Mormon Church, and for the next two months he worked to expose Joseph as a fallen prophet. Meetings of the Anointed Quorum became less frequent as church leaders dealt with these latest challenges. After meeting more than twenty times in January and February, the quorum only met four

---

57. Smith, *Intimate Chronicle,* 125.
58. Smith, "Recollections of Joseph Smith," 360.
59. See Kenney, *Wilford Woodruff's Journal,* 2:344, 348, and 346.

times in March, once in April, and six times from May to June 1844. Meetings apparently became less focused on spiritual matters as the situation with dissidents and reformers became increasingly critical. This is reflected in prayer circle meetings such as the one held on April 28: "We united [in prayer] for President Joseph[,] the church, the presidency[,] contest[ant]s [in] the Lawsuits. The apostates, the sick &c. &c." Despite the problems, William Clayton added, "We had a good time."[60] The friendship, trust, and unity experienced within the quorum was a welcome respite from the difficulties facing members on the outside.

On June 7, 1844, William Law and others published the first (and only) issue of the *Nauvoo Expositor,* which detailed Joseph's teachings on plural marriage and advocated repeal of the Nauvoo city charter. Joseph, as mayor, together with the city council, declared the *Expositor* a nuisance and ordered its destruction. The move was immediately denounced by outsiders, and Joseph was soon charged with inciting a riot and other treasonous activities. While awaiting trial in a jail in Carthage, Illinois, Joseph and Hyrum Smith were killed by a mob on June 27.

Joseph's death set apart those who had joined the Anointed Quorum during his lifetime from those who joined during the next year and a half, prior to the completion of the Nauvoo temple. To be sure, plural marriage continued to play an important role in the quorum. Initiates—especially those receiving the second anointing—were not only aware of the doctrine, but endorsed its practice. Of the thirty-seven men and twenty-nine women (sixty-six total) initiated into the quorum during Joseph's lifetime, sixteen men and twenty-two women (58 percent of those early members) were polygamists either before or after initiation. The sixteen men represented 43 percent of male initiates (24 percent of the initial sixty-six members), the twenty-two women 76 percent of female initiates (33 percent of initial members). Still, many polygamists were not admitted into the quorum during Joseph's lifetime. Of the twenty-eight men who are presumed to have entered plural marriage during Joseph's lifetime, sixteen (57 percent) joined the quorum prior to Joseph's death; twelve (43 percent) did not. Acceptance of plural marriage did not automatically assure admission into the quorum.[61] (See Table 2.)

---

60. Smith, *Intimate Chronicle,* 131.

61. See the list of Nauvoo polygamists in Smith, "Nauvoo Roots," 37-69; and Gary James Bergera, "The Earliest Mormon Polygamists, 1841-1844," *Dialogue: A Journal of Mormon Thought* (Fall 2005).

TABLE 2. Quorum membership and plural marriage during Joseph Smith's lifetime

Husbands	Initiated wives	Uninitiated wives
James Adams	Harriet Denton Adams	Roxena Repshire
Reynolds Cahoon	Thirza Stiles Cahoon	Lucina Roberts
William Clayton	Ruth Moon Clayton	
	Margaret Moon	
Orson Hyde	Marinda Nancy Johnson Hyde	Martha Rebecca Browett
		Mary Ann Price
Heber C. Kimball	Vilate Murray Kimball	Sarah Peak Noon
Vinson Knight	Martha McBride Knight	Philinda Clark Eldredge Myrick
Isaac Morley	Lucy Gunn Morley	Abigail Leonora Snow Leavitt
		Hannah Blakeslee Finch Merriam
Parley P. Pratt	Mary Ann Frost Stearns Pratt	Elizabeth Brotherton
Willard Richards	Jennetta Richards Richards	Sarah Longstroth
		Nanny Longstroth
		Susanna Lee Liptrot
Hyrum Smith	Mary Fielding Smith	Catherine Phillips
	Mercy R. Fielding Thompson	
John Smith	Clarissa Lyman Smith	Julia Ellis Hills
	Mary Aikens	
Joseph Smith	Emma Hale Smith	Louisa Beaman
	Agnes M. Coolbrith	Prescindia L. H. Buell
	Elizabeth Davis Durfee	Sarah Kinsley Cleveland
	Marinda Nancy Johnson Hyde	Hannah Ells
	Fanny Young Murray	Olive G. Frost
	Mary Ann Frost Sterns Pratt	Desdemona Fullmer
	Phebe Watrous Woodworth	Lucinda Pendleton Morgan Harris
		Elvira Cowles Holmes
		Mary Houston
		Zina D. H. Jacobs
		Almera W. Johnson
		Helen Mar Kimball
		Martha McBride Knight
		Maria Lawrence
		Sarah Lawrence
		Mary E. Rollins Lightner
		Melissa Lott
		Sarah Scott Mulholland
		Emily Dow Partridge
		Eliza Maria Partridge
		Rhoda Richards
		Ruth Vose Sayers
		Patty Bartlett Sessions

TABLE 2. *(continued)*

Husbands	Initiated wives	Uninitiated wives
		Sylvia Porter Sessions
		Vienna Jacques Shearer
		Delcena Johnson Sherman
		Eliza Roxcy Snow
		Lucy Walker
		Sarah Ann Whitney
		Nancy M. Winchester
		Flora Ann Woodworth
William Smith		Caroline Amanda Grant Smith
		Mary Ann Covington Sheffield
		Mary Jones
John Taylor	Leonora Cannon Taylor	Elizabeth Kaighan
		Jane Ballantyne
Lyman Wight		Harriet Benton
		Jane Margaret Ballantyne
		Mary Hawley
		Mary Ann Hobart
Brigham Young	Mary Ann Angell Young	Augusta Adams
	Lucy Ann Decker	Harriet Elizabeth Cook
		Clarissa Decker

Plural husbands not initiated during Joseph Smith's lifetime

Ezra T. Benson	Joseph Bates Noble
Joseph W. Coolidge	John E. Page
Howard Egan	Erastus Snow
William Felshaw	Theodore Turley
William D. Huntington	Edwin D. Woolley
Joseph A. Kelting	Lorenzo Dow Young

Of the men and women initiated during Joseph's lifetime, nineteen men and seventeen women (56 percent of all) received the second anointing prior to Joseph's death (see Table 3). These nineteen men represented 51 percent of male members (29 percent of all), the seventeen women 59 percent of female members (26 percent of all members). In addition, of the nineteen husbands who received the second anointing during Joseph's lifetime, eleven (58 percent) were polygamists, eight (42 percent) monogamists. No plural wife received the ordinance prior to Joseph's death. "[D]uring the lifetime of Joseph Smith," Quinn concluded, "polygamy was only an appendage 'to the highest order of the priesthood' [the second anointing] established on 28 September 1843."[62] Had Joseph lived, the requirements for initiation into the quorum, as well as the ordinances themselves, would have probably evolved further, especially considering the changes that had taken place in defining and bestowing the endowment between 1831 and 1843.

TABLE 3. The second anointing and plural marriage

Husband	Wife	Marital status
Members who received the second anointing during Joseph Smith's lifetime		
Reynolds Cahoon	Thirza Stiles Cahoon	polygamist
Alpheus Cutler	Lois Lathrop Cutler	monogamist
Orson Hyde	(anointed without wife)	polygamist
Heber C. Kimball	Vilate Murray Kimball	polygamist
Cornelius P. Lott	Permelia Darrow Lott	monogamist
William Marks	Rosannah Robinson Marks	monogamist
Isaac Morley	Lucy Gunn Morley	polygamist
William W. Phelps	Sally Waterman Phelps	monogamist
Orson Pratt	(anointed without wife)	monogamist
Parley P. Pratt	(anointed without wife)	polygamist
Willard Richards	Jennetta Richards Richards	polygamist
George A. Smith	Bathsheba Bigler Smith	monogamist
Hyrum Smith	Mary Fielding Smith	polygamist
John Smith	Clarissa Lyman Smith	polygamist
Joseph Smith	Emma Hale Smith	polygamist
(husband deceased)	Lucy Mack Smith	monogamist
John Taylor	Leonora Cannon Taylor	polygamist
Newel K. Whitney	Elizabeth Ann Smith Whitney	monogamist
Wilford Woodruff	Phoebe Carter Woodruff	monogamist
Brigham Young	Mary Ann Angell Young	polygamist

With Joseph's and Hyrum's deaths on June 27, 1844, church leaders faced the issue of presidential succession, and the Anointed Quorum became the principal stage on which this drama unfolded. As Quinn points out, during the five weeks after Joseph's death, "the primary format for discussing succession was at meetings of the Quorum of Anointed. Three-fourths of the apostles and other leaders were weeks of travel from Nauvoo. Unlike all other quorums, the Quorum of Anointed had no requirement that a majority be present to conduct business."[63] However, the issue of ap-

62. Quinn, "Latter-day Saint Prayer Circles," 88.
63. Quinn, *Origins,* 149.

pointing a trustee for the church divided quorum members, some of whom wanted to act immediately, while others, including Willard Richards, wanted to await the return of the apostles before deciding.[64]

Following the arrival in Nauvoo of a majority of apostles, Sidney Rigdon, Joseph's first counselor, offered to act as "guardian" of the church. Rigdon presented his case at a public meeting on August 8. However, most church members favored the leadership of the Quorum of the Twelve with Brigham Young as its president. At Rigdon's excommunication the next month, Elder Orson Hyde denounced Rigdon's revelations and observed that the dilemma could have been resolved elsewhere: "There is a quorum organized where revelations can be tested." Although he did not identify the Anointed Quorum by name, he clearly had in mind the quorum's prayer circles.[65] The day after Rigdon's public offer to assume guardianship of the church, Brigham Young assembled the Anointed Quorum, whose members voted to stop admitting new initiates "till times would admit."[66]

The remainder of 1844 saw only two meetings of the Anointed Quorum in October, none in November, and one in December. On December 22, quorum members voted to admit three women, although they would actually enter the quorum at a later date. Brigham dramatically increased quorum membership in 1845, the final year before the temple was finished, at which time the Anointed Quorum stopped meeting as a separate body. Not only did Young add over twenty people, but in the process he helped "make polygamy an institution instead of furtive practice" by increasing the percentage of plural wives within the quorum. In comparison to the women admitted under Joseph Smith, of whom less than 10 percent practiced polygamy, among the women Brigham admitted in 1845, close to 60 percent were plural wives.[67] Brigham also resumed administration of second anointings and proxy marriage sealings and began the adoption of men to men in father/son relationships.

When not admitting or advancing members, the Anointed Quorum held prayer circles. Not only did they pray for deliverance from their enemies outside the church, as for example when they asked God that Thomas Sharp, editor of the *Warsaw Signal* and one of the accused mur-

64. Ibid., 150.
65. Ibid., 171.
66. Richards, Diary, Aug. 9, 1844.
67. Quinn, *Origins,* 176.

derers of Joseph Smith, "be visited with judgements," but also for trou-
blemakers inside the church such as Presiding Patriarch William Smith
(Joseph's younger brother), who "is endeavoring to ride the Twelve
down."[68] At a time when the Saints were both struggling to complete the
temple and dealing with internal and external strife, it is no surprise that
many of the quorum's meetings lasted late into the night. On May 18,
1845, quorum members met until 2:00 a.m.; on May 22, they dispersed
at midnight; on the 29th they did not return home until 1:30 a.m. Only
the power they held as a result of their endowment, quorum members
believed, enabled them to unite together to open the temple, bless the
Saints, and eventually leave Nauvoo for the Rocky Mountains.

The Anointed Quorum met in the Nauvoo temple for the first time
on December 7, 1845. Three days later, they began the monumental process of endowing the general adult membership of the church. The temple was unfinished, but the attic level was completed, allowing ordinances
to be performed for over 5,000 men and women daily until February 8,
1846.

While the Nauvoo era of Latter-day Saint history is remembered, in
part, for the doctrinal and other developments associated with the temple,
the Anointed Quorum set the stage for those teachings. It was the
Anointed Quorum that met together for three and a half years, participating in the sacred rites of the temple and receiving instruction directly
from Joseph Smith, Brigham Young, and other church officials. Any study
of Nauvoo must treat the Anointed Quorum as Joseph's contribution to
temple-related theology. The quorum should be recognized for its com-
forting and invigorating spiritual power, acting as a separate, yet comple-
mentary, body from those governing the church administratively.

The entries that follow, arranged chronologically, contain every known
primary source regarding the meetings and activities of the quorum from
May 4, 1842, to December 10, 1845. While it is unavoidable that some
misreadings may exist, we have tried to present the original documents as
accurately as possible. These documents reveal the beginnings of what
Latter-day Saints experience today as they participate in the temple ceremonies. Hopefully, this compilation will help to generate continuing appreciation for this aspect of LDS history and theology. For a documentary
history of the endowment and related ceremonies following completion

---

68. Smith, *Intimate Chronicle,* 167.

of the Nauvoo temple, readers may wish to consult the companion to the present book, *The Nauvoo Endowment Companies, 1845-1846: A Documentary History*.

APPENDIX. Members of the Quorum of the Anointed, 1842-1845 (42 men, 48 women)

Name	First anointing	Marriage sealing[a]	Second anointing
Harriet Denton Adams	Oct. 8, 1843	May 28, 1843	N.A.
James Adams	May 4, 1842	May 28, 1843	died
Joseph S. Allen	Mar.-Dec. 1845?[b]	?	?
Lucy Morley Allen	Mar.-Dec. 1845?	?	?
Almon W. Babbitt	May 12, 1844	Jan. 24, 1846	Jan. 24, 1846
Louisa Beman*	Jan. 26, 1845	Apr. 5, 1841	Jan. 14, 1846
John M. Bernhisel	Sept. 28, 1843	Jan. 20, 1846	Jan. 20, 1846
Reynolds Cahoon	Oct. 12, 1843	1842[c]	Nov. 12, 1843
Thirza Stiles Cahoon	Oct. 29, 1843	Nov. 12, 1843?	Nov. 12, 1843
Ruth Moon Clayton	Mar. 29, 1845	July 22, 1843	Jan. 26, 1846
William Clayton	Feb. 3, 1844	Apr. 27, 1843[d]	Jan. 26, 1846
Agnes M. Coolbrith*	by Feb. 3, 1844	Jan. 6, 1842[e]	Jan. 28, 1846
Alpheus Cutler	Oct. 12, 1843	Nov. 15, 1843	Nov. 15, 1843
Lois Lathrop Cutler	Oct. 29, 1843	Nov. 15, 1843	Nov. 15, 1843
Harriet P. W. Decker	Jan.-Mar. 1845	Mar. 9, 1843[f]	Jan. 26, 1846
Lucy Ann Decker	Jan. 26, 1845	June 15, 1842	Mar. 21, 1845
Elizabeth Davis Durfee*	Oct. 1, 1843	by June 1842	?

*A plural wife of Joseph Smith prior to her entrance into the Quorum of the Anointed. For additional information, see the brief biographies at the end of this book.

[a]Eternal marriage sealings joined an already civilly married husband and wife or husband and intended plural wife "so long as you both shall live ... and also throughout eternity" (qtd. in *The Essential Joseph Smith* [Salt Lake City: Signature Books, 1995], 165). These unions were reinforced through the second anointing during which a wife, who may or may not have already been sealed for eternity to her husband, was anointed a "queen and Priestess unto her Husband" whom she subsequently washed and anointed "that [she] may have claim upon him in the morning of the first Reserrection" (qtd. in the Book of Anointings, entry no. 1, copy in editors' possession, original in LDS Archives; and Heber C. Kimball, Diary, following entry dated Oct. 19, 1843). A few sealings were for time only and, in the case of monogamous unions, functioned as *de facto* civil marriages whether or not such unions were recognized by civil law.

[b]Although no primary source supports Joseph Allen's and Lucy Allen's membership in the Anointed Quorum, Ehat ("Introduction of Temple Ordinances," 103) identifies them as possible members and Quinn, *Origins,* 402n165) does not dispute this.

[c]Sealed to Lucina Roberts as a plural wife. His first wife, Thirza Stiles Cahoon, was joined to him when both received the second anointing.

[d]Sealed to Margaret Moon as a plural wife. He was subsequently sealed to his first wife, Ruth Moon Clayton, on July 22, 1843.

[e]Sealed as a plural wife to Joseph Smith, probably for time only; perhaps at the same time sealed for eternity to her deceased first husband by proxy.

[f]Sealed as a plural wife to Lorenzo Dow Young.

APPENDIX. *(continued)*

Name	First anointing	Marriage sealing	Second anointing
Hannah Greenwood Fielding	by Feb. 3, 1844	Jan. 23, 1846	by Dec. 7, 1845?
Joseph Fielding	Dec. 9, 1843	by July 1845[g]	by Dec. 7, 1845?
Olive Grey Frost*	Jan. 26, 1845	mid-1843	?
John P. Greene	May 11, 1844	?	Jan. 31, 1846
Charles Hyde	May 2, 1845	?	?
Marinda Nancy Johnson Hyde*	Feb. 18, 1844	Apr. 1842	Jan. 12, 1846[h]
Orson Hyde	Dec. 2, 1843	Feb.-Mar. 1843?[i]	Jan. 25, 1844
Zina D. H. Jacobs*	Jan. 30, 1845	Oct. 27, 1841	?
Heber C. Kimball	May 4, 1842	1842[j]	Jan. 20, 1844
Helen Mar Kimball*	Jan. 26, 1845	May 1843	?
Vilate Murray Kimball	Nov. 1, 1843	Jan. 20, 1844	Jan. 20, 1844
Joseph C. Kingsbury	Jan. 26, 1845	Mar. 23, 1843[k]	Jan. 28, 1846

[g] Sealed to Mary Ann Peake, a plural wife. His first wife, Hannah Greenwood Fielding, was joined to him when both received the second anointing.

[h] There is some question about whether Marinda Nancy Johnson Hyde received the second anointing.

[i] Sealed to Martha Rebecca Browett, a plural wife. He received the second anointing alone and was later joined to his wives when they received the second anointing in the Nauvoo temple on January 12, 1846.

[j] Sealed to Sarah Peak Noon, a plural wife. His first wife, Vilate Murray Kimball, was apparently sealed to him for eternity around the same time as his sealing to Sarah, also when Vilate and he received their second anointings.

[k] Joseph C. Kingsbury was sealed to his deceased wife, Caroline Whitney (d. Oct. 10, 1842), daughter of Newel K. and Elizabeth Ann Whitney and sister of Sarah Ann Whitney, in appreciation for agreeing to civilly marry his sister-in-law, Sarah Ann, one of Joseph's plural wives. In sealing Kingsbury and Whitney, the prophet added:

> I Seal thee up [Kingsbury] to Come forth in the first resurrection unto eternal life—And thy Companion Caroline who is now dead thou shalt have in the first Resurrection for I seal thee up for and in her behalf to come forth in the first Resurrection unto eternal lives (and it shall be as though She was present herself) and thou Shalt have her and She Shall be thine & no one Shall have power to take her from thee, And you both Shall be crowned and enthroned to dwell together in a Kingdom in the Celestial Glory in the presents [presence] of God And you Shall enjoy each other['s] Society & embraces in all the fulness of the Gospel of Jesus Christ wourds [worlds] without End And I Seal these blessings upon thee and thy Companion in the name of Jesus Christ for thous shalt receive the holy annointing & Endowment in this Life to prepare you for all these blessings even So Amen.

Kingsbury wrote that one month later, on April 29,

> according to President Joseph Smith Couscil & others, I agreed to Stand by Sarah Ann Whitny as supposed to be her husband & had a prete[n]ded marriage for the purpose of Bringing about the purposes of God in these last days as Spoken by the mouth of the Prophets Isiah Jeremiah Ezekiel and also Joseph Smith, & Sarah Ann Should Recd a Great Glory, Honour & eternal lives to the full desire of my heart in having my Companion Caroline in the first Resurrection to claim her & no one have power to take her from me & we both shall be Crowned & enthroned together in the Celestial Kingdom of God Enjoying Each other's Society in all of the fulness of the Gospel of Jesus Christ & our little ones with us as is Received in th[e] blessing that President Joseph Smith Sealed upon my head on the Twenty third day of March 1843 ...

APPENDIX. *(continued)*

Name	First anointing	Marriage sealing	Second anointing
Vinson Knight	by July 31, 1842	by July 31, 1842	died
Jane Silverthorn Law	Oct. 1, 1843	?[l]	N.A.
William Law	May 4, 1842	?	N.A.
Mary E. Rollins Lightner*	Jan. 30, 1845	late Feb. 1842	Jan. 15, 1846
Cornelius P. Lott	Dec. 9, 1843	Sept. 20, 1843	Feb. 4, 1844
Permelia Darrow Lott	Dec. 23, 1843	Sept. 20, 1843	Feb. 4, 1844
Amasa Lyman	Sept. 28, 1843	Sept. 6, 1844[m]	Apr. 18, 1845
Mary Louisa Tanner Lyman	Dec. 22, 1844	Apr. 18, 1845?	Apr. 18, 1845
Rosannah Robinson Marks	Oct. 1, 1843	Oct. 22, 1843?	Oct. 22, 1843
William Marks	May 4, 1842	Oct. 22, 1843?	Oct. 22, 1843
George Miller	May 4, 1842	Aug. 15, 1844?	Aug. 15, 1844
Mary Fry Miller	by Feb. 3, 1844	Aug. 15, 1844?	Aug. 15, 1844
Margaret Moon	Mar. 29, 1845	Apr. 27, 1843	Jan. 26, 1846
Isaac Morley	Dec. 23, 1843	Jan. 14, 1844[n]	Feb. 26, 1844
Lucy Gunn Morley	Dec. 23, 1843	Feb. 26, 1844	Feb. 26, 1844
Fanny Young Murray*	Dec. 23, 1843	Nov. 2, 1843	?
Joseph Bates Noble	Mar. 20, 1845	Apr. 5, 1843[o]	Jan. 23, 1846
Mary Beman Noble	Mar. 20, 1845	Jan. 23, 1846	Jan. 23, 1846
John E. Page	Jan. 26, 1845	by June 27, 1844?[p]	N.A.
Mary Judd Page	Jan. 26, 1845	by June 27, 1844?	N.A.
Sally Waterman Phelps	Dec. 23, 1843	Feb. 2, 1844	Feb. 2, 1844
William W. Phelps	Dec. 9, 1843	Feb. 2, 1844	Feb. 2, 1844
Mary Ann Frost Sterns Pratt	Dec. 22, 1844	June 23, 1843?[q]	Jan. 12, 1846
Orson Pratt	Dec. 23, 1843	ca. Fall 1844[r]	Jan. 26, 1844

Two years later on March 4, 1845, the proxy sealing of Joseph Kingsbury to Caroline Whitney was repeated by Heber C. Kimball, with Dorcas Adelia Moore standing in for Caroline. Immediately afterwards, Kimball sealed Kingsbury and Moore as husband and wife "for time & eternity" ("History of Joseph C. Kingsbury," under entries dated Apr. 29, 1843, and Jan. 1845, Special Collections, Western Americana, Marriott Library, University of Utah, Salt Lake City).

[l]It is not clear if William and Jane Law were ever sealed.

[m]Sealed to Caroline Ely Partridge as a plural wife. His first wife, Maria Louisa Tanner Lyman, was joined to him when they received their second anointings.

[n]Sealed to Hannah Blakeslee Finch Merriam as a plural wife. His first wife, Lucy Gunn Morley, was joined to him when they received their second anointings.

[o]Sealed to Sarah B. Alley as a plural wife. His first wife, Mary Adeline Beaman Noble, was joined to him when both received the second anointing.

[p]May have been sealed to his first wife and/or to plural wives before June 27, 1844.

[q]Soon thereafter, the sealing to her husband, Parley P. Pratt, was apparently cancelled by Joseph Smith. Subsequently sealed to husband, possibly for time only and to Joseph Smith for eternity, on July 24, 1843; then resealed and anointed to Joseph Smith (deceased) on February 7, 1846, in the Nauvoo temple.

[r]Sealed to Charlotte Bishop as a plural wife. Sealed to first wife on November 12, 1844.

APPENDIX. *(continued)*

Name	First anointing	Marriage sealing	Second anointing
Parley P. Pratt	Dec. 2, 1843	June 23, 1843[s]	Jan. 21, 1844
Sarah M. Bates Pratt	Dec. 1844	Nov. 22, 1844	Jan. 13, 1846
Jennetta Richards Richards	Nov. 1, 1843	May 29, 1843	Jan. 27, 1844
Levi Richards	Dec. 9, 1843	Jan. 27, 1846	by Dec. 7, 1845?
Rhoda Richards*	Mar.-Dec. 1845?	June 12, 1843	Jan. 31, 1846
Willard Richards	May 4, 1842	Jan. 18, 1843[t]	Jan. 27, 1844
Sidney Rigdon	May 11, 1844	N.A.	N.A.
Sylvia Porter Sessions*	Jan.-Mar. 1845	Feb. 8, 1842	Apr. 26, 1845?[u]
Bathsheba W. Bigler Smith	Dec. 23, 1843	Jan. 20, 1844	Jan. 31, 1844
Clarissa Lyman Smith	Oct. 8, 1843	Feb. 26, 1844?	Feb. 26, 1844
Emma Hale Smith	Sept. 28, 1843	May 28, 1843	Sept. 28, 1843
George A. Smith	Dec. 2, 1843	Jan. 20, 1844	Jan. 31, 1844
Hyrum Smith	May 5, 1842	May 29, 1843	Oct. 8, 1843
John Smith	Sept. 28, 1843	Aug. 11, 1843[v]	Feb. 26, 1844
Joseph Smith	May 5, 1842	May 28, 1843	Sept. 28, 1843
Lucy Mack Smith	Oct. 8, 1843	?	Nov. 12, 1843
Mary Fielding Smith	Oct. 1, 1843	May 29, 1843	Oct. 8, 1843
Samuel H. Smith	Dec. 17, 1843	N.A.	N.A.
William B. Smith	May 12, 1844	N.A.	N.A.
Eliza Roxcy Snow*	Jan. 26, 1845	June 29, 1842	Feb. 6, 1846
Catherine Curtis Spencer	Dec. 23, 1843	Jan. 15, 1846	by Dec. 7, 1845?
Orson Spencer	Dec. 2, 1843	Jan. 15, 1846	by Dec. 7, 1845?
John Taylor	Sept. 28, 1843	Dec. 12, 1843[w]	Jan. 30, 1844
Leonora Cannon Taylor	Nov. 1, 1843	Jan. 30, 1844	Jan. 30, 1844
Mercy R. Fielding Thompson	Nov. 1, 1843	May 29, 1843	Jan. 23, 1846
Elizabeth Ann Smith Whitney	Oct. 8, 1843	Aug. 21, 1842	Oct. 27, 1843
Newel K. Whitney	May 4, 1842	Aug. 21, 1842	Oct. 27, 1843
Sarah Ann Whitney*	Jan. 26, 1845	July 27, 1842	Mar. 27, 1845
Lyman Wight	May 14, 1844	ca. May 14, 1844[x]	N.A.

[s]Soon thereafter, the sealing to his wife, Mary Ann Frost Stearns Pratt, was apparently cancelled by Joseph Smith. Sealed for eternity to deceased first wife, Thankful Halsey Pratt, with Mary Ann acting as proxy; then to Mary Ann, possibly for time only; and finally to first plural wife, Elizabeth Brotherton, for time and eternity on July 24, 1843.

[t]Sealed to Sarah and Nanny Longstroth as plural wives. Subsequently sealed to first wife, Jennetta Richards, on May 29, 1843.

[u]According to Quinn (*Origins,* 505), "Sylvia P. Sessions (Lyon, Smith, Kimball) received her second anointing with Heber C. Kimball, but apparently not [at] a meeting of the Anointed Quorum."

[v]Sealed to Mary Aikens as a plural wife, his first wife, Clarissa Lyman Smith, was joined to him when they received their second anointings.

[w]Sealed to Elizabeth Kaighan as a plural wife. First wife, Leonora Cannon Taylor, joined to him when they received their second anointings.

[x]May have been sealed to the following women: Harriet Benton (first wife) and Jane Margaret

APPENDIX. *(continued)*

Name	First anointing	Marriage sealing	Second anointing
Phoebe Carter Woodruff	Dec. 23, 1843	Nov. 11, 1843	Jan. 28, 1844
Wilford Woodruff	Dec. 2, 1843	Nov. 11, 1843	Jan. 28, 1844
Lucien Woodworth	Sept. 28, 1843	Jan. 17, 1846	Jan. 17, 1846
Phebe Watrous Woodworth*	Oct. 29, 1843	Jan. 17, 1846	Jan. 17, 1846
Brigham Young	May 4, 1842	June 15, 1842[y]	Nov. 22, 1843
Jane Bicknell Young	Feb. 3, 1844	Jan. 12, 1845	Jan. 12, 1845
Joseph Young	Feb. 3, 1844	Jan. 12, 1845	Jan. 12, 1845
Mary Ann Angell Young	Nov. 1, 1843	May 29, 1843	Nov. 22, 1843

Ballantyne, Mary Hawley, and May Ann Hobart (plural wives) around the time of his entrance into the Quorum of the Anointed.

[y]Sealed to Lucy Ann Decker as a plural wife. Subsequently sealed to first wife, Mary Ann Angell Young, on May 29, 1843.

ABBREVIATIONS
FOR FREQUENTLY CITED SOURCES

"Book of the Law of the Lord"
: "The Book of the Law of the Lord," in *The Papers of Joseph Smith, Volume 2: Journal, 1832-1842*, ed. Dean C. Jessee (Salt Lake City: Deseret Book, 1992), 334-506; and in *History of the Church*, various dates.

Brigham Young, Diary
: The diary of Brigham Young, LDS Archives. Young's scribes included William Clayton, Evan Greene, John D. Lee, Willard Richards, and Brigham Young.

Ehat, "Introduction of Temple Ordinances"
: Andrew F. Ehat, "Joseph Smith's Introduction of Temple Ordinances and the 1844 Mormon Succession Question," M.A. thesis, Brigham Young University, 1982.

George A. Smith, "History of George Albert Smith"
: "The History of George Albert Smith," typescript, LDS Archives; also in *Selected Collections from the Archives of*

The Church of Jesus Christ of Latter-day Saints (Provo, UT: Brigham Young University Press, 2002).

Heber C. Kimball, Diary

The diary of Heber C. Kimball, published in part in *On the Potter's Wheel: The Diaries of Heber C. Kimball*, ed. Stanley B. Kimball (Salt Lake City: Signature Books and Smith Research Associates, 1987). The original is housed in LDS Archives.

Historian's Office Journal

The journal of the Historian's Office of the LDS church, maintained by various clerks, LDS Archives; also in *Selected Collections from the Archives of The Church of Jesus Christ of Latter-day Saints* (Provo, UT: Brigham Young University Press, 2002).

History of the Church

History of the Church of Jesus Christ of Latter-day Saints. Period I. History of Joseph Smith, the Prophet, by Himself, 6 vols., ed. B. H. Roberts (Salt Lake City: Published by the Church/ Deseret Book, 1902-12), with a seventh volume, *Period 2: Apostolic Interregnum,* published in 1932; and in *Selected Collections from the Archives of The Church of Jesus Christ of Latter-day Saints* (Provo, UT: Brigham Young University Press, 2002). The original is housed in LDS Archives.

John Taylor, Diary

The Nauvoo, Illinois, diary of John Taylor (George Q. Cannon, scribe), published in "The John Taylor Nauvoo Journal, January 1845-September

1845," ed. Dean C. Jessee, *BYU Studies* 23 (Summer 1983): 1-96.

Joseph Smith, Diary	The diary of Joseph Smith (various scribes, principally Willard Richards), published in *An American Prophet's Record: The Diaries and Journals of Joseph Smith*, ed. Scott H. Faulring (Salt Lake City: Signature Books and Smith Research Associates, 1986); in *The Papers of Joseph Smith, Volume 2: Journal, 1832-1842*, ed. Dean C. Jessee (Salt Lake City: Deseret Book, 1992); in *History of the Church*, various dates; and in *Selected Collections from the Archives of The Church of Jesus Christ of Latter-day Saints* (Provo, UT: Brigham Young University Press, 2002). The original is housed in LDS Archives.
LDS Archives	Archives, Church of Jesus Christ of Latter-day Saints, Salt Lake City, Utah.
Manuscript History of Brigham Young	"Manuscript History of Brigham Young," published in *Manuscript History of Brigham Young, 1801-1844*, ed. Elden Jay Watson (Salt Lake City: Author, 1968). The original, compiled in the 1850s, is housed in LDS Archives.
"Meetings of Anointed Quorum"	"1843[-]4 Meetings of anointed Quorum Journalizings[—]Journal kept for Joseph Smith the Prophet." Transcript in D. Michael Quinn Papers, Beinecke Library, Yale University, New Haven, Connecticut. The original is housed in LDS Archives.
Quinn, *Origins*	D. Michael Quinn, *The Mormon Hierar-*

chy: Origins of Power (Salt Lake City: Signature Books and Smith Research Associates, 1994).

Wilford Woodruff, Diary

The diary of Wilford Woodruff, published in *Wilford Woodruff's Journal*, ed. by Scott G. Kenney, 9 vols. (Midvale, UT: Signature Books, 1983-85). The original is housed in LDS Archives.

Willard Richards, Diary

The diary of Willard Richards, LDS Archives; and in *Selected Collections from the Archives of The Church of Jesus Christ of Latter-day Saints* (Provo, UT: Brigham Young University Press, 2002).

William Clayton, Diary

The Nauvoo, Illinois, diary of William Clayton, published in part in *An Intimate Chronicle: The Journals of William Clayton*, ed. George D. Smith (Salt Lake City: Signature Books and Smith Research Associates, 1991). Additional excerpts in D. Michael Quinn Papers, Beinecke Library, Yale University, New Haven, Connecticut. The original is in possession of the LDS church.

William Clayton, Diary, kept for Heber C. Kimball

The Nauvoo, Illinois, diary of William Clayton, kept for Heber C. Kimball, published in part in *An Intimate Chronicle: The Journals of William Clayton*, ed. George D. Smith (Salt Lake City: Signature Books and Smith Research Associates, 1991), 199-258. The original is housed in LDS Archives.

I.

The Year

1842

"INSTRUCTIONS CONCERNING THE PRIESTHOOD"

Sunday, May 1, 1842

The Grove, Nauvoo, Illinois

[Joseph Smith speaking:] There are signs in heaven, earth, and hell. The Elders must know them all to be endowed with power, to finish their work and prevent imposition. The devil knows many signs but dos not know the sign of the Son of Man, or Jesus. No one can truly say he knows God until he has handled something, and this can only be in the Holiest of Holies.

—Joseph Smith, Diary, in "Book of the Law of the Lord."

Tuesday, May 3, 1842

Joseph Smith's Red Brick Store

[W]ith his [Joseph Smith's] family [1]

—Joseph Smith, Diary, in "Book of the Law of the Lord."

---

1. While this uncharacteristically brief entry is silent on the preparations underway at the Red Brick Store, the scribe may have been unaware of the purpose of the renovation or decided not to report on it.

Passed the day mostly with my [Joseph Smith's] family.

—*History of the Church*, 5:1.[2]

... I [Lucius N. Scovil(le)][3] can testify that on the 3rd day of May, 1842, Joseph Smith the Prophet called upon five or six, viz: Shadrack Roundy,[4] Noah Rogers,[5] Dimick B. Huntington, Daniel Cairns,[6] and myself (I am not certain but that Hosea Stout[7] was there also) to meet with him (the Prophet) in his business office (the upper part of his brick store). He told us that the object he had was for us to go to work and fit up that room preparatory to giving endowments to a few Elders that he might give unto them all the keys of power pertaining to the Aronic and Melchisedec Priesthoods.

We therefore went to work making the necessary preparations, and everything was arranged representing the interior of a temple as much as the circumstances would permit, he being with us dictating everything. He gave us many items that were very interesting to us, which sank with deep weight upon my mind, especially after the temple was finished at Nauvoo [Illinois], and I had received the ordinances in which I was

---

2. The published *History of the Church* is preferred when it does not differ significantly from its manuscript versions.

3. Lucius Nelson Scovil[le] (1806-89) was junior warden (or junior assistant to the worshipful master) of Nauvoo's Masonic lodge. He served a mission to Britain in 1846 and later served in the Eastern States. He was never a member of the Quorum of the Anointed.

4. Shadrack Roundy (1788-1872) converted to Mormonism in 1831. He was a member of the Nauvoo Legion beginning in 1841 and later served as a policeman and bodyguard to Joseph Smith. He entered the Salt Lake Valley in 1847, where he served on the Salt Lake High Council (1847-48) and later as bishop of the Salt Lake City 16th Ward (1849-56). He was never a member of the Quorum of the Anointed.

5. Noah Rogers (1797-1846) was baptized into the LDS church in 1837 and served a mission to Vermont with Addison Pratt. He was also a missionary to Tahiti and president of the Society Islands Mission from 1844 to 1845. He died while traveling west with the Saints. He was never a member of the Quorum of the Anointed.

6. Daniel Carn (1802-72) resided in Nauvoo, Illinois, where he became bishop of the first German-speaking branch of the LDS church. In 1851 he was called as a mission president in Germany. He was never a member of the Quorum of the Anointed.

7. Hosea Stout (1810-89) fought in the Battle of Crooked River in Ray County, Missouri (October 1838), and after settling with the LDS church in Nauvoo, Illinois, was clerk of the high council and chief of police. He occupied the latter position again in Winter Quarters and later in the Salt Lake Valley. He was never a member of the Quorum of the Anointed.

among the first, as I had been called upon to work in the [Nauvoo] Temple as one of the hands during the winter. Some weeks previous to the dedication he told us that we should have the privilege of receiving the whole of the ordinances in due time. The history of Joseph Smith speaks for itself. But I can and do testify that I know of a surety that room was fitted up by his order which we finished in the forenoon of the said 4th of May, 1842. ...

—Lucius N. Scovil[le], Letter to the Editor, "The Higher Ordinances," dated January [February] 2, 1884, *Deseret News Semi-Weekly*, February 15, 1884, p. 2.

....

In Nauvoo [Illinois] In [18]40 or [18]41 W[illia]m Felshaw,[8] Samuel R[o]lfe,[9] [and] Dimick B Huntington[10] prepared the masonic lodge room in the brick store chamber for the first endewments[;] took some bars of lead to hold up the tre[e]s of the garden and a piece of carpet for a curtain[,] Joseph Smith giving directions how to prepare all things[.] the masonic lodge met nights and he [Joseph Smith] used the room days for endewments[.] one night after work was over in the lodge [and he] was through working old brother [Asahel] Perry[11] the tyler sayed a brother wishes to enter let him enter[;] George A Smith was the master[.] Joseph Smith entered strode up and down the lodge saying hallahjuh halolujah hullahujah sayed h[e] I have done what king Solamon King Hiram & Hiram Abbif[12] could not do[:] I have set up the Kingdom no more to be

8. William Felshaw (1800-67) was a member of Nauvoo's Masonic lodge, a member of Nauvoo's 4th Ward, and an early Mormon polygamist. He traveled with his family to Salt Lake City in 1851 and settled in Fillmore, Utah. He was never a member of the Quorum of the Anointed.

9. Samuel Rolfe (1794-1867) was a founding member of Nauvoo's Masonic lodge. He later helped to settle Lehi, Utah. He was never a member of the Quorum of the Anointed.

10. Dimick (also Dimmock) Baker Huntington (1808-79) was official tyler (doorkeeper) of Nauvoo's Masonic lodge and brother to two of Joseph Smith's plural wives: Zina D. H. Jacobs (m. October 27, 1841) and Prescendia L. H. Buell (m. Dec. 11, 1841). He served as a missionary to Native American tribes for forty years. After the Latter-day Saints moved west, he was one of the first settlers in Provo, Utah. He was never a member of the Quorum of the Anointed.

11. Asahel Perry (1784-1869) was a member of Nauvoo's Masonic lodge. He subsequently settled in Springville, Utah. He was never a member of the Quorum of the Anointed.

12. According to Masonic teachings, Hiram Abiff, also known as the widow's son, was the master builder of King Solomon's temple. Because he was murdered for

thrown down forever nor never to be given to another people ...
D[imick] B Huntington's words the night of 12 of Dec[ember] 1878
S[alt] L[ake] City.

> —Statement, undated, photocopy in Mary Brown Firmage
> Papers, L. Tom Perry Special Collections, Harold B. Lee
> Library, Brigham Young University, Provo, Utah.

Wednesday, May 4, 1842
Joseph Smith's Red Brick Store

In council in the Presidents & General offices with Judge [James] Adams. Hyram Smith Newel K. Whitney. William Marks. W[illia]m Law. George Miller. Brigham Young. Heber C. Kimball & Willard Richards.[13] & giving certain instructions concerning the priesthood. &c on the Aronic Priesthood to the first continuing through the day.

> —Joseph Smith, Diary, in "Book of the Law of the Lord."

Strange Events, June [May] 1842. I [Heber C. Kimball] was aniciated [initiated] into the ancient order[,] was washed and annointed and Sealled and ordained a Preast, and so forth in company with nine others, Viz. Jos[e]ph Smith, Hiram Smith, W[illia]m. Law, W[illia]m. Marks, Judge [James] Adams, Brigham Young, Willard Richards, George Miller, N[ewel]. K. Whitney.

> —Heber C. Kimball, Diary, following entry dated October 19,
> 1843 (written after January 17, 1847).

4 Wednesday May 4— I [Joseph Smith] spent the day in the upper part of the Store (IE.[,] in my private office[,] so called, because in that room I keep the my sacred writings, translated ancient records, and re-

---

refusing to reveal the secret with which he had been entrusted, his death is commemorated in various Masonic rituals.

13. Of the ten men present, only William Law and William Marks never accepted plural marriage. "About 4 years ago next May," Heber C. Kimball stated in December 1845, "nine [actually ten] persons were admitted in to the Holy order 5 are now living—B[righam]. Young—W[illard]. Richards George Miller—N[ewel]. K. Whitney & H[eber]. C. Kimball two [actually three] are dead [i.e., James Adams, Hyrum Smith, and Joseph Smith], and two are worse then dead [i.e., William Law and William Marks]" (William Clayton, Diary, Kept for Heber C. Kimball, Dec. 21, 1845).

ceived revelations) and in my general business office, or Lodge room (IE[,] where the Masonic fraternity met occasionally for want of a better place), in council with Gen[eral] James Adams, of Springfield [Illinois], Patriarch Hyrum Smith, Bishops Newel K. Whitney, & Geo[rge]. Miller, (leave these blank) W[illia]m Marks, W[illia]m Law & & Pres[iden]ts Brigham Young Heber C. Kimball & Willard Richards,[14] instructing them in the principles and order of the priesthood, attending to washings & anointings, & endowments, and the communications of keys, pertaining to the Aaronic Priesthood, and so on to the highest order of the Melchisedek Priesthood, setting forth the order pertaining to the Ancient of days & all those plans & principles by which any one is enabled to secure the fulness of those blessings which has been prepared for the church of the firstborn, and come up into and abide in the presence of God in the Eloheim in the eternal worlds. In this council was instituted the Ancient order of things for the first time in these last days. And the communications I made to thiese council brethr [this] Council were of things spiritual, and to be received only by the spiritual minded: and there was nothing made known to these men but what will be made known to all Saints, of the last days, so soon as they are prepared to receive, them and a proper place is prepared to communicate them, even to the weakest of the Saints; therefore let the Saints be diligent in building the [Nauvoo] temple and all the houses which they have been or shall hereafter be commanded of god to build, and wait their time with patience, in all meekness and faith, & perserverance unto the end. knowing assuredly that all these things referred to in this council are always governed by the principles of Revelation.

—Rough Draft, "Manuscript History of the Church," Willard Richards, scribe (written ca. 1845), LDS Archives.

....

I [Joseph Smith] spent the day in the upper part of the store, that is in my private office (so called because in that room I keep my sacred writings, translate ancient records, and receive revelations) and in my general business office, or lodge room (that is where the Masonic fraternity meet occasionally, for want of a better place), in council with General James Adams, of Springfield [Illinois], Patriarch Hyrum Smith, Bishops Newel

---

14. By the time this narrative was composed, both William Law and William Marks had left the LDS church.

K. Whitney and George Miller, and President Brigham Young and Elders Heber C. Kimball and Willard Richards, instructing them in the principles and order of the Priesthood, attending to washings, anointings, endowments, and the communications of keys pertaining to the Aaronic Priesthood, and so on to the highest order of the Melchisedek Priesthood, setting forth the order pertaining to the Ancient of Days, and all those plans and principles by which any one is enabled to secure the fullness of those blessings which have been prepared for the Church of the First Born, and come up and abide in the presence of the Eloheim in the eternal worlds. In this council was instituted the ancient order of things for the first time in these last days. And the communications I made to this council were of things spiritual, and to be received only by the spiritual minded: and there was nothing made known to these men but what will be made known to all the Saints of the last days, so soon as they are prepared to receive, and a proper place is prepared to communicate them, even to the weakest of the Saints; therefore let the Saints be diligent in building the [Nauvoo] Temple, and all the houses which they have been, or shall hereafter be, commanded of God to build; and wait their time with patience in all meekness, faith, perserverance unto the end, knowing assuredly that all these things referred to in this council are always governed by the principles of revelation.

—*History of the Church,* 5:1-2.

I [Brigham Young] met with Joseph [Smith], Hyrum [Smith], Heber [C. Kimball], Willard [Richards], Bishops [Newel K.] Whitney and [George] Miller, and Gen[eral]. James Adams, in Joseph's private office, where Joseph taught the ancient order of things for the first time in these last days, and received my washings, anointings and endowments.

—*Manuscript History of Brigham Young,* p. 116.

Pres[iden]t [Brigham] Young was filled with the spirit of God & revelation & said when we got our washings and anointings under the hands of the Prophet Joseph [Smith] at Nauvoo [Illinois] we had only one room to work in with the exception of a little side room or office where we were washed and anointed had our garments placed upon us and received our New Name. and after he [Joseph Smith] had performed these ceremonies[,] he gave the Key Words signs, togkens [tokens] and penalties.[15]

---

15. This refers to several specific elements of the endowment ceremony. Simi-

then after we went into the large room over the store in Nauvoo. Joseph divided up the room the best that he could[,] hung up the veil, marked it gave us our instructions as we passed along from one department to another giving us signs, tokens, penalties with the Key words pertaining to those signs and after we had got through Bro[ther] Joseph turned to me [Brigham Young] and said Bro[ther] Brigham this is not arranged right but we have done the best we could under the circumstances in which we are placed ...

—L. John Nuttall, Diary, entry dated February 7, 1877,
Archives and Manuscripts, L. Tom Perry Special Collections,
Harold B. Lee Library, Brigham Young University,
Provo, Utah.

Thursday, May 5, 1842
Joseph Smith's Red Brick Store

Judge [James] Adams left for Springfield [Illinois] the others continued in Council as the day previous & Joseph [Smith] & Hyrum [Smith] were [blank][.]

—Joseph Smith, Diary, in "Book of the Law of the Lord."

General [James] Adams started for Springfield [Illinois], and the remainder of the Council of yesterday continued their meeting at the same place, and myself [Joseph Smith] and Brother Hyrum [Smith] received in turn from the others, the same that I had communicated to them the day previous.

—*History of the Church,* 5:2–3.

I [Brigham Young] attended Council as yesterday, and we administered to brother Joseph [Smith] the same ordinances.

—*Manuscript History of Brigham Young,* p. 116.

Many of the Apostles and Elders having returned from England, Joseph [Smith] washed and anointed as Kings and Priests to God, and over the House of Israel, the following named persons, as he said he was commanded of God, viz: James Adams (of Springfield [Illinois]), William Law,

---

larities between the endowment and early nineteenth-century Masonic ritual are most evident in these symbols. The particulars of these elements were viewed as especially sacred by endowment initiates.

Joseph Smith's Red Brick Store (also known as the General Store) on the south side of Water Street near Granger Street was constructed in 1841. The Quorum of the Anointed first formed here on the second floor in May 1842. Quorum members assembled here more than thirty times from 1842 to 1844. Photograph ca. 1855.

William Marks, Willard Richards, Brigham Young, Heber C. Kimball, Newel K. Whitney, Hyrum Smith and myself [George Miller]; and conferred on us Patriarchal Priesthood. This took place on the 5th and 6th [sic; 4th and 5th] of May, 1842.

> —George Miller, Autobiography, in "De Tal Palo Tal Astilla," compiled by H. W. Mills, *Annual Publications, Historical Society of Southern California* 10 (1917), Part 3:120-21.

....

Brother Joseph [Smith] feels as well as I [Heber C. Kimball] Ever see him. one reason is he has got a Small company. that he feels safe in thare ha[n]ds. and that is not all[,] he can open his bosom to[o] and feel him Self safe[.] I wish you was here so as to see and hear fore your Self. we have received some pressious things through the Prophet [Joseph Smith] on the preasthood that would caus your Soul to rejoice[.] I can not give them to you on paper fore they are not to be riten. So you must come and get them fore your Self. ... Thare is a similarity of preast Hood in masonary.[16] Bro[ther] Joseph ses masonary was taken from preasthood but has become degenerated but menny things are perfect.[17]

> —Heber C. Kimball, Letter to Parley and Mary Ann Pratt, dated June 17, 1842, LDS Archives.

---

16. Willard Richards wrote some three months earlier: "MARCH 15th. This day the Masonic lodge of Nauvoo was installed on the hill near the Temple, in the grove. Thousands of people present. [March] 16th President Joseph [Smith] and Sidney [Rigdon] are initiated by Grand Master Jonas, of the Grand Lodge of Illinois. Masonry had its origin in the Priesthood. A hint to the wise i[s] sufficient" (Letter to Levi Richards, dated March 7, 1842, but reporting events after that date, in Joseph Grant Stevenson, ed., *Richards Family History* [Provo, UT: Stevenson's Genealogical Center, 1991], 3:90, courtesy H. Michael Marquardt).

17. "Many have joined the masonic Institution," recorded Joseph Fielding, who subsequently joined the Quorum of the Anointed, and "this seems to have been a Stepping Stone or Preparation for something else, the true Origin of Masonry, this I have also seen and rejoice in it" (Diary, Dec. 1843, LDS Archives). One of Joseph's confidants, Benjamin F. Johnson, added that "[h]e [Joseph Smith] told me Freemasonry, as at present, was the apostate endowments" (*My Life's Review: Autobiography of Benjamin Franklin Johnson* [Provo: Grandin Book, 1997; 1st ed., 1947], p. 85). "Those who were recipients of these ordinances," explains Ehat ("Introduction of Temple Ordinances," 24-25), "were aware that these ordinances resembled non-Mormon rituals. In fact, the resemblance to Freemasonry was one case of which Joseph Smith made particular mention. Joseph Smith taught that these ordinances would serve as a standard by which the subcelestial impurities of surviving remnants of earlier Gospel dispensations could be judged. To quorum members, therefore, parallels (such as Freemasonry) provided confirmation of the breadth of the restoration impulse and

Sunday, June 26, 1842
Joseph Smith's Homestead

Joseph [Smith] attended meeting, & council at his house at 6 o clock P.M. present Hyrum Smith. Geo[rge] Miller N[ewel]. K. Whitney. W[illia]m Marks. Brigham Young. Heber C. Kimball. & Willard Richards. To take into consideration the situation of the pine country & Lumbering business and other subjects of importance in the church; after consulation thereon the Brethren united in Solemn prayer that God would make known his will concerning the pine country, & that he would deliver his anointed, his people from all the evil designs of [Missouri] Governor [Lilburn W.] Boggs,[18] & the powers of the state of Missouri, & of [Illinois] Governor [Thomas] Carlin.[19] & the authorites of Illinois, & of all presidents, governors. Judges Legislators & all in authority, and of John C. Bennett.[20] & all mobs & evil designing persons.—so that his people might

---

was an evidence of Joseph Smith's divine calling as a prophet. The endowment was a new and everlasting way of entering covenants with God, a new revelation renewing an ancient order of priesthood covenants and power." David John Buerger agreed that "[w]hile it is uncertain exactly why Freemasonry was initially embraced, its activities undoubtedly provided fraternal benefits and its ceremonies clearly provided part of the specific wording for the Nauvoo temple endowment, although most nineteenth-century Masonic rituals have no resemblance to early temple ceremonies. It is significant that, following conferral of endowment rites on Nauvoo adults and their subsequent relocation to Utah, Masonry never regained the prominence among Mormons it received in Nauvoo" *(The Mysteries of Godliness: A History of Mormon Temple Worship* [San Francisco: Smith Research Associates, 1994], 58).

18. Lilburn W. Boggs (1796-1860) was fifth governor of Missouri (1837-41). In 1838 he expelled the Mormons from Missouri and issued an extermination order against them. In 1842 he was shot and wounded at home by an unknown assailant. Orrin Porter Rockwell was charged with the crime, with Joseph Smith as an accessory. Rockwell was jailed for a time and released. Four years later Boggs left Missouri and settled in California.

19. Thomas Carlin (1789-1852) served as governor of Illinois (1838-42) during the earliest years of the Latter-day Saint sojourn in Nauvoo.

20. John Cook Bennett (1804-67) held several professorships and helped to found a medical college at Willoughby University in 1834 before joining the Mormons in Nauvoo six years later. In 1841 he was elected mayor of Nauvoo, appointed acting Assistant President to Joseph Smith, chancellor of the University of Nauvoo, and major general of the Nauvoo Legion. In 1842 he was charged with adultery, withdrew from the church, and became disaffected from Joseph Smith. That same year he published an attack on Mormonism titled *History of the Saints; or, An Exposé of Joe Smith and Mormonism.* For a time he affiliated with James J. Strang, one of several would-be successors to Joseph Smith. Bennett died in Iowa. For more, see Andrew F. Smith, *Saintly Scoundrel: The Life and Times of Dr. John Cook Bennett* (Urbana: University of Illinois Press, 1997).

continue in peace & build up the city of Nauvoo [Illinois]. & that his chosen might be blessed & live to man's appointed age. & that their households. & the household of faith might. continually be blessed with the fost[er]ing care of heaven.—& enjoy the good things of the earth abundantly.—adjourned to monday evening[.]

—Joseph Smith, Diary, in "Book of the Law of the Lord."

....

I [Joseph Smith] attended meeting and council at my house at six o'clock p.m.; present Hyrum Smith, George Miller, Newel K. Whitney, William Marks, Brigham Young, Heber C. Kimball, and Willard Richards, to take into consideration the situation of the Pine country, and lumbering business, and other subjects of importance to the Church; after consultation thereon the brethren united in solemn prayer that God would make known His will concerning the Pine country, and that He would deliver His anointed, His people, from all the evil designs of Governor [Lilburn W.] Boggs, and the powers of the state of Missouri, and of Governor [Thomas] Carlin and the authorities of Illinois, and of all Presidents, Governors, Judges, Legislators, and all in authority, and of John C. Bennett, and all mobs and evil designing persons, so that His people might continue in peace and build up the city of Nauvoo [Illinois], and that His chosen might be blessed and live to man's appointed age, and that their households, and the household of faith might continually be blest with the fostering care of heaven, and enjoy the good things of the earth abundantly. Adjourned to Monday evening.

—*History of the Church,* 5:44–45.

....

Six, p.m., I [Brigham Young] attended Council at brother Joseph [Smith]'s, to take into consideration the situation of the pine country and lumbering business, and other subjects of importance to the Church; after which we spent a season in prayer that the Lord would deliver us from the power of our enemies, and provide means for us to build houses as he had commanded his people.

—*Manuscript History of Brigham Young,* p. 118.

Monday, June 27, 1842
Joseph Smith's Homestead

[W]hen the council assembled in the evening Brothers. [Edward]

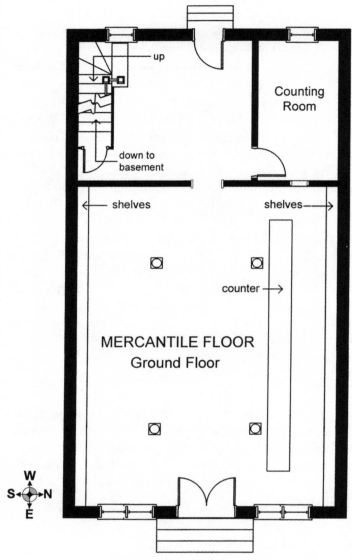

The ground floor of Joseph Smith's store. Drawing by Lisle G.
Brown; original in private possession, used by permission.

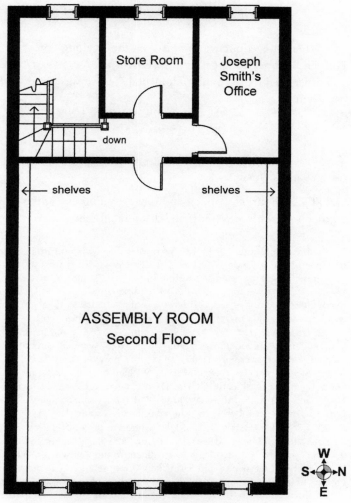

The second floor of Joseph Smith's store. On the second floor, those initiated into the Anointed Quorum were first washed and anointed in Joseph's office. The endowment ceremony/ritual was then presented in the Assembly Room, which was divided by curtains into different departments required for the ritual. Drawings by Lisle G. Brown; originals in private possession, used by permission.

Hunter.[21] [Charles or James] Ivins[22] [Edwin D.] Wooley.[23] [Robert] Pierce[24] & others being present. the adjourned council was pos[t]poned till tuesday evening[.][25]

—Joseph Smith, Diary, in "Book of the Law of the Lord."

....

When the council assembled in the evening, Brothers [Edward] Hunter, [Charles or James] Ivins, [Edwin D.] Woolley, [Robert] Pierce and others being present, the adjourned council was postponed till Tuesday evening ...
—*History of the Church,* 5:45.

Tuesday, June 28, 1842
Joseph Smith's Homestead

[T]he adjourned council of Sunday evening met at the upper Room at Joseph [Smith]s & were agreed that a reinforcement go immediately to

---

21. Edward Hunter (1793-1883), converted to Mormonism in 1840 and was a member of the Nauvoo City Council that closed down the *Nauvoo Expositor* in early June 1844. He served as a bishop in Nauvoo, Winter Quarters, and Salt Lake City. In 1851 he was appointed third Presiding Bishop of the LDS church and remained in office until 1883, also serving as a counselor to Brigham Young for one year. He was never a member of the Quorum of the Anointed.

22. James Ivins (1797-1877) was born in New Jersey and became a prominent land owner in Nauvoo. Charles Ivins (1799-1875) was excommunicated from the LDS church for apostasy in May 1844. The previous month, he was appointed bishop of a splinter group established by William Law, Joseph Smith's former counselor. According to Willard Richards, Ivins "aided and abetted" the mob that killed Joseph and Hyrum Smith in late June 1844 (*History of the Church,* 7:146). Neither Ivins was ever a member of the Quorum of the Anointed.

23. Edwin D. Woolley (1807-81) converted to the LDS church in 1837 and was an early settler in Nauvoo. He arrived in the Salt Lake Valley in 1848 and for several years served as business manager to Brigham Young. He was also a member of the Utah territorial legislature and Salt Lake County recorder. He helped organize the Deseret Telegraph Company and served as bishop of the Salt Lake City 13th Ward from 1853 until his death. He was never a member of the Quorum of the Anointed.

24. Robert Pierce (1797-1884) resided in the Nauvoo 4th Ward. He was never a member of the Quorum of the Anointed.

25. Quinn (*Origins,* 493) does not believe this was a meeting of the Quorum of the Anointed since Edward Hunter, Edwin D. Woolley, Charles or James Ivins, and Robert Pierce had not yet been initiated. Ehat ("Introduction of Temple Ordinances," 52) feels that the quorum intended to meet but abandoned its plans when the above uninitiated men showed up at the same time.

the pine country Led by Bro[ther] Ezra Chase.[26] & after uniting in Solemn prayer. to God. for a blessing on themselves & famiilies & the church
in general. & for the building up of the [Nauvoo] Temple. & Nauvoo
House. & city: for deliverance from their enemies. & the spread of the
work of Righteousness: & that Bro[ther] [Willard] Richards (who was
expecting to go east tomorrow for his family,) that he might have a prosperous Journey. have power of [and?] over the winds & elements, & all
opposition & dangers, his life & health be preserved & be speedily returned to this place with his family. that their lives & he[a]lth might be
preserved & that they might come up in peace to this place. & that
Bro[ther] Richards might be prospered according to the desire of his
heart in all things in relation to his household. & the church. & that the
spirit of God might rest upon him ~~continually~~ so that he may act according to the wisdom of heaven, continually, the council disposed.

—Joseph Smith, Diary, in "Book of the Law of the Lord."

The adjourned council of Sunday evening met in my [Joseph Smith's]
upper room, and were agreed that a reinforcement go immediately to the
Pine country, led by Brother Ezra Chase. The council dispersed after uniting in solemn prayer to God for a blessing on themselves and families, and
the Church in general, and for the building up of the [Nauvoo] Temple
and Nauvoo House and city; for deliverance from their enemies, and the
spread of the word of righteousness; and that Brother [Willard] Richards
(who was expected to go East tomorrow for his family) might have a prosperous journey, have power over the winds and elements, and all opposition and dangers, his life and health be preserved, and be speedily returned
to this place with his family, that their lives and health might be preserved,
and that they might come up in peace to this place, and that Brother
Richards might be prospered according to the desire of his heart, in all
things in relation to his household, and the Church, and that the Spirit of

26. Ezra Chase (1796-1873) converted to the LDS church in 1839 and was later
a member of the Nauvoo 3rd Ward. He was called in July 1843 as one of several
missionaries to preach throughout Illinois in an attempt to "disabuse the public
mind over my [Joseph Smith's] arrest" on charges of complicity in the attempted assassination of Lilburn W. Boggs (*History of the Church,* 5:484-85). He was endowed
in the Nauvoo temple on December 15, 1845, and later came to Utah with Lorenzo
Snow's company of immigrants.

God might rest upon him continually, so that he may act according to the wisdom of heaven.[27]

—*History of the Church,* 5:46.

Wednesday, September 21, 1842
Joseph Smith's Red Brick Store

In the large room over the store.[28]

—Joseph Smith, Diary, in "Book of the Law of the Lord."

....

In the large room over the store.

—*History of the Church,* 5:165.

Monday, September 26, 1842
Joseph Smith's Red Brick Store

In the large room over the Store.[29]

—Joseph Smith, Diary, in "Book of the Law of the Lord."

---

27. "By July 1842," notes Ehat ("Introduction of Temple Ordinances," 53-54), "while the other members of the [Anointed] Quorum had accepted eternal and plural marriage, Hyrum Smith, William [Smith,] and William Marks had resisted Joseph Smith's effort to broach the subject with them. Their crusade against the embarrassing activities of [John C.] Bennett narrowed their perspective, and Joseph Smith soon learned that he should not try then to convert them. This helps explain why in the year after Joseph Smith first gave these endowment blessings to the Quorum he did not invite others to become members of the group, did not yet invite the wives of these men to receive these ordinances, and did not administer any of the more advanced ordinances. The reason Joseph Smith held back can only be understood by appreciating the indirect effect Bennett had on the Quorum. This story is the key to why the Quorum for a year remained on such a plateau."

28. This may or may not imply a meeting of the Quorum of the Anointed.

29. This may or may not imply a meeting of the Quorum of the Anointed.

II.

The Year

1843

"THE HIGHEST
AND HOLIEST ORDER"

Friday, May 26, 1843
Joseph Smith's Homestead

5 P.M. I [Joseph Smith] and Hiram [Smith] and Judge [James] Adams and Bishop [Newel K.] Whitney, B[righam] Young, H[eber] C. Kimball, W[illard] Richards, and W[illia]m Law in council in upper room receiving instructions on the priesthood, the new and everlasting covenant, &c. &c.[1] Adjourned to Sunday 5 P.M.

—Joseph Smith, Diary.

---

1. This apparently marks the date of Hyrum Smith's acceptance of the doctrines of eternal and plural marriage. (This entry also suggests that plural marriage was discussed—at least by the brethren—in meetings of the Quorum of the Anointed.) Hyrum had previously opposed his younger brother's teachings: "If an angel from heaven should come and preach such doctrine," he had told church members on May 14, 1843, "[you] would be sure to see his cloven foot and cloud of blackness over his head" (qtd. in Levi Richards, Diary, under date, LDS Archives). Brigham Young also recalled: "We had heard him [i.e., Joseph Smith] say hard things. I recollect in one counsel where Joseph undertook to teach the brethren and sisters, William Law was there, and William and Hyrum and a few others was met and assembled counseled together and they were against Joseph. William Law madethis expression, 'If an angel from heaven was to reveal to me that a man should have more than one wife, if it were in my power I would kill him'. That was pretty

5 P.M. I [Joseph Smith] & Hyrum [Smith] & Judge [James] Adams & Bishop [Newel K.] Whitney, B[righam]. Young. H[eber]. C. Kimball. W[illard]. Richards & W[illia]m Law, in Council in Upper room, receiving instructions on the priesthood, the new & everlasting covenant &c., &c., adjourned to Sunday, 5 P.M.

—"Meetings of Anointed Quorum."

President [Joseph Smith] in meeting with the Twelve [Apostles] and Judge [James] Adams. Hyrum [Smith] received the doctrine of priesthood.[2]

—William Clayton, Diary.

At five p.m. I [Joseph Smith] met in counsel in the upper room, with my brother Hyrum [Smith], Brigham Young, Heber C. Kimball, Willard Richards, Judge James Adams, Bishop Newel K. Whitney and William Law, and gave them their endowments and also instructions in the priesthood on the new and everlasting covenant, &c.

—*History of the Church,* 5:409.

P.M. Meeting Joseph [Smith.]

—Willard Richards, Diary.

Met with the Prophet Joseph [Smith], the Patriarch Hyrum [Smith], brothers [Heber C.] Kimball and [Willard] Richards, Judge James Adams, and Bishop N[ewel] K. Whitney, and William Law receiving our endow-

---

hard, but Joseph had to submit for it. The brethren were not prepared to receive the doctrine. Brother [Heber C.] Kimball and others were in that Counsel. Hyrum agreed with him, and they preached and talked and had meetings, and Joseph had meeting in his house time after time, and month after month every Sunday evening. Joseph was worn out with it, but as to his denying any such thing I never denied knew that he denied the doctrine of polygamy. Some have said that he did, but I do not believe he ever did" (Brigham Young, Sermon, 8 Oct. 1866, LDS Archives). According to Ehat ("Introduction to Temple Ordinances," 55): "Hyrum could not accept eternal marriage because he also had to accept plural marriage. Hyrum's first wife, Jerusha Barden, died in 1837. Later, when the doctrine of eternal marriage was first revealed to him, the fact that he had remarried created a stumbling block. As he subsequently explained, the doctrine of eternal marriage had imposed on him the demand to answer a plural marriage question: How can a man be married to two women in eternity?" (endnotes omitted).

2. The term "doctrine of the priesthood" was often employed by William Clayton as code for plural marriage. Clayton was a polygamist, but not yet a member of the Quorum of the Anointed; it is not clear if Hyrum Smith accepted plural marriage before, during, or after a meeting of the quorum.

ments and instructions in the Priesthood.[3] The Prophet Joseph administered to us the first ordinances of endowment, and gave us instructions on
the Priesthood and the new and everlasting covenant.[4]

—*Manuscript History of Brigham Young,* p. 129.

Sunday, May 28, 1843
Joseph Smith's Homestead

5 P.M. Adjourned council met in the upper room. Attended to ordinances and counselled and prayed that James Adams might be delivered
from his enemies, that O[rrin] P. Rockwell[5] [be released from prison in
Missouri], and [that] the Twelve [Apostles] be prospered in collecting
means to build the Nauvoo House. ^Joseph [Smith] and J[ames]. Adams
<were married>^[6] ~~Adjourned to 9 o'clock Monday Morning~~[.]

—Joseph Smith, Diary.

---

3. Brigham Young's published manuscript history does not note that William
Law was also present. By the time Brigham's history was being compiled, William
had come out in opposition to the church.

4. As Quinn (*Origins,* 494) observes, "Thus, Joseph Smith re-performed the
endowment ceremony he had originally given these same men a year ago. ... Smith
reconferred the endowment for two reasons. First, to prepare for the next day's sealing of marriages for time and eternity, which he explained to the men in attendance.
Second, because the Presiding Patriarch [Hyrum Smith] had stopped his opposition
to polygamous marriages."

5. Orrin Porter Rockwell (ca. 1813-78) was born in Belchertown, Hampshire
County, Massachusetts. He converted to Mormonism as a teenager with his family
in June 1830, just two months after the organization of the church. He helped in the
Mormon exodus from Missouri in 1839 and accompanied Joseph Smith to Washington, D.C., to seek redress for damages suffered by the Saints in Missouri. In 1842
he was charged and briefly imprisoned in the attempted assassination of former
Missouri governor Lilburn W. Boggs. After arriving in Salt Lake City in 1847, he
served as deputy marshal from 1849 until his death. He also fought in the Utah War
of 1857-58 in the Echo Canyon Campaign. He was never a member of the Quorum of the Anointed.

6. As used throughout this book, angled brackets < > indicate text originally
recorded in shorthand, carets ^ ^ text added interlinearly. Joseph and Emma Smith
were sealed for time and eternity on this date, as were James and Harriet Adams.
Their sealings were the first between living, civilly married couples. Quinn (*Origins,*
494) speculates that "because of his recent conversion to polygamy, Hyrum Smith
may have been the one who performed the sealing of Emma Hale Smith to Joseph
Smith for time and eternity on this date." Emma, too, had recently accepted her husband's teachings, personally participating in the resealing of sisters Emily and Eliza
Partridge as plural wives to Joseph Smith earlier in the month. (The young women

5 P.M. Adjourned Council met in the Upper Room—attended to Ordinances Counselled & prayed that James Adams might be delivered from his enemies & O[rrin]. P[orter]. Rockwell [be released from prison in Missouri] & the Twelve [Apostles] be prospered in collecting means to build the Nauvoo House. Joseph [Smith] & J[ames]. Adams. [blank]

—"Meetings of Anointed Quorum."

[A]t Br[other] Joseph Smith in councel with Br[other]s J[oseph]. Smith H[yrum] Smith H[eber]. C. Kimball N[ewel]. K. Whitney Judge [James] Adams & W[illard]. Richards.

—Brigham Young, Diary.

[A]t Joseph [Smith']s— upper Room[.]

—Willard Richards, Diary.

At five p.m. I [Joseph Smith] met with brother Hyrum [Smith], Brigham Young, Heber C. Kimball, Willard Richards, Newel K. Whitney, and James Adams,[7] in the upper room to attend to ordinances and coun-

---

had been sealed to Joseph the previous March without Emma's knowledge; the re-sealing was for Emma's benefit.) In recognition of her support, Emma was sealed to her husband for eternity on this date. "It is a well-known fact," explains Lyndon W. Cook, "that the Mormon leader [Joseph Smith] required all who were eternally married or sealed to accept the doctrine of 'spiritual wives' or plural marriage (either in fact or in theory) before an eternal sealing could be effected" (*William Law* [Orem, UT: Grandin Book, 1996], 27n84). Perhaps Harriet Adams had also acceded to her husband's decision to marry Roxena Repshire as a plural wife seven weeks later on July 11, 1843.

7. Ehat ("Introduction to Temple Ordinances," 74) speculates that William Law did not attend this and the next meeting of the Quorum of the Anointed because Joseph Smith had very recently informed him that he and his wife, Jane, could not be sealed for eternity, presumably because William would not accept plural marriage. William would attend subsequent meetings, and Jane, beginning in October 1843, would also participate as a member of the quorum. "[T]hese ordinances [i.e., sealings and the second anointing]," Ehat ("Introduction to Temple Ordinances," 74–75) writes, "were being administered to those who were at least willing to believe in the divinity of plural marriage. In the background of Joseph's introduction of the temple ordinance was the principle of plural marriage. True, the practice of plural marriage was never a prerequisite to receiving these, the highest ordinances of salvation; however, Joseph Smith believed that God told him to employ this principle as a means of testing the faith of those selected to receive these temple blessings. Acceptance of plural marriage was a demonstration that they would obey the actual laws that God taught were absolutely prerequisite to such blessings—the laws of obedience, sacrifice, and consecration. No higher sacrifice could be asked of those in that day" (endnotes omitted).

seling. Prayed that James Adams might be delivered from his enemies, and that Orrin P. Rockwell might be delivered from prison, and that the Twelve [Apostles] be prospered in collecting means to build the Nauvoo House ...

—*History of the Church,* 5:412.

....

I [Brigham Young] met with brothers Joseph [Smith], Hyrum [Smith], Heber [C. Kimball], Willard [Richards], Bishop [Newel K.] Whitney and Judge [James] Adams when we administered to brother Joseph the same ordinances of Endowment, and of the holy priesthood which he administered unto us.

—*Manuscript History of Brigham Young,* p. 129.

Monday, May 29, 1843
Joseph Smith's Homestead

9 A.M. Met pursuant to adjournment. ~~Joseph~~ Hyrum [Smith], Brigham [Young], Willard [Richards], and Sis[ter] [Mercy Rachel Fielding] Thompson <were married> and Heber and Newel K. [Whitney] present. Also Joseph [Smith] and James Adams.[8] Singing and prayer by Elder

---

8. This marks the eternal sealings of the following couples: Hyrum and Mary Smith, Brigham and Mary Ann Young, and Willard and Jennetta Richards. In addition, the following sealings were performed for the dead: Hyrum and Jerusha (deceased) Smith, with Mary Smith acting as proxy for Jerusha; Brigham and Miriam (deceased) Young, with Mary Ann Young as proxy for Miriam; and Mercy Rachel Fielding and Robert Thompson (deceased), Hyrum Smith as proxy for Robert. "Such a wedding I am quite sure [was] never witnessed before in this generation," remembered Mercy Rachel; "... perhaps some may think I could envy Queen Victoria in some of her glory. Not while my name stands first on the list in this Dispensation of women seal[e]d to a Dead Husband through devine Revelation" ("Reminiscence of Mercy Rachel Fielding Thompson," in Carol Cornwall Madsen, ed., *In Their Own Words: Women and the Story of Nauvoo* [Salt Lake City: Deseret Book, 1994], 195).

Hyrum Smith would marry his sister-in-law Mercy Rachel Fielding Thompson as a plural wife the following month. "On the 11 of August 1843," Mercy recalled in an untitled autobiographical sketch dated December 20, 1880, in LDS Archives, "I was called by direct revelation from Heaven through Brother Joseph the Prophet to enter into a state of Plural Marriage with Hyrum Smith the Patriarch. This subject when first communicated to me tried me to the very core of my former traditions and every natural feeling of my Heart rose in opposition to this Principle but I was convinced that it was appointed by him who is too wise to err and too good to be unkind. Soon after Marriage I became an inmate with my sister [Mary Fielding Smith] in the House of Hyrum Smith where I remained until his

Brigham Young. Conversation and instruction &c. teaching concerning the things of God. Had a pleasant interview.

—Joseph Smith, Diary.

9 A.M. Monday met pursuant to adjournment Hyrum [Smith], Brigham [Young], Willard [Richards], & Sis[ter]. [Mercy Rachel Fielding] Thompson [blank] & Heber [C. Kimball] & Newel K. [Whitney] present also Joseph [Smith] & James Adams. Singing & prayer by Elder Brigham Young. Conversation & instruction & teaching concerning the things of God, had a pleasant interview.

—"Meetings of Anointed Quorum."

At nine a.m., I [Joseph Smith] met in council with brother Hyrum [Smith], Brigham Young, Heber C. Kimball, Willard Richards, Newel K. Whitney, and James Adams.

Singing, and prayer by Elder Brigham Young. Conversation, instruction and teaching concerning the things of God. Had a pleasant interview.

—*History of the Church*, 5:412-13.

Met at 9 a.m., with the same brethren, when Joseph [Smith] instructed us further in principles pertaining to the holy Priesthood.

—*Manuscript History of Brigham Young*, p. 129.

Thursday–Friday, July 6–7, 1843
Location unknown; no details available.[9]

Sunday, August 27, 1843
Joseph Smith's Mansion House

Evening Joseph [Smith], W[illia]m Law,[10] W[illia]m Marks, Hyrum [Smith], N[ewel] K. Whitney, and Willard Richards were in Joseph's new

---

Death sharing with my sister the care of his numerous family[,] I had from the time I moved to his House acted as scribe Recording Patriarchal Blessings."

9. Quinn (*Origins*, 495) theorizes, based on "Meetings of Anointed Quorum," that the quorum may have met on these two days, although the entries for these two dates are otherwise blank.

10. "If Joseph [Smith] and William [Law] were at tremendous odds with one another," observes Ehat ("Introduction to Temple Ordinances," 95), "it was not manifest at this prayer circle."

house prayed that W[illia]m Law's father[11] might live and receive the gospel and our families believe and rejoice and be saved.

—Joseph Smith, Diary.

....

Meeting. at Joseph [Smith's] new home in the evening.

—Willard Richards, Diary.

....

In the evening I [Joseph Smith] attended council and prayer meeting with my brother Hyrum [Smith], Newel K. Whitney, Willard Richards, William Law and William Marks.

—*History of the Church*, 5:556.

Sunday, September 3, 1843
Joseph Smith's Mansion House

6 [o'clock] Eve[ning] Joseph [Smith], Hyrum [Smith], W[illiam]. Marks, N[ewel] K. Whitney, W[illia]m Law and [George] Miller in council at Joseph [Smith's house] prayed for Hiram['s] sick child[12] and Whitney's[13] &c. Much instruction from the President [Joseph Smith] on future things.

—Joseph Smith, Diary.

....

6 o Clock evening. Joseph [Smith], Hyrum [Smith], W[illiam] Marks, N[ewel]. K. Whitney, W[illia]m Law & Willard [Richards] in council at Joseph [Smith]'s prayed for Hyrum's sick child & Whitney's &c. much instruction from the President [Joseph Smith] on future things.

—"Meetings of Anointed Quorum."

....

I [Joseph Smith] attended council with my brother Hyrum [Smith], Newel K. Whitney, Willard Richards, William Law and William Marks, and gave instructions to the brethren in relation to things in futurity.[14]

—*History of the Church*, 6:2.

---

11. Richard Law, of Ireland, married Mary Wilson and immigrated to the United States with his family in 1818.

12. At the time, Hyrum Smith had five living children, three of whom were under the age of five. The child in question was either Mary Ann Smith (1841-1923), two years old, Joseph Fielding Smith (1838-1918), four, or Sarah Smith (1837-76), five.

13. Likely Don Carlos Whitney (1841-?), born in Nauvoo and two years old at the time.

14. Note that the *History of the Church* places William Marks's and William Law's

Joseph Smith's Mansion House, built in 1842 on the corner of Main Street and Water Street, was site to some twelve or more meetings of the Anointed Quorum the next year. These included the initiation of women beginning with Joseph Smith's wife, Emma Hale Smith. The Mansion House also served as Joseph's and Emma's residence, a hotel, and a public meeting hall. Photograph ca. 1885.

Monday, September 11, 1843
Joseph Smith's Mansion House

6 P.M. Joseph [Smith], Hyrum [Smith], W[illia]m Law, N[ewel] K. Whitney and Willard [Richards] had a season of prayer in Joseph's east room New House for [William] Laws little daughter who was sick and Emma [Smith] who was some better.
—Joseph Smith, Diary.

6 P.M. Joseph [Smith], Hyrum [Smith], W[illiam] Law, N[ewel]. K. Whitney & Willard [Richards] had a season of prayer in Joseph's Court Room New House for [William] Law's little daughter who was sick & Emma [Smith] who was some better. —"Meetings of Anointed Quorum."

6 P.M. prarer of the quorum for [William] Laws Daughter.
—Willard Richards, Diary.

Six, p.m., I [Joseph Smith] met with my Brother Hyrum [Smith], William Law, Newel K. Whitney, and Willard Richards in my private room, where we had a season of prayer for Brother [William] Law's little daughter, who was sick, and Emma [Smith], who was somewhat better.
—*History of the Church,* 6:31.

Thursday, September 28, 1843
Joseph Smith's Red Brick Store/Mansion House

11½ A.M. Council over the store. Hyrum [Smith], Newell [K. Whitney], Geo[rge] M[iller]., Wa<she>d. and An<oi>nt<e>d and J[ohn] S[mith], J[ohn] T[aylor], A[masa] L[yman], L[ucien] W[oodworth], J[ohn] M. B[ernhisel] an[oin]t[ed].

At 7 eve[ning] met at the Mansion's upper room front with W[illiam] L[aw] [and] W[illiam] M[arks]. Beurach Ale [code for Joseph Smith] was by common consent and unanimous voice chosen President of the quorum and anointed and ord[ained] to the highest and holiest order of the priesthood (and companion [Emma Hale Smith])[15] Joseph Smith, Hyrum

names after the other members of the Quorum of the Anointed. By the time the *History of the Church* was being compiled, both men had left the church.

15. Joseph and Emma Smith received the second anointing; presumably on this same day, if not earlier, Emma was also initiated into the quorum and received her endowments as the first woman to enter the quorum. According to Heber C.

Smith, Geo[rge] Miller, N[ewel] K. Whitney, Willard Richards, John Smith, John Taylor, Amasa Lyman, Lucien Woodworth, J[ohn] M. Bernhisel, W[illia]m Law, W[illia]m Marks. President [Joseph Smith] led in prayer that his days might be prolonged, have dominion over his enemies, all the households be blessed and all the church and world.[16]

—Joseph Smith, Diary.

11½ A.M. Council over the Store Hyrum [Smith], Newell [K. Whitney], Geo[rge]. M[iller]., Willard [Richards], J[ohn] S[mith], J[ohn]. T[aylor]., A[masa]. L[yman], L[ucien]. W[oodworth], J[ohn] M. B[ernhisel] at 7 evening we met at the Mansion Upper Room Front with W[illiam] L[aw]. W[illiam] M[arks]. Baurak Ale [Joseph Smith] was by common consent & unanimous voice chosen president of the Quorum & anointed & ordained to the highest & holiest order of the priesthood (& Companion) D[itt]o

Joseph Smith, Hyrum Smith, Geo. Miller, N[ewel]. K. Whitney Willard Richards, John Smith, John Taylor, Amasa Lyman Lucien Woodworth, J[ohn]. M. Bernhisel, W[illiam]m Law, W[illiam]m Marks. President led in prayer that his days might be prolonged have dominion over his enemies, all their households be blessed & all the church & world.

—"Meetings of Anointed Quorum."

The Council met over the store Also at 7 oclock in the Evening met in an upper Room in the mansion, there were present Joseph Smith Hyram Smith, George Miller N[ewel]. K. Whitney, Willard Richard[s] John Smith John Taylor, Amasa Lyman, Lucian Woodworth, J[ohn] M

Kimball, speaking two years later: "Females were not received when we first received the Holy order—Men apostatized, being led by their wives—if any such cases occur again—no more women will be admitted" (William Clayton, Diary, kept for Heber C. Kimball, entry dated December 21, 1843).

16. "[T]his was the occasion," writes Ehat ("Introduction to Temple Ordinances," 95-96), "when for the first time in the history of the Church the fulness of the priesthood was conferred. These ordinances, depending on the person's ecclesiastical position, made the recipient a 'king and priest,' 'in,' 'in and over,' or (as only in Joseph Smith's case) 'over' the Church. Moreover, the recipient had sealed upon him the power to bind and loose on earth as Joseph explained in his definition of the fulness of the priesthood. Another blessing, growing out of the promise of the sealing power was the specific blessing that whatever thing was desired[,] it would not be withheld when sought for in diligent prayer. ... Combined in one ordinance, all these blessings (as Joseph Smith from the earliest stages of his ministry taught) were the highest powers available to mortals."

Bernhisel W[illia]m Law, W[illia]m Marks, Joseph Smith led in prayer he prayed that his days might be lengthened out & have dominion over his Enemies, and all thare Households be blessed & all the Church Than by common Consent *Joseph Smith the Prophet* received *his second* Anointing of the Highest & Holiest order.

—Wilford Woodruff, Historian's Private Journal, entry dated 26 February 1867, LDS Archives.[17]

Meeting. Council of [holy] order.

—Willard Richards, Diary.

At 11 W[illiam] Walker came and said President Joseph [Smith] wanted me to go to Macedonia [Illinois]. I went immediately to see him and he requested me to go with him. ... After we had got on the road he began to tell me that E[mma] [Smith] was turned quite friendly and kind. She had been anointed and he also had been a[nointed] K[ing].

—William Clayton, Diary, entry dated October 19, 1843.

At half-past eleven, a.m., a council convened over the store, consisting of myself [Joseph Smith], my brother Hyrum [Smith], Uncle John Smith, Newel K. Whitney, George Miller, Willard Richards, John Taylor, Amasa Lyman, John M. Bernhisel, and Lucien Woodworth; and at seven in the evening we met in the front upper room of the Mansion, with William Law and William Marks. By the common consent and unanimous voice of the council I was chosen president of the special council.

The president [Joseph Smith] led in prayer that his days might be prolonged until his mission on the earth is accomplished, have dominion over his enemies, all their households be blessed, and all the Church and the world.

—*History of the Church,* 6:39.

Sunday, October 1, 1843
Joseph Smith's Mansion House

Eve[ning] Council met same as Thursday previous except [Jane] Law,

---

17. This entry is preceded by the notation: "While reading Dr [Willard] Richards Journal we Found the Account of the Second Anointing of President Joseph Smith, & By the Council of G[eorge]. A. Smith His[toria]n[.] I [Wilford Woodruff] record the Account in this Journal." It is not clear what source Wilford Woodruff consulted in copying this account of Joseph Smith's second anointing.

[Rosannah] Marks, [Elizabeth] Durphy, Hiram's wife [Mary],[18] Joseph [Smith] &c. reanointed. [William] Law[19] &c. anointed counselors. Prayer and singing. Adjourned to Wednesday eve[ning].

—Joseph Smith, Diary.

....

Evening. Council met, same as Thursday previous[.]

Joseph [Smith] reanointed [William] Law & anointed Councillors. prayer & singing. Adj[ourned] to Wednesday even[in]g.

—"Meetings of Anointed Quorum."

....

Council met in the evening same as on Thursday previous.

—*History of the Church,* 6:41.

Wednesday, October 4, 1843
Joseph Smith's Mansion House

Council of the quorum adjourned to Sunday eve[ning], Hiram's child being sick.[20]

—Joseph Smith, Diary.

....

Council of the quorum [special council, see p. 39][21] met and ad-

---

18. Ehat ("Introduction to Temple Ordinances," 119) suggests that these women, the next female members of the Quorum of the Anointed after Emma Smith, were washed and anointed by Emma prior to this meeting.

19. Ehat ("Introduction to Temple Ordinances," 119) speculates that Joseph Smith anointed William Law and Amasa Lyman as his first and second counselors in the First Presidency. Quinn (*Origins,* 496) asserts that Joseph reanointed William Law a member of the Quorum of the Anointed "due to Law's confession of adultery committed since his 1842 endowment." (This problematic allegation is discussed in Cook, *William Law,* 25-27 and notes.) Quinn continues that "Smith also anointed Law as first counselor and Amasa M. Lyman as second counselor in anticipation of dropping the unendowed Sidney Rigdon as first counselor at the upcoming general conference. These priesthood ordinances were not otherwise announced or repeated." It is possible that William was reanointed because he had not been present on May 28, 1843, when all of the other founding members of the quorum were reanointed.

20. See note 12 for the child's possible identification. Ehat ("Introduction to Temple Ordinances," 120) believes that Hyrum Smith was to have received the second anointing on this date, but because of his child's illness was unable to attend the meeting.

21. This is B. H. Roberts's bracketed editorial notation in his edition of the *History of the Church.*

journed to Sunday evening; my [Joseph Smith's] Brother Hyrum [Smith]'s child being sick.

—*History of the Church,* 6:45.

Sunday, October 8, 1843
Joseph Smith's Mansion House

Prayer Meeting at Joseph [Smith]'s. Quorum present also in addition Sis[ters] [Harriet] Adams, [Elizabeth Ann] Whitney,[22] Uncle John's wife [Clarissa Smith], Mother [Lucy Mack] Smith. Hiram and his wife [Mary] were blessed, ord[ained], and anointed.[23] Prayer and singing.

—Joseph Smith, Diary.

....

Prayer Meeting at Joseph [Smith]'s.

—"Meetings of Anointed Quorum."

....

Prayer-meeting at my [Joseph Smith's] house in the evening. Quorum present; also, in addition, Sisters [Harriet] Adams, Elizabeth Ann Whitney, my aunt Clarissa Smith, and my mother [Lucy Mack Smith].

My brother Hyrum [Smith] and his wife [Mary] were blessed, ordained and anointed.

—*History of the Church,* 6:46.

Thursday, October 12, 1843
Joseph Smith's Mansion House

Eve[ning] prayer Meeting at Joseph [Smith]'s. Prayed for W[illia]m Marks sick. A[masa] Lyman John Taylor absent. [Alpheus] Cutler and [Reynolds] Cahoon present.

—Joseph Smith, Diary.

....

Evening—Prayer Meeting at Joseph [Smith]s—prayed for W[illia]m Marks sick. A[masa]. Lyman John Taylor absent. [Alpheus] Cutler & [Reynolds] Cahoon present.

—"Meetings of Anointed Quorum."

---

22. Harriet Adams and Elizabeth Ann Whitney had already been sealed to their husbands for eternity. The previous year, Elizabeth Ann and Newel K. Whitney had given their daughter, Sarah Ann, to Joseph Smith as a plural wife.

23. This would have been a second anointing.

Prayer-meeting in my room. We prayed for William Marks, who was sick.

—*History of the Church,* 6:54.

Sunday, October 22, 1843
Joseph Smith's Mansion House

Prayer meeting at Mansion [at] 2 P.M. W[illia]m Marks and <wife [Rosannah] anointed>[24] 24 present.

—Joseph Smith, Diary.

....

[P]rayer Meeting at Mansion [at] 2 P.M. W[illia]m Marks & Wife [Rosannah] anointed—24 present[.]

—"Meetings of Anointed Quorum."

....

[F]ound my famely pirty well[.] Br[other] J[oseph]. Smith feels well was glad to see us went in to counsel with the Bretheren in the afternoon[.][25]

—Brigham Young, Diary.

....

I [Joseph Smith] remained at home all day, and held a prayer-meeting at my house at two, p.m.; twenty-four persons present.

—*History of the Church,* 6:60.

....

[A]rrived on the 22nd, and went into council with Joseph [Smith], Hyrum [Smith] and others, when ordinances were administered to William Marks and wife [Rosannah].

—*Manuscript History of Brigham Young,* p. 154.

....

Mr. [William] Marks then told me ... he (Marks) was ordained to the same office ["prophet, priest, and king"] under the hands of Joseph Smith.

—Samuel James, Letter to Sidney Rigdon, dated January 28, 1845, in *Latter Day Saints' Messenger and Advocate* 1 (March 1, 1845): 130.

Friday, October 27, 1843
Joseph Smith's Mansion House

---

24. A second anointing.
25. Brigham Young, and other members of the Quorum of the Twelve Apostles, had just returned home that day from a mission to the East.

30

Prayer Meeting in the evening at Joseph [Smith's]. Bis[hop] [Newel K.] Whitney and <wife [Elizabeth Ann] anointed>.[26] Hiram [Smith] ^said his voice should be heard in the streets.^ Joseph spoke and [Reynolds] Cahoon.

—Joseph Smith, Diary.

....

Prayer Meeting in the Evening at Joseph [Smith]'s, Bishop [Newel K.] Whitney & Wife [Elizabeth Ann] anointed. Hyrum [Smith] said his voice sho[ul]d. be heard in the Streets. Joseph spoke and [Reynolds] Cahoon.

—"Meetings of Anointed Quorum."

....

Prayer-meeting at my [Joseph Smith's] house in the evening.

—*History of the Church,* 6:61.

....

I [Brigham Young] attended prayer-meeting in the evening at President Joseph Smith's. Bishop N[ewel]. K. Whitney and [Elizabeth Ann] wife were anointed.

—*Manuscript History of Brigham Young,* entry dated November 27, 1843.

Sunday, October 29, 1843
Joseph Smith's Mansion House

2 P.M. or near 4 [P.M.], before all were ready prayer meeting at the mansion. 25 present Sis[ters] [Lois] Cutler, [Thirza] Cahoon, [Phoebe] Woodworth. Adjourned Wednesday over Brick store. Joseph [Smith] taught.

—Joseph Smith, Diary.

....

2 P.M. or near 4 before all were ready. Prayer Meet[in]g. at the Mansion 25 present, Sister[s] [Lois] Cutler, [Thirza] Cahoon, [Phoebe] Woodworth. adj[ourne]d. to Wednesday even[in]g.

—"Meetings of Anointed Quorum."

....

[S]isters [Thirza] cahoon [Lois] Cutler & [Phoebe] woodworth was taken in to the order of the Priesthood[.]

—Brigham Young, Diary.

---

26. A second anointing.

Two, p.m., prayer-meeting in my [Joseph Smith's] house; twenty-five present. I gave instructions on the priesthood.

—*History of the Church,* 6:62.

Wednesday, November 1, 1843
Joseph Smith's Mansion House

Eve[ning]. Prayer Meeting of Mansion. 29 present. (Sister[s] [Mercy R.] Fielding,[27] [Jennetta] Richards, [Leonora] Taylor, [Mary Ann] Young, [Vilate] Kimball <anointed> &c.

—Joseph Smith, Diary.

Evening Prayer Meeting at Mansion. 29 present. Sist[ers] [Mercy R.] Fielding, [Jennetta] Richards, [Leonora] Taylor, [Mary Ann] Young, [Vilate] Kimball, anointed, &c.

—"Meetings of Anointed Quorum."

Mary A. young admited in to the p[r]iest orderer Priesthood[.][28]

—Brigham Young, Diary.

My wife Vilate and menny feemales was recieved in to the Holy Order, and was washed and inointed [anointed] by Emma [Smith].

—Heber C. Kimball, Diary, following entry dated October 19, 1843.

[M]eeting eve[ning,] prepared for meeting in the Hall. but went [to the] Mansion.

—Willard Richards, Diary.

In the evening there was a prayer-meeting in the mansion; twenty-nine present.

—*History of the Church,* 6:62.

I received my endowments by the direction of the Prophet Joseph

---

27. Mercy Rachel Fielding Thompson had married Hyrum Smith as his plural wife on August 11, 1843.

28. Brigham Young also recorded in his diary on this date an eight/nine-line entry, which was later erased. However, from subsequent statements, he may have noted his plural marriages to Harriet Cook and August Adams Cobb, both performed by Joseph Smith. (Appreciation to D. Michael Quinn for pointing this out.)

[Smith], his wife Emma [Smith] officiating in my case.

> —Mercy Fielding Thompson, in "Recollections of the Prophet Joseph Smith," *Juvenile Instructor* 27 (July 1, 1892): 400.

Q[uestion]:— Now you did not take any obligation did you Mrs. [Mercy R.] Thompson, not to say at any time whether you changed your clothing or not [in receiving the endowment]? [Answer:—] No sir, but at the same time I do feel that I would be able to answer that question.

Q:— Well did you change your clothing in the taking of the endowments? A:— Yes sir.

Q:— You did? A:— Yes sir, we did.

Q:— And you did yourself? A:— Yes sir.

Q:— How many rooms were in the building? A:— There was always two rooms.

Q:— There was always two rooms? A:— Yes sir, no I was mistaken about that, there was always three rooms I think. Yes it was three rooms.

Q:— Two of them were ante rooms, and the other one was the main room where the ceremonies were conducted? A:— Yes sir.

Q:— There was a place in one of the ante rooms where you were washed and a[n]ointed with oil? A:— Yes sir.

Q:— Did they anoint the whole body with oil, or just the head? A:— Well now there it is, you are asking these questions and I have answered them as far as I can, but these are questions, or that is a question that I do not feel that I am called on to answer.

> —Mercy R. Thompson, Testimony, in "Respondent's Testimony, Temple Lot Case," 1892, pp. 279-80, Library/Archives, Community of Christ, Independence, Missouri.

Thursday, November 2, 1843
Location unknown

Joseph [Smith], Hyrum [Smith], [Brigham] Young, [Heber C.] Kimball, [John] Taylor, and [William] Clayton had council at 10.[29] Agreed to write a letter to the 5 Candidates for the [U.S.] Presidency to enquire

---

29. Quinn (*Origins,* 497) feels this was a "prayer circle ... despite the fact that [William Clayton] was not yet endowed." It could also have been a meeting of ranking church leaders with Clayton acting as scribe.

what their feeling[s] were or what their course would be towards the Saints if they were elected.

—Joseph Smith, Diary.

....

Joseph [Smith], Hyrum [Smith], [Brigham] Young, [Heber C.] Kimball, [John] Taylor, & [William] Clayton had council at 10 agreed to write a letter to the 5 candidates for the [U.S.] Presidency to enquire what their feelings were, or what their course would be towards the Saints if they were elected.

—"Meetings of Anointed Quorum."

....

Sitting in council with Hyrum [Smith], Brigham Young, Heber C. Kimball, Willard Richards, John Taylor, William Law, and William Clayton, at ten, a.m., on the subject of the following letter from Joseph L. Heywood[30]:— ...

We agreed to write a letter to the five candidates for the Presidency of the United States, to inquire what their feelings were towards us as a people, and what their course of action would be in relation to the cruelty and oppression that we have suffered from the State of Missouri, if they were elected.

—*History of the Church,* 6:62-63.

Sunday, November 5, 1843
Joseph Smith's Red Brick Store

Prayer Meeting eve[ning] at the Hall over the store. <Joseph [Smith] did not dress nor Emma [Smith]>[.][31]

—Joseph Smith, Diary.

....

[P]repared room & had meet— in Hall[.]

—Willard Richards, Diary.

....

In the evening a prayer-meeting in the hall over the store.

—*History of the Church,* 6:65.

---

30. Joseph Leyland Heywood (1815-1910) was baptized in 1842 and later helped to dispose of the church's property in Nauvoo at the time of the Saints' exodus west in 1846. He remained in Nauvoo until 1848 and arrived in Salt Lake City that fall. In 1849 he was appointed acting postmaster of Salt Lake City.

31. Quinn speculates (*Origins,* 497) that Joseph and Emma Smith did not dress in the endowment robes "due to his assumption that he [Joseph Smith] had been poisoned at dinner earlier in the day ..."

Wednesday, November 8, 1843

Joseph Smith's Red Brick Store

(Prayer Meeting in eve[ning] over store. Joseph [Smith] not present.)
—Joseph Smith, Diary.

....

Prayer Meeting in Evening over Store Joseph [Smith] not present.
—"Meetings of Anointed Quorum."

....

Prayer metting eve[ning].
—Willard Richards, Diary.

Sunday, November 12, 1843

Joseph Smith's Homestead

Prayer Meeting in the evening at S[outh] E[ast] Room [of] Jos[eph Smith's] old house. R[eynolds] Cahoon and <wife [Thirza] anointed and Mother [Lucy Mack] Smith>.[32]
—Joseph Smith, Diary.

....

Prayer Meet[ing] in the even[in]g. at S[outh]. E[ast]. Room, Joseph [Smith]'s old house. R[eynolds]. Cahoon & Wife [Thirza] anointed.
—"Meetings of Anointed Quorum."

....

[P]rayer Meeting at J[oseph Smith's]. old house.
—Willard Richards, Diary.

....

Prayer-meeting in the evening, in the south-east room of my [Joseph Smith's] old house.
—*History of the Church*, 6:71.

Wednesday, November 15, 1843

Joseph Smith's Homestead

Prayer Meeting at the old house. A[lpheus]. Cutler and <wife [Lois]

---

32. Reynolds and Thirza Cahoon and apparently Lucy Mack Smith received their second anointings. Lucy's deceased husband may have been anointed by proxy (Quinn, *Origins*, 497).

anointed>.[33] Spoke of Proclamation to the kings.[34] Letter to [James A.] Bennet[35] and Petition to Congress[36] &c.

—Joseph Smith, Diary.

Prayer Meet[in]g at the old house. A[lpheus]. Cutler & Wife [Lois] anointed. Spoke of Proclamation to the Kings. Letter to [James A.] Bennet. Petition to Congress, &c.

—"Meetings of Anointed Quorum," entry dated November 14, 1843.

[P]rayer meeting[.]

—Willard Richards, Diary.

Prayer-meeting at the old house, I [Joseph Smith] spoke of a petition to Congress, my letter to [James A.] Bennett, and intention to write a proclamation to the kings of the earth.

—*History of the Church*, 6:79.

---

33. A second anointing.

34. The idea for this public declaration came first in a revelation dated January 19, 1841: "Let him [Sidney Rigdon] assist my servant Joseph, and also let my servant William Law assist my servant Joseph, in making a solemn proclamation unto the kings of the earth, even as I have before said unto you" (D&C 124:107). Six days after the above-mentioned meeting of the quorum, Joseph Smith assigned Willard Richards, Orson Hyde, John Taylor, and William W. Phelps to compose such a proclamation (*History of the Church*, 6:80). Joseph's later "Appeal to the Green Mountain Boys" was similar in spirit. However, after Joseph's death, Parley P. Pratt (on behalf of the Twelve Apostles) wrote the kind of proclamation Joseph's revelation originally proposed. In October 1845, in Liverpool, England, Wilford Woodruff oversaw the printing of 20,000 copies of Pratt's *A Proclamation of the Twelve Apostles of the Church of Jesus Christ of Latter-day Saints To All the Kings of the World; To the President of the United States of America; To the Governors of the Several States and to the Rulers and Peoples of all Nations.*

35. James Arlington Bennett (1788-1865) was a lawyer who joined the Latter-day Saints in 1843. Previous to his conversion, he had been appointed inspector-general of the Nauvoo Legion in 1842. In 1844 he was Joseph Smith's first choice as vice-presidential running mate in the upcoming U.S. election, but declined to run. He left the church soon after Joseph's death.

36. By this time, the Latter-day Saints had sent two petitions to Congress in an attempt to seek redress for the wrongs committed against them in Missouri. A third would follow. The first, submitted in 1839-40, consisted of hundreds of affidavits and a twenty-eight-page memorial signed by Joseph Smith, Sidney Rigdon, and Elias Higbee. The petition was rejected by the U.S. Senate Judiciary Committee in March 1840. A second attempt was made and subsequently rejected by Congress in 1842. A third attempt in 1844 met with the same results.

Sunday, November 19, 1843
Joseph Smith's Homestead

11 A.M. to 2 P.M. Prayer and fasting at the old house. Prayer meeting in the eve[ning] breaking bread[37] &c.
—Joseph Smith, Diary.

....

[F]asting & prayer in the quorum. &c eve[ning] Prayer[.]
—Willard Richards, Diary.

....

Eleven a.m. to two p.m., prayer-meeting at the old house, and fasting. In the evening, prayer-meeting and breaking of bread, &c.
—*History of the Church,* 6:79.

Wednesday, November 22, 1843
Joseph Smith's Homestead

Prayer Meeting in the eve[ning] at old house. B[righam] Young <anointed and wife [Mary Ann]>[38] &c.
—Joseph Smith, Diary.

....

Prayer Meet[in]g. in even[in]g at old house. B[righam] Young ~~anoint-ed~~ <anointed and wife [Mary Ann]>[.]
—"Meetings of Anointed Quorum."

....

Prayer Metting[.]
—Willard Richards, Diary.

....

Prayer-meeting in the evening at the old house.
—*History of the Church,* 6:80.

....

Mr. [William] Marks then told me he was present when the twelve were ordained, and Brigham Young was ordained under Hyrum Smith, to the office of prophet, priest, and king, and Brigham Young ordained the

37. This refers to the eucharist—blessing and partaking of bread and wine in remembrance of Jesus Christ—as adopted by Joseph Smith in 1830.

38. This was their second anointing. Quinn (*Origins,* 497) notes: "Later statements by Young, Heber C. Kimball, and George A. Smith ... claim Young's second anointing was on 14 Jan. 1844, which indicates that this ceremony was performed again on Young's behalf the day before the other apostles began receiving the second anointing."

rest of the twelve [apostles] to the same office.

—Samuel James, Letter to Sidney Rigdon, dated January 28,
1845, in *Latter Day Saints' Messenger and Advocate* 1 (March 1,
1845): 129-30.

....

Pres[iden]t. [George A.] Smith, on rising ... alluded to councils which had been held in Nauvoo [Illinois], and to the fact of the Prophet Joseph [Smith] calling the Twelve together, and, at a meeting called for that purpose, of Joseph and Hyrum [Smith] the Patriarch administering to Brigham Young, then President of the Twelve Apostles, what is known as the Second Anointing, and instructing him to administer in like manner to his brethren of the Twelve, which he did to the nine of the Twelve who were then at home. He stated that the Twelve were then instructed to administer in the ordinances of the Gospel for the dead, beginning with baptism and the laying on of hands. This work was at once commenced. It soon became apparent that some had long records of their dead, for whom they wished to administer. This was seen to be but the beginning of an immense work, and that to administer all the ordinances of the Gospel to the hosts of the dead was no light task. The Twelve asked Joseph if there could not be some shorter method of administering for so many. Joseph in effect replied—"The laws of the Lord are immutable, we must act in perfect compliance with what is revealed to us. We need not expect to do this vast work for the dead in a short time. I expect it will take at least a thousand years."

Brother George A. Smith, in the foregoing recital incidentally remarked that Elder Sidney Rigdon had never received the Second Anointing, nor the keys pertaining to baptism for the dead.

—George A. Smith, Discourse, December 25, 1874, recorded by
James G. Bleak, clerk and historian of the Southern Mission, in
the "St. George [Utah] Stake Historical Record," 3:28, LDS
Archives; subsequently published in *Latter-day Saints'*
Millennial Star 37 (February 2, 1975): 66-67.

Saturday, December 2, 1843

Joseph Smith's Red Brick Store

Prayer Meeting at the assembly room (room over the store). P[arley] P. Pratt, O[rson] Hyde, W[ilford] Woodruff, Geo[rge] A. Smith, O[rson] Spencer ^were anointed preparatory^ and A[lpheus]. Cutler and [Reynolds] Cahoon were all present at the meeting which continued from 1 to 5 P.M. About 35 present. Adjourned to 10 next morning.

—Joseph Smith, Diary.

Received into the Quorum Orson Hyde P[arley]. P. Pratt W[ilford]. Woodruff G[eorge]. A. Smith Orson Spencer Runald [Reynolds] Cahoon Thades [Alpheus] Cutlar[.]

—Brigham Young, Diary.

I [Wilford Woodruff] felt quite unwell yet I met with the quorum & conversed upon a variety of subjects among which were the progress of the work of God & the emegration of the Saints. The light blessings & glory that awaiteth Zion & the blessings that approach those who keep the Law of God. Truth & Virtue will bring exhaltation to the soul in the security of knowledge while Bigotry & superstition will Join vice in debasing man in ignorance untill he degrages humanity & looses the obje[c]t for which he was created. ^P[arley] P. Pratt Orson Hyde W[ilford] Woodruff G[eorge] A Smith & O[rson] Spencer all of us received our Anointing preperitory for further Blessings from 1 oclk to 6 PM.^[39]

—Wilford Woodruff, Diary.

Prayer-meeting from one to six p.m., in the assembly room over the store. Orson Hyde, Parley P. Pratt, Wilford Woodruff, George A. Smith, and Orson Spencer received their endowments and further instructions in the Priesthood. About thirty-five persons present.

—*History of the Church*, 6:98.

Met in the Assembly Room with Joseph [Smith], Hyrum [Smith] and the Twelve [Apostles], when the ordinances of endowment were administered to Elders Orson Hyde, Parley P. Pratt, W[ilford]. Woodruff,

---

39. Three weeks earlier, on November 11, 1843, Wilford and Phebe Woodruff were sealed for eternity: "During the evening I walked over to Br[other] [John] Taylors & spent some time in conversing about the principle of the Celestial world or some of them. Br[other] Hiram Smith was in with us & presented som ideas of much interest to me concerning Baptism for the dead, the resurrection redemption & exhaltation in the New & everlastig covenant [i.e., plural marriage] that reacheth into the eternal world. He sealed the marrige covenant between me & my wife Phebe W Carter for time & eternity & gave us the principle of it which was interessting to us. After spending the evening pleasantly we returned home & spent the night" (Wilford Woodruff, Journal, under date).

Geo[rge]. A. Smith and Orson Spencer. We received instructions on the Priesthood from Joseph.

—*Manuscript History of Brigham Young,* pp. 155-56.

Sunday, December 3, 1843

Joseph Smith's Red Brick Store

I [Joseph Smith] arrived at the assembly room about 12 noon. Found all present, except Hyrum [Smith] and his wife [Mary?]. He had slipped and turned his knee joint in backwards and sprained his large muscle, and I had been ministering to him, and Emma [Smith] had been unwell during the night. Meeting organized. W[illiam] W. Phelps read Appeal to "Green Mountain Boys"[40] which was dedicated by prayer after all had spoken upon it and prayed for Nathan Pratt,[41] who was very sick. Hyrum and others.[42]

—Joseph Smith, Diary.

....

I [Joseph Smith] arrived at the Assembly Room about 12 noon, found all present except Hyrum [Smith] & his Wife [Mary?], he had slipped & turned his knee joint in backwards & sprained his large muscel & I had been ministering to him, & Emma [Smith] had been unwell during the night. Meeting organized. W[illiam] W Phelps read "Appeal to Green Mountain Boys" which was dedicated by prayer after all had spoken upon it prayer for Nathan Pratt who was very sick, Hyrum & others.

—"Meetings of Anointed Quorum."

....

[H]ad a meeting in the upper room[.] Br[other] [William W.] Phelps read Joseph [Smith's] a Peal to the g[r]eene mountn Boys[.]

—Brigham Young, Diary.

---

40 The Green Mountain Boys were vigilantes from Vermont, originally led by Ethan Allen in the eighteenth century. They had used threats, intimidation, and violence to suppress land grants in New York. In the Revolutionary War, they captured Fort Ticonderoga from the British. As a Vermont native, Joseph Smith appealed to this group to use "all honorable means help to bring Missouri to the bar of justice." The appeal was printed and circulated.

41. Nathan Pratt (1838-43) was the five-year-old son of Parley P. and Mary Ann Frost Pratt. He died nine days after the above-mentioned prayer in his behalf.

42. "Instead of ordinances," observes Quinn (*Origins,* 497), "this was a political meeting ..."

I met with the quorum & herd an address deliverd by President Joseph Smith. The fore part of the day was taken up on the appeal to the green mountain boys. It was read by W[illiam] W Phelps & consecrated & [was] dedicated unto God by the quorum. The latter part of the day was taken up by instructions from President [Joseph] Smith & remarks from others. President Hiram Smith injured his leg by a fall. I was quite unwell. We were both prayed for I received a blessing.

—Wilford Woodruff, Diary.

....

I [Joseph Smith] arrived at the assembly room about noon: found all present, except Hyrum [Smith] and his wife [Mary]. He had slipped and turned his knee-joint backward, and sprained the large muscle of his leg, and I had been ministering unto him. Emma [Smith] had been unwell during the night. After the meeting was organized, William W. Phelps read my "Appeal to the Green Mountain Boys," which was dedicated by prayer after all had spoken upon it. We also prayed for Nathan Pratt, who was very sick, Hyrum, and others. I afterwards instructed them in the things of the Priesthood.

—*History of the Church*, 6:98-99.

....

Met in the Assembly Room and received instructions from Joseph [Smith]. His appeal to the Green Mountain Boys was read and dedicated by prayer.

—*Manuscript History of Brigham Young*, p. 156.

Saturday, December 9, 1843
Joseph Smith's Red Brick Store

Prayer Meeting over the store. W[illia]m W. Phelps, L[evi] Richards, [Cornelius P.] Lot, and Joseph Fielding.

—Joseph Smith, Diary.

....

Prayer meet[in]g over Store, W[illiam]. W. Phelps L[evi]. Richards, [Cornelius P.] Lott & Joseph Fielding.

—"Meetings of Anointed Quorum."

....

We met in counsel at the store with the quorum. Elders W[illiam] W Phelps Levi Richards & C[ornelius] Lott met with us. ^& received their Anointing.^

—Wilford Woodruff, Diary.

Some also beside the 12 [apostles] had received their Endowment, which was expected at the completion of the [Nauvoo] Temple[.] I myself [Joseph Fielding] and my Wife [Hannah] had had this Privilege granted us in part ... it is necessary that they [who are dead] as well as we who are now alive should be made acquainted with the Ordinances, Signs and Tokens of the Priesthood and the Terms of Admission into the Kingdom in Order that they may come forth with those who have received it here.
—Joseph Fielding, Diary, entry dated June 1844, LDS Archives.

....

Prayer-meeting in the assembly room.
—*History of the Church,* 6:107.

....

Met with the Quorum in the Assembly Room. Elders W[illiam]. W. Phelps, Levi Richards and C[ornelius]. P. Lott received ordinances.
—*Manuscript History of Brigham Young,* p. 156.

Sunday, December 10, 1843
Joseph Smith's Red Brick Store

Eve[ning] prayer Meeting over the store. Joseph [Smith] not present.
—Joseph Smith, Diary.

....

Evening Prayer Meeting over the Store, Joseph [Smith] not present[.]
—"Meetings of Anointed Quorum."

....

In the evening I met with the quorum. Br[other] Joseph [Smith] was not present. B[righam] Young was Called to the Chair[43] who addressed the meeting in a vary feeling manner & interesting to our minds. He reasoned Clearly that we should follow our file leader & our Savior in all his law & commandments without asking any questions why they were so. He was followed by P[arley]. P. Pratt & others who expressed their minds freely. Several sick were Prayed for.
—Wilford Woodruff, Diary.

....

[A]ttended meeting ove[r] Store eve[ning.]
—Willard Richards, Diary.

---

43. This may mark the first time Brigham Young presided at a meeting of the Quorum of the Anointed, although he may have presided at a November 8, 1843, meeting in Joseph Smith's absence.

A prayer-meeting held this evening in the assembly room. I [Joseph Smith] was not present. Brigham Young presided. Several sick persons were prayed for.

—History of the Church, 6:108.

....

I [Brigham Young] attended prayer-meeting in the Assembly Room. President Joseph Smith being absent, I presided and instructed the brethren upon the necessity of following our file leader, and our Savior, in all his laws and commandments, without asking any questions why they were so. I was followed by P[a]r[ley]. P. Pratt and others, who expressed their minds freely. Several sick persons were prayed for.

—Manuscript History of Brigham Young, p. 156.

Saturday, December 16, 1843
Joseph Smith's Red Brick Store

16th [blank]

—"Meetings of Anointed Quorum."

....

I [Wilford Woodruff] met with the quorum. President [Brigham] Young & others took the lead of the meeting.

*—*Wilford Woodruff, Diary.

....

Prayer meeting in the evening.

—History of Joseph Smith, 6:117.

....

Evening, attended prayer-meeting; I [Brigham Young] took the lead.

—Manuscript History of Brigham Young, p. 156.

Sunday, December 17, 1843
Joseph Smith's Red Brick Store

4 P.M. prayer meeting at the Store Assembly room. Samuel Harrison Smith admitted. Returned home at 7.

*—*Joseph Smith, Diary.

....

4. P.M. Prayer Meeting at the Store Assembly Room[.] Samuel Harrison Smith admitted— returned home at 7.

—"Meetings of Anointed Quorum."

I [Wilford Woodruff] met with the quorum. Br[other] Samuel Smith met with us. ^Received his first anointing.^ President Joseph Smith met with us also. We received good instruction.

—Wilford Woodruff, Diary.

....

[I]n assembly room from 4 to 7 S[amuel]. H[arrison]. Smith[.]

—Willard Richards, Diary.

....

At home till 4 p.m.; attended prayer meeting at the assembly room. Samuel Harrison Smith admitted. Returned home at 7.

—*History of the Church,* 6:117.

....

I [Brigham Young] met in the Assembly Room with the Quorum. Brother Samuel H. Smith received his endowments. Brother Joseph [Smith] preached to us.

—*Manuscript History of Brigham Young,* pp. 156-57.

Saturday, December 23, 1843
Joseph Smith's Mansion House/Red Brick Store

Prayer Meeting in the Assembly room Isaac Morl[e]y and wife [Lucy]. O[rson] Pratt,[44] Sister [Permelia] Lot, Fanny Murray, Sister [Phoebe] Woodruff, Geo[rge] A. Smith's wife [Bathsheba], Sister O[rson] Spencer [Catherine], [and] Sister [Sally] Phelp[s].

—Joseph Smith, Diary.

....

Prayer Meet[in]g. in Assembly Room. Isaac Morley & Wife [Lucy], O[rson]. Pratt, Sister [Permelia] Lott, Fanny Murray, Sister [Phoebe] Woodruff, Geo[rge]. A. Smiths Wife [Bathsheba], Sister O[rson]. Spencer [Catherine], Sister [Sally] Phelps[.]

—"Meetings of Anointed Quorum."

....

I [Wilford Woodruff] met with the quorum through the day. Mrs [Phoebe W.] Woodruff & several other sisters were present. Br[other] [Isaac] & sister [Lucy] Morley &c.

---

44. Orson Pratt was the ninth apostle to be initiated into the Quorum of the Anointed. "All nine," notes Ehat ("Introduction to Temple Ordinances," 123), "had accepted, in principle, the doctrines of eternal and plural marriage, and six of the nine had entered the practice of plural marriage." The six were: Brigham Young, Heber C. Kimball, Willard Richards, John Taylor, Orson Hyde, and Parley P. Pratt.

^O[rson] Pratt[,] Sisters [Permelia] Lot Fanny M[urray] P[hoebe Woodruff]. W[ilford]. Woodruff Bathsheba W. Smith Sister O[rson]. Spencer [Catherine] Sister [Sally] Phelps received their Anointing.^

—Wilford Woodruff, Diary.

Meeting in the Assembly Room. O[rson] Pratt. I[saac]. Morley[.]

—Willard Richards, Diary.

Prayer meeting in the Assembly Room.

—*History of the Church*, 6:133.

I [Brigham Young] spent the day with the Quorum in the Assembly Room. Brother Isaac Morley and wife [Lucy] received their endowments.

—*Manuscript History of Brigham Young*, p. 157.

... [I]n company with my [Bathsheba W. Smith's] husband [George A. Smith] I received my endowments and my anointing in sister Emma [Smith]'s bed room [in Nauvoo, Illinois], and then we went in the lodge room over Joseph [Smith]s' store, and he gave us lectures there ...

Q[uestion]:— What subject,—upon what subject were these lectures? ... A[nswer]:—They were on religious subjects ...

Q:— She [Mary Fielding Smith] poured oil on your head? A:— Yes sir.

Q:— What else did she do? A:— She blessed me.

Q:— What else did she do, if any thing? A:— That was all. ...

Q:— ... How much change was there in your clothing at the time you were anointed by Mary Smith, the wife of Hyrum Smith? ... A:— Well we have different clothing to put on, but it is not always the same or just alike.

Q:— Where was the Lodge room there in Nauvoo? A:— It was over Joseph Smith's store,—in the Masonic Hall. ...

Q:— Who was the chief man in the room? A:— Joseph Smith, the prophet.

Q:— Was he sitting or standing? A:— Why both.

Q:— Did he have his hat on, or off? A:— Off.

Q:— All of the time? A:— Yes sir, all of the time,—that is all of the time he was in the room.

Q:— Was there any body else in the room? A:— Yes sir ... a dozen or two.

Q:— All ladies? A:— No sir.

Q:—About what proportion of them were ladies? A:— About half of them were ladies. ...

[Q: Who gave the lectures?] A:— ... It was brother Joseph who gave the lectures. ...

Q:— Was she [Emma Smith] present at the time of this anointing? A:— Yes sir.

Q:— Did she do the anointing? A:— No sir.

Q:— Did she help in the performance in any way? A:— No sir, but she was sitting there.

Q:— How many were in the bed room at the time you were anointed? A:— There was seven of us I think.

Q:— Any other ladies beside yourself and the one that did the anointing, and sister Emma [Smith]? A:— Yes sir, there was two or three sisters in there. ...

Q:— Well I believe you stated that sister Hyrum Smith performed the ordinance of anointing? A:— Sister Mary Smith, who was brother Hyrum Smiths wife was the one that did it. There was no bath room there I think, for in those days we did not have many bath rooms. ...

Q:— Did you take an oath there then not to disclose any thing that occurred there at that time? A:— Yes sir. ... I held up my hand and promised solemnly that I would not reveal it ...

[Q: Was there a dramatization of Adam and Eve?] A:— ... I never saw any one playing Adam and Eve any place,—I will say that much.

Q:— In Nauvoo you did not? A:— No sir, nor here or any other place.

Q:— And did you not represent Eve when you went through the endowments? A:— No sir.

Q:— Who did you represent? A:— I represented myself.

> —Bathsheba W. Smith, Testimony, in "Respondent's Testimony, Temple Lot Case," 1892, pp. 292, 300, 301–302, 303, 305, 330, Library/Archives, Community of Christ, Independence, Missouri.

....

[I]t was in the lodge room over the [Red Brick] store ... there were two rooms over the store. In one room they had a sheet hung up as a vail, and the first endowments were given there. ... Joseph [Smith] gave me permission to stand by the vail and listen to the ceremony, which I did. ... Joseph said that Masonry was taken from the priesthood. Our brethren used to belong to these societies, but since the priesthood had been more fully established the brethren have withdrawn from these societies.

—Bathsheba W. Smith, Remarks, Salt Lake Temple Sisters' Meeting, Minutes, June 16, 1899, LDS Archives.

I know that the endowments are given now the same as they were given by Joseph Smith the Prophet. He was present with us and lectured and talked with us after we had received our first ordinances, and I have met him many times at councils which were held and he told us many things and explained them to us, showed us how to pray, and how to detect them when true or false angels come to us, and many other true things he taught us, and he instituted the endowments through the Lord, and it was not Brigham Young or any one else. I know he was a true Prophet of God and this knowledge could not be stronger if angels were to come and talk to me. I know he never taught a thing that was wrong, and if we obey him we will receive celestial glory and without we will not. I bear this testimony and it is true ...

—Bathsheba W. Smith, Remarks, Weber (Utah) Stake Reunion, June 12, 1903, in the *Deseret Evening News,* June 23, 1903.

Near the close of the year 1843, or in the beginning of the year 1844, I [Bathsheba W. Smith] received the ordinance of anointing in a room in Sister Emma Smith's house, in Nauvoo [Illinois], and the same day, in company with my husband [George A. Smith], I received my endowments in the lodge upper room over the Prophet Joseph Smith's store. The endowments were given under the direction of the Prophet Joseph Smith, who afterwards gave us lectures, or instructions, in regard to the endowment ceremonies. ... A short time after I received my anointings I was sealed to my husband, George A. Smith, for time and for eternity, by President Brigham Young, in the latter's house, according to the plan taught, to my knowledge, by the Prophet Joseph Smith.[45]

—Bathsheba W. Smith, Affidavit dated November 19, 1903, LDS Archives.

The following is a Statement by Sister Maria Dougal. "Aunt B[a]thsheba Smith told me that she helped Emma Smith and Aunt Eliza R. Snow make the original Endowment clothes for the Prophet Joseph

45. George A. and Bathsheba W. Smith were sealed for eternity on January 20, 1844. They received the second anointing on January 31, 1844.

Smith. I asked her why they made strings for the garments instead of buttons. She said they were too poor to buy buttons, so they tore strips of the cloth for strings. I asked her the meaning of the Collar. She said that in making the garment they did not know just how to finish them at the top. Emma suggested that a small collar be put on which was done. She said that the first cap that was made, looked like a crown. The Prophet Joseph told them it should be more like the Baker's cap."

—Maria Dougal, Statement, in George F. Richards, Diary, October 11, 1922, LDS Archives.

Sunday, December 24, 1843
Joseph Smith's Red Brick Store

In the evening I [Wilford Woodruff] again met with the quorum in Company with Mrs [Phoebe] Woodruff. We recieved some instruction concerning the Priesthood.

—Wilford Woodruff, Diary.

....

Meeting eve[ning.]

—Willard Richards, Diary.

....

Attended a prayer-meeting with the [First] Presidency and Twelve in the Assembly Room.

—*Manuscript History of Brigham Young*, p. 157.

Monday, December 25, 1843
Location unknown; no details available.[46]

Saturday, December 30, 1843
Joseph Smith's Red Brick Store

P.M. with the Quorum in Assembly room. W[illia]m Law and wife [Jane] were not present.[47]

—Joseph Smith, Diary.

---

46. Quinn (*Origins*, 498-99) notes that Brigham Young performed a civil marriage for quorum member Levi Richards on this day. While the Quorum of the Anointed apparently did not meet, "perhaps members ... held a prayer circle as part of the marriage ceremony."

47. Ehat ("Introduction to Temple Ordinances," 125) feels that William Law "had just made his decision against plural marriage ..."

I [Wilford Woodruff] met in council in the afternoon & herd a lecture deliverd on principle which was truly interesting & edifying.

—Wilford Woodruff, Diary.

[P]rayer Meeting W[illia]m Law and wife [Jane] absent.

—Willard Richards, Diary.

In the afternoon, met in the assembly room with the quorum. William Law and wife [Jane] were not present.

—*History of the Church,* 6:153.

I attended a meeting with the Quorum in the Assembly Room. President Joseph Smith preached on the principles of integrity, and showed that the lack of sustaining this principle led men to apostasy.[48]

—*Manuscript History of Brigham Young,* pp. 157–58.

Sunday, December 31, 1843
Joseph Smith's Red Brick Store

To meeting early candle light till ten o'clock. Prayer Meeting. Sacrament after I [Joseph Smith] retired.

—Joseph Smith, Diary.

I [Wilford Woodruff] met in council In the evening & was interested.

—Wilford Woodruff, Diary.

Meeting eve[ning] Lecture on tatling &c— Sacrament[.]

—Willard Richards, Diary.

At early candle-light, went to prayer-meeting; administered the sacrament; after which I [Joseph Smith] retired.

—*History of the Church,* 6:153.

Evening, attended prayer-meeting in the Assembly Room.

—*Manuscript History of Brigham Young,* p. 158.

---

48. Quinn (*Origins,* 499) believes this refers to William Law's disaffection from the church.

III.

The Year

1844

SEALINGS AND ANOINTINGS

Saturday, January 6, 1844

Location unknown; no details available.[1]

Sunday, January 7, 1844

Joseph Smith's Red Brick Store

6 P.M. attended the prayer meeting in the assembly room. [William] Law absent.[2] [William] Marks not present.

—Joseph Smith, Diary.

....

6 P.M. Attended the Prayer Meet[in]g. in Assembly Room. [William] Law & [William] Marks absent.

—"Meetings of Anointed Quorum."

....

Mrs [Phoebe] Woodruff and myself [Wilford Woodruff] met with the quorum and we had an interesting time of instruction.

—Wilford Woodruff, Diary.

---

1. Ehat ("Introduction of Temple Ordinances," 99) asserts that the Quorum of the Anointed met on this date.

2. William Law became the first member to be expelled from the Quorum of the Anointed.

[M]eeting of Quorum[.]

—Willard Richards, Diary.

....

At six p.m. attended prayer-meeting with the quorum in the assembly room. [William] Law and [William] Marks absent.

—*History of the Church,* 6:171.

....

I [Bathsheba W. Smith] was present when William Law, Joseph Smith's counselor, was dropped from that quorum by each one present voting yes or no in his turn. He was the first member that was dropped who had received his endowments. One member hesitated to vote,[3] which called forth earnest remarks from the Prophet Joseph [Smith]. He [Joseph Smith] showed clearly that it would be doing a serious wrong to retain him longer. After his explanation the vote was unanimous.

—Bathsheba W. Smith, "Recollections of Joseph Smith,"
Juvenile Instructor 27 (June 1, 1892): 345.

....

I [William Law] was passing along the street near my house, when call'd to by Joseph Smith, he said I was injuring him by telling evil of him, he could not name any one that I talked to, he said my wife [Jane] was injuring him and that Wilson Law[4] was doing so too; he could not give any authority but was very angry, and told me I had no longer a place in the Quorum, and that he had cut me off from the first Presidency and appointed another[5] in my place. Some unpleasant words ensued. I told him his cause was not only unjust but dishonourable, &c. &c.

—William Law, Diary, entry dated January 8, 1844, in "Record
of Doings at Nauvoo [Illinois] in 1844," published in
Lyndon W. Cook, *William Law* (Orem, Utah:
Grandin Book Co., 1994), pp. 35-61.

Sunday, January 14, 1844
Joseph Smith's Red Brick Store

---

3. As Quinn (*Origins,* 499) points out, this hesitant member could not have been William Marks since he did not attend this meeting of the quorum.

4. Wilson Law (1807-77) was brigadier general of the Nauvoo Legion and a member of the Nauvoo City Council. He was excommunicated with his younger brother William, became involved with the Reformed Mormon Church, and helped to publish the *Nauvoo Expositor.* He was accused in the murders of Joseph and Hyrum Smith but never arrested despite a warrant being issued.

5. This was probably Amasa Lyman.

Prayer meeting at the assembly room. Did not go.[6] ^H[eber]
C. K[imball] and G[eorge] A. S[mith] in history office G[reat] S[alt]
L[ake] City, Jan[uar]y 4[th] 1857 say ~~that~~ B[righam] Y[oung] and wife
Mary Ann anointed[.]^7

—Joseph Smith, Diary.

Prayer Meet[in]g. at Assembly Room—did not go.

—"Meetings of Anointed Quorum."

In the evening I [Wilford Woodruff] met with the quorum of the
Twelve. Conversed upon a variety of subjects building the [Nauvoo]
Temple, the endowment &c. Some good ideas advanced.

—Wilford Woodruff, Diary.

P[rayer]. meeting eve[ning.]

—Willard Richards, Diary.

He [George A. Smith] alluded to councils which had been held in
Nauvoo [Illinois], and to the fact of Joseph [Smith] the Prophet calling
the Twelve together, and as contained in Par[agraph]. 40 Sec[tion]. 103
D[octrine] & C[ovenants] [i.e., 124:127] placeing Brigham Young as
President of the Twelve. The speaker stated that the Prophet and Patriarch
Hyrum [Smith], in one of those meetings, had administered to Brigham
Young what is known as the Second Anointing, and instructed him to ad-
minister in like manner to his brethren of the Twelve; which he did to the
nine of the Twelve then at home.

—St. George, Utah, Historical Stake Record, entry dated
December 25, 1874, LDS Archives.

A prayer-meeting was held in the assembly room. I [Joseph Smith]
did not attend.

—*History of the Church,* 6:176.

In the evening attended prayer-meeting at the Assembly Room. My
[Brigham Young's] wife Mary Ann and I received our second anointing.

—*Manuscript History of Brigham Young,* p. 158.

---

6. Presumably Brigham Young conducted the meeting.

7. If this account is accurate, Brigham and Mary Ann Young's second anointing duplicated the ordinance they received on November 22, 1843. Also, someone
other than Joseph Smith performed this repeat ordinance.

Saturday, January 20, 1844

Joseph Smith's Red Brick Store

Eve[ning] 6 Prayer Meeting. H[eber] C. Kimball and wife [Vilate] present.[8] I [Joseph Smith] was at home.

—Joseph Smith, Diary.

....

6 Evening Prayer Meet[in]g. H[eber] C Kimball & wife [Vilate] present—I [Joseph Smith] was at home.

—"Meetings of Anointed Quorum."

....

My self [Heber C. Kimball] and wife Vilate was announted Preast and Preastest [Priestess] unto our God under the Hands of B[righam]. Young and by the voys [voice] of the Holy Order.

—Heber C. Kimball, Diary, entry dated February 1, 1844, but following entry dated October 19, 1843.[9]

....

I [Vilate Kimball] am yours in time, and ~~in~~ throughout all eternity. this blessing has be[e]n sealed upon us, by the holy spirit of promis; and cannot be broken only through transgression or, commiting a grocer [grosser] crime than your heart or mine is capable of, that is murder.

—Vilate Kimball, Letter to Heber C. Kimball, dated June 8, 1844, in Heber C. Kimball, Diary, following poem dated May 28, 1844.

....

In the evening I [Wilford Woodruff] met with the quorum in the evening & had an interesting time. {H[eber]. C. K[imball]} {V[ilate].

---

8. Heber C. and Vilate Kimball received the second anointing, administered by Brigham Young.

9. The second part of the fullness of the priesthood ordinance occurred some ten weeks later as noted in Heber C. Kimball's diary following the entry dated October 19, 1843:

> Apriel the first 4 day 1844. I Heber C. Kimball recieved the washing of my feet, and was annointed by my wife Vilate fore my burial, that is my feet, head, Stomach. Even as Mary did Jesus, that she mite have a claim on Him in the Reserrection. In the City of Nauvoo.
> In 1845 [sic] I recieved the washing of my feet by[:]
> I Vilate Kimball do hereby certify that on the first day of April 1844 I attended to washing and anointed the head, ^Stomach^ and feet of my dear companion Heber C. Kimball, that I may have claim upon him in the morning of the first Reserrection.
> Vilate Kimball.

K[imball].} Received their second Anointing &c.

—Wilford Woodruff, Diary.

[M]eeting eve[ning]. H[eber] C. Kimball & wife [Vilate].

—Willard Richards, Diary.

At six, p.m., prayer-meeting in the assembly room. I [Joseph Smith] was at home.

—*History of the Church,* 6:181.

Met with the Quorum: Heber C. Kimball and his wife Vilate received their second anointing.

—*Manuscript History of Brigham Young,* p. 158.

Sunday, January 21, 1844
Joseph Smith's Red Brick Store

Prayer meeting over store. Parley P. Pratt present. Joseph [Smith] not there.[10]

—Joseph Smith, Diary.

Prayer Meet[in]g over the Store—Parley P. Pratt present; Joseph [Smith] not there.

—"Meetings of Anointed Quorum."

I [Wilford Woodruff] met with the quorum in the evening. Had an interestin[g] time. Many good exhortation[s] were given by the brethren concerning the things of God. {P[arley]. P. P[ratt].} Received his 2d Anointing. Joseph [Smith] said Concerning Parley P Pratt that He had no wife sealed to him for Eternity and asked if their was any harm for him to have another wife for time & Eternity as He would want a wife in the Resurrection or els his glory would be Cliped. Many arguments He used upon this subject which were rational & consistant. B̶r̶[̶o̶t̶h̶e̶r̶]̶ ̶J̶o̶s̶e̶p̶h̶ ̶s̶a̶i̶d̶ ̶n̶o̶w̶ ̶w̶h̶a̶t̶ ̶w̶i̶l̶l̶ ̶w̶e̶ ̶d̶o̶ ̶w̶i̶t̶h̶ ̶E̶l̶d̶e̶r̶ ̶P̶[̶a̶r̶l̶e̶y̶]̶ ̶P̶ ̶P̶r̶a̶t̶t̶?̶ ̶H̶e̶ ̶h̶a̶s̶ ̶n̶o̶ ̶w̶i̶f̶e̶ ̶s̶e̶a̶l̶e̶d̶ ̶t̶o̶ ̶h̶i̶m̶ ̶f̶o̶r̶ ̶E̶t̶e̶r̶n̶i̶t̶y̶.̶ ̶H̶e̶ ̶h̶a̶s̶ ̶o̶n̶e̶ ̶l̶i̶v̶i̶n̶g̶ ̶w̶i̶f̶e̶ ̶b̶u̶t̶ ̶s̶h̶e̶ ̶h̶a̶d̶ ̶a̶ ̶f̶o̶r̶m̶e̶r̶ ̶H̶u̶s̶b̶a̶n̶d̶

---

10. Parley P. Pratt received the second anointing. Quinn (*Origins,* 500) writes that Parley's deceased wife, Thankful Halsey Pratt, also received her endowments and second anointing on this date by proxy. However, Apostles Orson Hyde and Orson Pratt both received the second anointing alone the following week, and it seems more likely that Parley was also anointed without a companion.

~~and did not wish to be sealed to Parly for Eternity. Now is it not right for Parley to have another wife that can [blank]?~~[11]

—Wilford Woodruff, Diary.

....

[M]eeting eve[ning]— P[arley] P. Pratt.

—Willard Richards, Diary.

....

Prayer-meeting in the Assembly Room.

—*History of the Church*, 6:185.

....

I [Brigham Young] met in the Assembly Room with the Quorum, and administered to Parley P. Pratt his second anointing.

—*Manuscript History of Brigham Young*, pp. 158-59.

Monday, January 22, 1844

Brigham Young House

Prayer Meeting at Pres[iden]t [Brigham] Young's, 10 present.

—Joseph Smith, Diary.

....

Prayer Meet[in]g at Pres[iden]t [Brigham] Youngs. 10 present—

—"Meetings of Anointed Quorum."

....

I [Wilford Woodruff] met with the quorum of the twelve [apostles] at President B[righam] Youngs house & spent the evening and conversed upon a variety of subjects. Had a good time in expressing our views upon religious subjects.

—Wilford Woodruff, Diary.

....

P.M. Brother [Reynolds] Cahoon came to my house to say that a vote

---

11. According to Ehat ("Introduction of Temple Ordinances," 66-71), Parley and Mary Ann Pratt had been sealed for eternity by Hyrum Smith on June 23, 1843; when Joseph Smith learned of the ceremony performed in his absence and without his permission, he cancelled it. Reportedly, Joseph wanted Mary Ann's sister, Olive Grey Frost, to be Parley's first plural wife whereas Parley was courting Elizabeth Brotherton. The following month, on July 24, 1843, Joseph married Parley and his first wife, Thankful Halsey Pratt (deceased), for eternity, with Mary Ann acting as proxy, then sealed (probably for time only) Parley and Mary Ann, and finally sealed Elizabeth Brotherton to Parley as his first plural wife. Since Joseph was not present at this meeting of the Quorum of the Anointed (Brigham Young performed the anointing), the prophet's explanation, recorded by Woodruff, must have occurred elsewhere.

had been taken on my being admitted into the quorum and I was accepted. This filled my heart with joy, and gratitude for truly the mercy of the Lord and the kindness of my brethren have been great to me.

—William Clayton, Diary.

Prayer-meeting at President [Brigham] Young's; ten present.

—*History of the Church*, 6:185.

I [Brigham Young] met with the Quorum of the Twelve [Apostles] at my house, for prayer and conversation.

—*Manuscript History of Brigham Young*, p. 159.

Thursday, January 25, 1844
Brigham Young House

Prayer meeting at at Bro[ther] Brigham [Young]'s. O[rson] Hyde present.[12] 8 of the 12 [Apostles].

—Joseph Smith, Diary.

Prayer Meet[in]g at Brother Brigham [Young]'s O[rson]. Hyde present—8 of the 12 [Apostles]—

—"Meetings of Anointed Quorum."

Met with the quorum of the Twelve [Apostles]: at President [Brigham] Youngs house. Had a good prayer meeting. {O[rson] H[yde]} Br[other] Orson Hyde was present. Had not met with us for some time. Orson Hyde Received his 2d Anointing.

—Wilford Woodruff, Diary.

[E]ve[ning] Brigham [Young']s[.]

—Willard Richards, Diary.

P.M. Sister [Elizabeth] Durphy came to make my Robe and Garment.[13]

—William Clayton, Diary.

---

12. Orson Hyde apparently received the second anointing alone. Quinn (*Origins*, 515) feels, however, that he received the ordinance in conjunction "with another woman (possibly deceased)."

13. This refers to clothing worn by those who receive the endowment. The robe is worn only during the endowment ceremony, while the underclothing ("garments") is thereafter worn by the initiate at all times.

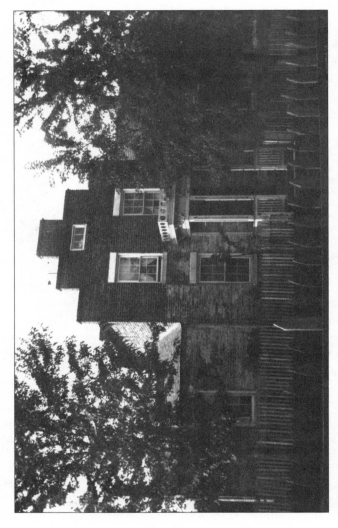

Brigham Young's house, near the southeast corner of Granger Street and Kimball Street in Nauvoo, was built in 1843-44. The Anointed Quorum met here several times, before and after Joseph Smith's death on June 27, 1844. Photograph ca. 1885.

Prayer-meeting at Brother Brigham [Young]'s; eight of the Twelve Apostles present.

—*History of the Church,* 6:185.

....

The Quorum met at my house: Orson Hyde received his second anointing.

—*Manuscript History of Brigham Young,* p. 159.

Friday, January 26, 1844
Brigham Young House

Prayer meeting at Bro[ther] [Brigham] Young's. 8 of the [12] [Apostles]. O[rson] Pratt present.[14]

—Joseph Smith, Diary.

....

Prayer Meet[in]g at Bro[ther] [Brigham] Youngs, Orson Pratt present—8 of the 12 [apostles]—

—"Meetings of Anointed Quorum."

....

I [Wilford Woodruff] met with the Twelve [Apostles] this evening Also at Br[other] B[righam]. Youngs time was spent in exhortation mostly. {O[rson] P[ratt]} Spoke & we were edefyed. Elder O[rson]. Pratt Received his 2d Anointing.

—Wilford Woodruff, Diary.

....

Bro[ther] Brigham [Young's.]

—Willard Richards, Diary.

....

Prayer-meeting at Brother [Brigham] Young's: eight of the Twelve Apostles present.

—*History of the Church,* 6:186.

....

The Twelve [apostles] met at my house: Orson Pratt received his second anointing.

—*Manuscript History of Brigham Young,* p. 159.

Saturday, January 27, 1844
Joseph Smith's Red Brick Store

Prayer Meeting at the Store chamber. W[illard] Richards present.[15]

—Joseph Smith, Diary.

---

14. Orson Pratt received the second anointing alone.
15. A second anointing.

Prayer Meet[in]g at the Store Chamber—W[illard]. Richards present[.]

—"Meetings of Anointed Quorum."

The quorum met for a meeting in the evening at Joseph [Smith's] Store. Had a number of prayers & exhortations upon the subject of holiness of h[e]art &c. {W[illard] R[ichards]} {&} {J[ennetta] R[ichards]} Br[other] & Sister [Willard and Jennetta] Richards were present. They had both been unwell for a number of days before but wer[e] able to attend meeting this evening & seemed to enjoy themselves well. They had received blessings by the prayer of faith. Willard & Jenette Richards Received their 2d *Anointing* and *sealing*.

—Wilford Woodruff, Diary.

Prayer Store[.]

—Willard Richards, Diary.

Prayer-meeting in the assembly room.

—*History of the Church*, 6:186.

We met at the Assembly Room: Willard Richards and his wife Jenetta were sealed and received their second anointing.

—*Manuscript History of Brigham Young*, p. 159.

Sunday, January 28, 1844
Joseph Smith's Red Brick Store

Prayer Meeting at the store. Present W[ilford] Woodruff.[16]

—Joseph Smith, Diary.

Prayer Meet[in]g at the Store present W[ilford]. Woodruff.

—"Meetings of Anointed Quorum."

I [Wilford Woodruff] met with the quorum of the Twelve [Apostles] and others for instruction. Mrs [Phoebe] Woodruff and myself were both some unwell from the effects of the coal [cold?] during the day. Yet we had an interesting time.

{W[ilford] W[oodruff]} {P[hebe] W[.] W[oodruff]} I Wilford Woodruff and Phoebe W. Woodruff both recieved a benefit by Prayers

---

16. A second anointing.

and laying on of hands. The Subject of Elijah's coming to seal the hearts of the fathers to the Children &c was spoken of. Seal the hearts of the children to the fathers Malachi IVth Ch[apter]. 6 vers[e].

^Wilford & Phoebe W Woodruff receivd our 2d Anointing & sealings.^

—Wilford Woodruff, Diary.

....

[A]t store.— meeting[.]

—Willard Richards, Diary.

....

Prayer-meeting in the assembly room.

—*History of the Church,* 6:186.

....

The Quorum met in the Assembly Room. Wilford Woodruff and his wife Phoebe W. were sealed and received their second anointing.

—*Manuscript History of Brigham Young,* p. 159.

....

There's Sister Bathsheba Smith, she and I both had our endowments under the hand of the Prophet Joseph Smith. I had my second anointings and sealings under his hands.

—Wilford Woodruff, quoted in *Young Women's Journal* 5 (August 1894): 513.

Monday, January 29, 1844
Brigham Young House

I [Wilford Woodruff] met in the evening at Elder B[righam] Youngs for a Prayer meeting but few of us to gether.

—Wilford Woodruff, Diary.

Tuesday, January 30, 1844
Brigham Young House

Prayer Meeting at B[righam] Young's. John Taylor and wife [Leonora] present.[17]

—Joseph Smith, Diary.

---

17. A second anointing.

Prayer Meeting at B[righam]. Youngs—John Taylor & Wife [Leonora] present.

—"Meetings of Anointed Quorum."

Met with the quorum at Elder [Brigham] Youngs for a meeting. {J[ohn] T[aylor]} {L[eonora] T[aylor]} Br[other] & Sister John [and Leonora] Taylor was with us. Br[other] Taylor made some appropriate remarks unto edifycation. ^J[ohn] Taylor & Leonora Taylor Received their 2d Anointing & sealing.^

—Wilford Woodruff, Diary.

Pr[ayer] meeting, Brigham [Young] John Taylor & wife [Leonora.]

—Willard Richards, Diary.

Prayer-meeting at Elder Brigham Young's.

—*History of the Church*, 6:190.

The Quorum met at my house. John and Leonora Taylor were sealed and anointed.

—*Manuscript History of Brigham Young*, p. 159.

Wednesday, January 31, 1844
Brigham Young House

Prayer meeting at B[righam] Young's. Geo[rge] A. Smith and wife [Bathsheba] present. ^Geo[rge] A. Smith and wife Bathsheba W. Bigler received their Second Anointing which was administered by Brigham Young, Pres[iden]t of the Twelve [Apostles.]^[18]

—Joseph Smith, Diary.

Prayer Meet[in]g. at B[righam] Youngs, Geo[rge] A Smith & Wife

---

18. "Thus," notes Ehat ("Introduction of Temple Ordinances," 147-48), "in the twelve days between 20 and 31 January 1844, the eight other members of the Quorum of the Twelve Apostles then residing in Nauvoo received the fulness of the priesthood under the hands of their President, Brigham Young. ... At the time of their anointings, these nine of the Twelve Apostles were the highest quorum of the Church (save Joseph of the First Presidency) to receive these blessings. In fact, they were the first and only quorum ever in the Church of Joseph's day, the majority of whom received these blessings[, and] ... at a time when no member of the publicly acknowledged First Presidency (except Joseph Smith) was even a member of the Anointed Quorum" (endnotes omitted).

[Bathsheba] present[.]

—"Meetings of Anointed Quorum."

Geo[rge] A Smith & Bathsheba W Smith Rec[ei]v[e]d our 2 anointing at B[righam] Young house.

—George A. Smith, Diary, LDS Archives.

I [Wilford Woodruff] met with the quorum of Twelve [Apostles] this evening at Elder [Brigham] Youngs & had a good time. {G[eorge] A[.] S[mith]} {B[athsheba] S[mith]} Br[other] & Sister G[eorge] A Smith was present this evening ^And Received their 2d Anointing & Sealing^. They have been quite unwell.

—Wilford Woodruff, Diary.

Prayer-meeting at Elder Brigham Young's in the evening. There seems to be quite a revival throughout Nauvoo [Illinois], and an inquiry after the things of God, by all the quorums and the Church in general.

—*History of the Church,* 6:191.

I [Brigham Young] met with the Quorum at my house. George A. and Bathsheba W. Smith were anointed, having been sealed on the 20th inst.

—*Manuscript History of Brigham Young,* p. 159.

Q[uestion]:— Now from whom did you receive your anointing? A[nswer]:— Well I think it was from President [Brigham] Young the first time, and in the Temple [the second time].

—Bathsheba W. Smith, Testimony, in "Respondent's Testimony, Temple Lot Case," 1892, p. 299, Library/Archives, Community of Christ, Independence, Missouri.

Friday, February 2, 1844
Brigham Young House

Prayer meeting at Br[igham] Young's. W[illiam] W. Phelps and wife [Sally].

—Joseph Smith, Diary.

Prayer Meet[in]g at B[righam] Young, W[illiam] W Phelps & Wife [Sally] present[.]

—"Meetings of Anointed Quorum."

I [Wilford Woodruff] met with the quorum for Prayer &c at Elders [Brigham] Youngs. {W[illiam] W[.] [Phelps]} {S[ally] P[helps]} Br[other] & Sister W[illia]m. W. Phelps attended with us. Br[other] Phelps spoke Concerning his appointment as a Lawyier in Israel.[19] ^Brother & Sister W[illia]m. W Phelps Received their 2d Anointing & sealing.^

—Wilford Woodruff, Diary.

Prayer-meeting at Elder Brigham Young's.

—*History of the Church,* 6:194.

Saturday, February 3, 1844
Joseph Smith's Red Brick Store

Prayer meeting over the Store in the P.M. Joseph [Smith] not present. W[illia]m Clayton and Joseph Young and wife [Jane] present.[20]

—Joseph Smith, Diary.

Prayer Meet[in]g P.M. over Store, Jos[ep]h. [Smith] not present W[illia]m Clayton & Jos[ep]h Young & wife [Jane] present[.]

—"Meetings of Anointed Quorum."

In the evening of this day the quorum met at Joseph [Smith's] store. Brothers W[illia]m. W Clayton & Joseph Young met with them But I [Wilford Woodruff] was not present. ... Joseph Young & wife [Jane] & W[illia]m. Clayton Received their 2d Endowments &c.[21]

—Wilford Woodruff, Diary.

---

19. On September 22, 1835, Joseph Smith had blessed William W. Phelps as follows: "He shall be a wise lawyer in Israel, for he shall understand the law of the Lord perfectly and the the [sic] renowned among men shall acknowledge his superior wisdom pertaining to the laws of nations and of kingdoms. Behold, he shall have understanding in all sciences and languages, and with his brother, Oliver, shall write and arrange many books for the good of the church, that the young may grow up in wisdom: these shall remain for a memorial unto their names, and the generations to come shall call them blessed" (qtd. in William W. Phelps, Diary, 30-34, LDS Archives).

20. A second anointing.

21. From Wilford Woodruff's diary, it would appear that William Clayton was both initiated into the Quorum of the Anointed and received the second anointing on this date. However, Woodruff notes that he was not present for these ceremonies, and Clayton's diary clearly recounts only his initiation, not his receipt of the second anointing.

P.M. was permitted to the ordinance of washing and anointing, and was received into the Quorum of Priesthood. This is one of the greatest favors ever conferred on me [William Clayton] and for which I feel grateful. May the God of Joseph [Smith] preserve me and mine house to walk in the paths of righteousness all the days of my life and oh that I may never sin against him or displease him. For thou oh God knowest my desire to do right that I may have eternal life.

—William Clayton, Diary.

Prayer-meeting in the assembly room.

—*History of the Church*, 6:195.

Sunday, February 4, 1844
Joseph Smith's Red Brick Store

Evening at the prayer meeting [at] Brick Store. Cornelius P. Lot and wife [Permelia] present.[22]

—Joseph Smith, Diary.

Attended in the even[in]g at Prayer Meet[in]g. [at] Brick Store, Cornelius P Lot & Wife [Permelia] present[.]

—"Meetings of Anointed Quorum."

I [Wilford Woodruff] met with the quorum in the evening. Br[other] & Sister [Cornelius and Permelia] Lott was present. We had a good time in prayer. Br[other] Joseph [Smith] gave us good instruction in meekness & humility. The revelator John remarks was quoted to in the evening Concerning the 144,000 of the tribes of Israel.[23] ^Cornelius P. Lott & wife [Lois] Received their 2d Anointing & sealing.^

—Wilford Woodruff, Diary.

Evening attended quorum.

—William Clayton, Diary.

I [Joseph Smith] attended prayer-meeting with the quorum in the assembly room, and made some remarks respecting the hundred and forty-four thousand mentioned by John the Revelator, showing that the

---

22. A second anointing.
23. Joseph's remarks were based on Revelation 7:4-8.

selection of persons to form that number had already commenced.[24]

> —*History of the Church,* 6:196.

Saturday, February 10, 1844
Joseph Smith's Red Brick Store

Prayer meeting assembly Room prayed for Sister [Jennetta] Richards and others.

> —Joseph Smith, Diary.

....

Prayer Meeting at Assembly Room—prayed for Sister [Jennetta] Richards & others.

> —"Meetings of Anointed Quorum."

....

Evening attended quorum.

> —William Clayton, Diary.

....

Prayer-meeting in the assembly room. Prayed for Sister [Jennetta] Richards and others, who were sick.

> —*History of the Church,* 6:211.

....

Attended prayer-meeting in the Assembly Room.

> —*Manuscript History of Brigham Young,* p. 160.

Sunday, February 11, 1844
Joseph Smith's Red Brick Store

Pr[ayer] Meeting adjourned till Saturday next.

> —Joseph Smith, Diary.

....

Prayer Meeting adj[ourne]d [blank] next [blank][.]

> —"Meetings of Anointed Quorum."

....

Evening I [William Clayton] attended quorum but we did not organize.

> —William Clayton, Diary.

Sunday, February 18, 1844
Joseph Smith's Red Brick Store

---

24. Joseph may have had in mind those of the quorum who had received the second anointing.

I attended Prayer Meeting at seven over the store. Sister [Marinda Nancy] Hyde was there.[25]

—Joseph Smith, Diary.

I attended Prayer Meet[in]g at 7 ove[r] the Store. Sister [Marinda Nancy] Hyde was there.

—"Meetings of Anointed Quorum."

On our return home I [Wilford Woodruff] met with the quorum President J[oseph] Smith with us. We had a good time. Sister Orson Hyde [Marinda Nancy Hyde] was present.

—Wilford Woodruff, Diary.

[P]rayer Meeting eve[ning] Sis[ter] [Marinda Nancy] Hyde.

—Willard Richards, Diary.

At seven, attended prayer-meeting in the assembly room.

—*History of the Church,* 6:221.

I met in the evening in the Assembly Room. Brother Joseph [Smith] and the Twelve [Apostles] were present.

—*Manuscript History of Brigham Young,* p. 160.

Sunday, February 25, 1844
Joseph Smith's Red Brick Store

Eve[ning] Prayer Meeting over the store. Prayed that Gen[eral] [Joseph] Smith's views of the ^power and policy of the U.S.^ United States[26] might be spread far and wide and be the means of op[en]ing the hearts of the people.[27]

—Joseph Smith, Diary.

Evening Prayer Meeting over Store, pra[y]ed that Gen[era]l. [Joseph]

---

25. Marinda Nancy Johnson Hyde was initiated into the quorum.

26. *General Joseph Smith's Views of the Powers and Policy of the Government of the United States* was a pamphlet published on February 25, 1844, containing the candidate's platform for the U.S. presidential campaign. Joseph produced the work with William W. Phelps between January 29 and February 4. After publication, copies were sent to the president of the United States and other officials.

27. Quinn (*Origins,* 501) points out that this was a political meeting since no ordinances were performed.

Smiths ["]views of the powers & policy of the Government of the United States" might be spread far & wide & be the means of opening the hearts of the people—

—"Meetings of Anointed Quorum."

In the evening I [Wilford Woodruff] met with the quorum and had an interesting time. We had received correct information concerning the death of Joseph Duncan[28] & Govornor [Thomas] Reynold[s] of Missouri. He Shot himself through the head. They were two of the most invenerate enemies against the latter Day Saints. President Joseph Smith Prophesyed that within five years we should be rid of our old enemies whether they were Apostates or of the world & wished us to record it that when it comes to pass that we need not say we had forgotten the saying.

—Wilford Woodruff, Diary.

Evening attended quorum. President Joseph [Smith] gave some important instructions. We had an interesting season.

—William Clayton, Diary.

Evening, I [Joseph Smith] attended prayer-meeting in the assembly room. We prayed that "General Joseph Smith's Views of the Powers and Policy of the United States," might be spread far and wide, and be the means of opening the hearts of the people. I gave some important instructions, and prophesied that within five years we should be out of the power of our old enemies, whether they were apostates or of the world; and told the brethren to record it, that when it comes to pass they need not say they had forgotten the saying.

—*History of the Church*, 6:225.

Monday, February 26, 1844
Joseph Smith's Red Brick Store

Prayer Meeting over store. P.M. John Smith there. Eve[ning] Father

---

28. Joseph Duncan (1794-1844) was governor of Illinois from 1834 to 1838. Prior to this, he had served in the army during the War of 1812, in the state House of Representatives (1825-29), and later in the U.S. House of Representatives (1827-34). Four years after serving as governor, he ran again for the same office as the Whig candidate. His promise to repeal Nauvoo's city charter, as well as an agenda generally hostile to Mormon interests, was the focus of his campaign. He lost the election to Thomas Ford.

[Isaac] Morley there. Had his second anointing in evening. John Smith and wife [Clarissa] had their second anointing.

—Joseph Smith, Diary.

....

Prayer Meeting over Store PM. John Smith there—Even[in]g. Father Morley there[.]

—"Meetings of Anointed Quorum."

....

I [Wilford Woodruff] met with the quorum in the evening but meeting Closed soon after we arived. Fathers John Smith & wife [Clarissa] & Isaac Morley & wife [Lucy] met with the quorum in the afternoon & evening. I took a severe Cold & had a sick night. ^Father John Smith & wife Isaac Morley & wife Rec[eive]d their 2d Anointing & sealings.^

—Wilford Woodruff, Diary.

....

I was living with Father [John] Smith, the Prophet's uncle and on one occasion the Prophet wrote a letter to his uncle [asking] him to meet him the next morning in Nauvoo, [they lived] twenty-five miles from [Nauvoo]. Mother [Clarissa] Smith ... was sick and [since] I was the hired girl I had to get these clothes and fix them in time for Father Smith to meet the Prophet Joseph in Nauvoo. Mother Smith told Father Smith to explain to me about this clothing, what they were for and what they did with them, the reason he had to have them and have them in good condition, before I got them out, and he did so. That was the first I knew about endowment clothes but they were the same as they are now. Sister Smith told me where they were and how to prepare them for him. They were in a chest locked up, inside of a little cotton bag made for the purpose and were all together. Then I got the clothes and pressed them out and put them in good condition and he went to meet the Prophet. These clothes were never put out publicly, in the washing or in any other way. When we washed them we hung them out between sheets, because we were in the midst of the Gentiles.

—Maria Jane Johnston Woodward, Statement, dated April 21, 1902, in George H. Brimhall, Letter to Joseph F. Smith, April 21, 1902, LDS Archives.

....

Maria J. Woodward came to Nauvoo from Middle, Tennessee when she was 17 in 1841. She was the only member of the Church in her father's family. While she worked in the home of the Prophet for 3 weeks she acquired the following testimony:

"[Joseph Smith] was always kind and often talked with me and asked about my [family] ... I ... can bear testimony that [Joseph] had had his endowments and wore garments, for the woman who washed for the family showed them to me."

—"Joseph Smith the Prophet ... Maria J. Woodward [Testimony]," *Young Woman's Journal* 17 (December 1906): 543-44.

Prayer-meeting in the assembly room in the afternoon. My [Joseph Smith's] uncle John Smith and lady [Clarissa] were present, were anointed, and received blessings; and in the evening Father [Isaac] Morley was also blessed.

—*History of the Church,* 6:225.

Wednesday, February 28, 1844
William W. Phelps House?

Eve[ning], I [Joseph Smith] sent Bro[ther] [Joseph W.] Coolidge[29] to Bro[ther] [William W.] Phelps to call the Brethren and pray for Bro[ther] Coolidge['s] sick child.[30] He thought [it] could not live till morning. Bro[ther] [John] Taylor, [William W.] Phelps, and [Willard] Richards prayed for him.

—Joseph Smith, Diary.

Evening I [Joseph Smith] sent Bro[ther] [Joseph W.] Coolidge to Bro[ther]. [William W.] Phelps to call the Brethren & pray for Bro[ther] Coolidge's sick child, he tho[ugh]t. could not live till morning Bro[ther]. [John] Taylor [William W.] Phelps & [Willard] Richards prayed for him—

—"Meetings of Anointed Quorum."

In the evening I [Joseph Smith] sent Brother [Joseph W.] Coolidge to Brother [William W.] Phelps, to call the brethren and pray for Brother Coolidge's sick child, as he thought it could not live till morning. Elder John Taylor and others prayed for him.

—*History of the Church,* 6:226.

---

29. Joseph Wellington Coolidge (1814-71), a carpenter, resided in Nauvoo and was the administrator of Joseph Smith's estate.

30. This child, Joseph S. Coolidge, died at the age of one year and eleven days, before March 29, 1844, of inflamation of the lungs. See Lyndon W. Cook, ed., *Nauvoo Deaths and Marriages* (Orem, UT: Grandin Book Co., 1994), 18.

Sunday, March 3, 1844
Joseph Smith's Red Brick Store

Prayer meeting a little while.[31]

—Joseph Smith, Diary.

During the evening I [Wilford Woodruff] met with the quorum. Had remarks from a number of the brethren.

—Wilford Woodruff, Diary.

Evening attended Q[uorum].

—William Clayton, Diary.

Attending prayer-meeting in the evening.

—*History of the Church,* 6:230.

Friday, March 15, 1844
Joseph Smith's Red Brick Store; no details available.[32]

Sunday, March 17, 1844
Joseph Smith's Red Brick Store

Prayer Meeting adjourned 1 week.

—Joseph Smith, Diary.

Attended prayer meeting.

—*History of the Church,* 6:267.

Attended prayer meeting.

—*Manuscript History of Brigham Young,* p. 164.

Before I [Orson Hyde] went east on the 4th of April last [1844], we were in council with Brother Joseph [Smith] almost every day for weeks, says Brother Joseph in one of those councils there is something going to happen; I dont know what it is, but the Lord bids me to hasten and give

31. Quinn (*Origins,* 501) notes that this was largely a political meeting. He adds that "the female members of the Anointed Quorum apparently attended this meeting without voicing views on its political agenda."

32. Ehat ("Introduction of Temple Ordinances," 99) asserts that the quorum met during the evening on this date.

you your endowment before the temple is finished. He conducted us through every ordinance of the holy priesthood, and when he had gone through with all the ordinances he rejoiced very much, and says, now if they kill me you have got all the keys, and all the ordinances and you can confer them upon others, and the hosts of Satan will not be able to tear down the kigndom, as fast as you will be able to build it up; and now says he on your shoulders will the responsibility of leading this people rest, for the Lord is going to let me rest a while.[33]

—Orson Hyde, quoted in "Trial of Elder [Sidney] Rigdon,"
Times and Seasons 5 (September 8, 1844): 651.

....

We, the undersigned, do hereby solemnly, sincerely, and truly testify before God, Angels, and men, unto all people unto whom this certificate may come, that we were present at a Council in the latter part of the Month of March last, held in the City of Nauvoo in the upper part of the brick building situate[d] upon Water Street, commonly known here as "Joseph's Store," in which Council Joseph Smith did preside; and the greater part of the Twelve Apostles were present. Namely, Brigham Young, Heber C Kimball, Orson Hyde, Parley P Pratt, Orson Pratt, John Taylor, Amasa Lyman, Willard Richards, and Wilford Woodruff. These we feel confident were all present on that occasion, besides many others who were of the quorum of high Priests to which we ourselves belong.

In this Council, Joseph Smith seemed somewhat depressed in Spirit, and took the liberty to open his heart to us concerning his presentiments of the future. His own language to us on that occasion, as nearly as we can recollect, was as follows.

Brethren, the Lord bids me hasten the work in which we are engaged. He will not suffer that you should wait for your endowment until the Temple is done. Some important Scene is near to take place. It may be that my enemies will kill me, and in case they should, and the Keys and power which rest on me not be imparted to you, they will be lost from the Earth;

---

33. This and the next excerpt may actually describe the Anointed Quorum's meeting of March 22, 1844, held in Brigham Young's house, or the meeting of the Council of Fifty held on March 26, 1844. The all-male Council of Fifty was another secret group that met in Nauvoo under Joseph Smith's leadership. It mostly concerned itself with political matters, however theoretical the deliberations may have been. There is evidence that the council was planning to move the church to Texas to establish a temporal Kingdom of God on Earth. Approximately 75 percent of the male members of the Quorum of Anointed were also members of the Council of Fifty. See Quinn, *Origins,* 136.

but if I can only succeed in placing them upon your heads, then let me fall a victim to murderous hands if God will suffer it, and I can go with all pleasure and satisfaction, knowing that my work is done, and the foundation laid on which the kingdom of God is to be reared in this dispensation of the fulness of times. Upon the shoulders of the Twelve must the responsibility of leading this Church hence forth rest until you shall appoint others to succeed you. Your enemies cannot kill you all at once, and should any of you be killed, you can lay your hands upon others and fill up your quorum. Thus can this power and these Keys be perpetuated in the Earth. Brethren, you have many storms to pass through, and many sore trials await you. You will know what it is to be bound with chains and with fetters for this cause sake. God knows I pity you and feel for you; but if you are called to lay down your lives, die like men, and pass immediately beyond the reach of your enemies. After they have killed you, they can harm you no more. Should you have to walk right into danger and the jaws of death, fear no evil; Jesus Christ has died before you.

After this appointment was made, and confirmed by the holy anointing under the hands of Joseph and Hyrum, Joseph continued his speech unto them, saying, while he walked the floor and threw back the collar of his coat upon his shoulders, "I roll the burthen and responsibility of leading this Church off from my shoulders on to yours. Now, round up your shoulders and stand under it like men; for the Lord is going to let me rest a while." Never shall we forget his feelings or his words on this occasion. After he had thus spoken, he continued to walk the floor, saying: "Since I have rolled the burthen off from my shoulders, I feel as light as a cork. I feel that I am free. I thank my God for this deliverance."

We gave our testimony on the 8th of September last before a special Conference in this City, at which Sidney Rigdon was tried and excommunicated from the Church; and altho' we declared it then in the presence of many thousand people, we now feel it a pleasure in reducing it to writing, and freely give our names to the world in confirmation of the above statements; and further, that Joseph Smith did declare that he had conferred upon the Twelve every key and every power that he ever held himself before God. This our testimony we expect to meet in a coming day when all parties will know that we have told the truth and have not lied, so help us God.

—Orson Hyde, undated, unsigned certificate of nine of the
Quorum of the Twelve Apostles, written ca. September 8, 1844,
and March 1845, typescript, LDS archives.

Friday, March 22, 1844

Brigham Young House

I [Wilford Woodruff] met with the quorum of the Twelve [Apostles] at B[righam]. Youngs for Prayer. We united together to pray for the Presidency[,] the Twelve[,] the sick[,] &c.

—Wilford Woodruff, Diary.

....

P.M. Met with the Twelve [Apostles] in prayer at B[righam]. Youngs.

—William Clayton, Diary.

....

In the afternoon, met with the Twelve [Apostles] in prayer at President Brigham Young's house.

—*History of the Church*, 6:271.

....

Attended prayer-meeting with the Prophet [Joseph Smith] and the Twelve [Apostles] in my [Brigham Young's] house.

—*Manuscript History of Brigham Young*, p. 164.

Sunday, April 28, 1844

Joseph Smith's Red Brick Store

Suddenly sick eve[ning] could not attend Prayer Meeting eve. Prayed for our enemies. Lawsuits &c. &c.

—Joseph Smith, Diary.

....

I [Wilford Woodruff] attended meeting in the evening with all the quorums of the elders to prepare for our missions.

—Wilford Woodruff, Diary.

....

[P]rayer Meeting eve[ning.]

—Willard Richards, Diary.

....

[E]vening attended quorum. We united for President Joseph [Smith,] the Church, the presidency [and] contest[ant]s [in] the Lawsuits. The apostates,[34] the sick &c. &c. We had a good time. President Joseph [Smith] was not there.

—William Clayton, Diary.

---

34. The immediate trouble was due to the activities of Robert D. Foster and brothers William and Wilson Law, excommunicated on April 18, 1844. Earlier in the day, before the quorum's April 28 meetings (above), Brigham Young had de-

Prayer meeting in the evening: the brethren prayed for the sick, a deliverance from our enemies, a favorable termination to lawsuits, &c., &c. I [Joseph Smith] had been suddenly taken sick and was therefore unable to attend.

—History of the Church, 6:346.

....

[E]vening, attended prayer-meeting.

—Manuscript History of Brigham Young, p. 166.

Saturday, May 11, 1844
Joseph Smith's Red Brick Store

6 a prayer Meeting. Elder [Sidney] Rigdon and J[ohn] P. Green[e] admitted. J[ohn] P. Green[e] complained of James Blakesly[35] and F[rancis] M. Higbee[36] for abusing Joseph [Smith] and the Twelve [apostles] at Quincy [Illinois] in court House.[37]

—Joseph Smith, Diary.

---

nounced Foster publicly. Two days previously, Foster had threatened to kill Joseph Smith. He was charged, arrested, fined one hundred dollars, and ordered to keep the peace for six months. The next day he accused Joseph of involvement with Mormon vigilantes and attempting to kill former Missouri governor Lilburn W. Boggs. Foster and the Laws had already accused Joseph of polygamy and other crimes and were gathering affidavits to support their allegations. Joseph wrote that on the evening of April 24, "Brother Ezra Thayer, Dr. Richards, and Dr. Williams were in my room, and a man who boarded at the Masonic hall. At their request, I gave them a history of the Laws' proceedings, in part, in trying to make a difficulty in my family, &c" (*History of the Church,* 6:343-47). Willard Richards brought a civil suit against Foster for slander. As described in one history of the period, "The verbal abuses turned into a series of lawsuits and legal proceedings exchanged between the ... group, whom Smith called the 'anties' (short for anti-Mormons') and church leaders" (Edwin Brown Firmage and Richard Collin Mangrum, *Zion in the Courts: A Legal History of the Church of Jesus Christ of Latter-day Saints, 1830-1890* [Urbana: University of Illinois Press, 1988], 106).

35. James Blakesley (1802-66) had served as an LDS missionary in New York, Illinois, and England. He was excommunicated in May 1844 and became a counselor to William Law in the Reformed Mormon Church. He later affiliated with James Strang and eventually joined the Reorganized Church of Jesus Christ of Latter Day Saints in 1859.

36. Francis Marion Higbee (1820-?) was a colonel in the Nauvoo Legion but later joined with the dissenters and was excommunicated in May 1844. He affiliated with William Law's Reformed Mormon Church and became one of its apostles. Along with the Law brothers and others, he helped to publish the *Nauvoo Expositor* in June 1844.

37. This refers to a public meeting Blakesley and Higbee convened (or at-

Prayer Meetings—[Sidney] Rigdon & [John P.] Green[e] admitted— 6 to 8 P.M.

—Willard Richards, Diary.

....

[A]t 6 p.m. attended prayer meeting: John P. Greene and Sidney Rigdon present.

—*History of the Church,* 6:363.

Sunday, May 12, 1844
Joseph Smith's Red Brick Store

3 P.M. Prayer Meeting at council room. W[illia]m Smith and Almon ^W.^ Babbit were present. A full room prayed for deliverance from our enemies and exaltation to such officers as will enable the Servants of God to execute Righteousness in the Earth.

—Joseph Smith, Diary.

....

[A]ttended prayer meeting Quorum[.]

—Willard Richards, Diary.

....

I [Joseph Fielding] and my Wife [Hannah] attended the Grand Quorum, as I shall call it when W[illia]m Smith and Alman Babbit were taken into it in the legal form[.]

—Joseph Fielding, Diary, entry dated December 1843, LDS Archives.

....

At 3 p.m. I [Joseph Smith] attended prayer meeting in the council room. William Smith and Almon W. Babbit were present. The room was full and we all prayed for deliverance from our enemies and exaltation to such offices as will enable the servants of God to execute righteousness in the earth.

—*History of the Church,* 6:367.

....

Three p.m.,: attended prayer-meeting in the Council room.

—*Manuscript History of Brigham Young,* p. 167.

---

tended) in Quincy, Illinois. According to the *Quincy Whig,* the men reportedly "made out that Joe Smith was pretty much of a rough customer, especially in relation to the 'spiritual wife' d[o]ctrine. Their whole aim was principally against the church—of which they still claimed to be members. They painted Smith, as any thing but the saint he claims to be—and as a man, to the last degree, corrupt in his morals and religion." The following Wednesday, Mormon elder John P. Greene addressed the citizens of Quincy in an attempt to rebut Blakesley's and Higbee's claims (see the *Quincy Whig,* qtd. in the *Nauvoo Expositor,* June 7, 1844).

In the year 1844, a short time before the death of the Prophet Joseph Smith, it was my privilege to attend a regular prayer circle meeting in the ~~lodge~~ upper room over the Prophet's store. There were present at this meeting most of the Twelve Apostles, their wives and a number of other prominent brethren and their wives. On that occasion the Prophet arose and spoke at great length, and during his remarks I heard him say that he had conferred on the heads of the Twelve Apostles all the keys and powers pertaining to the Priesthood, and that upon the heads of the Twelve Apostles the burden of the Kingdom rested, and that they would have to carry it.

—Bathsheba W. Smith, Affidavit, dated November 19, 1903, LDS Archives.

Tuesday, May 14, 1844
Joseph Smith's Red Brick Store

4 P.M. Prayer Meeting, few present. Prayed for Bro[ther] [Lucien] Woodworth's daughter[38] who was sick. Lyman Wight was present.

—Joseph Smith, Diary.

Instructing Lyman Wight. — on Quorum.

—Willard Richards, Diary.

At 4 p.m. prayer meeting; few present. Prayed for Elder [Lucien] Woodworth's daughter, who was sick. Elder Lyman Wight was present.

—*History of the Church,* 6:377.

Sunday, May 19, 1844
Joseph Smith's Red Brick Store

Prayer Meeting at P.M. Was dispensed with. So muddy and rainy. About 12 men 2 women attending.

—Joseph Smith, Diary.

2 P.M. meeting. rain — few come — no meeting.

—Willard Richards, Diary.

---

38. Flora Ann Woodworth (1826-ca. 1851) married Joseph Smith as a plural wife in 1843. Soon after Joseph's death in 1844, she married non-Mormon Carlos Gove.

The usual prayer meeting at 2 p.m. was dispensed with on account of the mud and rain.

—*History of the Church*, 6:398.

Saturday, May 25, 1844
Joseph Smith's Mansion House

2 P.M. Council in my [Joseph Smith's] north Room.[39] Letter from [Orson] Hyde.[40] Ordered an answer.[41] Also made arrangements to have me have post office.[42] Adjourned ^to Friday next^ week 2 o'clock. W[illard] Richards writes to [Orson] Hyde for Council.

—Joseph Smith, Diary.

....

[C]ouncil of Kingdom[?] in the P.M.

—Willard Richards, Diary.

....

P.M. in council with the quorum.

—William Clayton, Diary.

....

At 2 p.m. I [Joseph Smith] was in council in my north room, and heard the letters from Elder O[rson]. Hyde read, and instructed Dr. [Willard] Richard[s] to write an answer ...

—*History of the Church*, 6:405.

Sunday, June 9, 1844
Joseph Smith's Mansion House

---

39. This may be a meeting of the recently organized Council of Fifty.

40. Letter from Orson Hyde, dated April 30, 1844. Hyde was then in Washington, D.C., with Orson Pratt and John E. Page, hoping to get "Joseph Smith's Memorial, asking to be appointed 'a member of the U.S. Army' and to be authorized to raise one hundred thousand armed volunteers to police the intermoutain and Pacific coast west from Oregon to Texas" (*History of the Church*, 6:286).

41. Willard Richards, Letter to Orson Hyde, dated May 26, 1844, in *History of the Church*, 6:405-407.

42. During the John C. Bennett scandal, Joseph came to distrust Sidney Rigdon, who served as Nauvoo's postmaster. In February 1843, Joseph had contacted U.S. senator Richard M. Young asking for Sidney's removal from office. Joseph wrote of the "dishonest conduct of the postmaster and those connected with the postoffice in this city," asserting that "letters had frequently been broken open, money detained, and letters charged twice over &c" (*History of the Church*, 5:266-76). Despite Joseph's urging, more than fifteen months passed before Sidney resigned and Joseph was named his successor. See Robert Bruce Flanders, *Nauvoo: Kingdom on the Mississippi*

Meeting at Mansion 6 o'clock.[43]

—Joseph Smith, Diary.

....

There was a meeting at the Mansion at 6 p.m.

—*History of the Church,* 6:405.

....

President Joseph Smith attended the meetings of that "[Holy] Order," which were held in the large room in the second story of his brick store building. One day in June, 1844,[44] the "Order" was in session from morning until evening. At the adjournment for dinner we saw Joseph Smith come from there, and again after dinner, he returned back to the same place, as in returning from dinner President Smith and the writer walked by ourselves, side by side in intimate conversation, but parted at the store.

Not long after parting with President Smith, wishing to speak with him, we ran hastily up the stairs to call him out when to our amazement we encountered John Taylor, one of the twelve Apostles, in a long white garment, with a white turban on his head, and a drawn sword in his hand, evidently representing the "cherubims and flaming sword which was placed at the east of the garden of Eden, to guard the tree of life." He informed us Bro[ther]. Joseph was in the room.

—Ebenezer Robinson, "Utah Not Responsible. Endowment Robes in Nauvoo, in 1843-44," in *The Return* 2 (April 1890): 252.

....

I was present at a prayer meeting held in the upper room of the brick store building, at a time when his enemies were seeking his life. At another time [June 9, 1844?]—a time never to be forgotten—I was present at a meeting when Joseph [Smith] knelt down with a small congregation surrounding him, when every sentence he uttered seemed to convey to my mind, and to the minds of others present, the impression that this was our last meeting togther—and so it was.

—Mercy Fielding Thompson, "Recollections of Joseph Smith," *Juvenile Instructor* 27 (July 1, 1892): 399.

_____

(Urbana: University of Illinois Press, 1965), 257; and Richard S. Van Wagoner, *Sidney Rigdon: A Portrait of Religious Excess* (Salt Lake City: Signature Books, 1994), 311.

43. This may be a meeting of the Council of Fifty and not of the Quorum of the Anointed.

44. Robinson gives an approximate date, which he may have misremembered.

Sunday, June 30, 1844
Location unknown.

A few of the Quorum assembled and agreed to send G[eorge]. J. Adams[45] to bear the news [of Joseph and Hyrum Smith's deaths] to the Twelve [Apostles].

—William Clayton, Diary.

....

A few of the brethren met in council, and agreed to send Brother George J. Adams to bear the news of the massacre [of Joseph and Hyrum Smith] to the Twelve [Apostles].

—"Manuscript History of Brigham Young,"
in *History of the Church,* 7:147.

Thursday, July 4, 1844
William Marks House

P.M. in Council with Brothers [William] Marks, [Alpheus] Cutler and [Reynolds] Cahoon at [William] Mark[s's] house. It seemed manifest to us that brother [William] Marks['s] place is to be appointed president, and Trustee in Trust and this accords with Emma [Smith]'s feelings.[46] Brother [John] Taylor is at Brother [William] Mark[s's]. I saw some of his [John Taylor's] wounds[47] which are bad but he is recovering.

—William Clayton, Diary.

Sunday, July 7, 1844
Council Chamber

---

45. George J. Adams (1810–80), a member of the Council of Fifty, was excommunicated in 1845. Beginning in 1846, he became a follower of James J. Strang until founding his own Church of the Messiah in 1861.

46. With financial worries in mind, Emma hoped that William Marks, then Nauvoo Stake president, would be appointed as trustee-in-trust for the church. He opposed plural marriage, and Emma wanted to purge the practice from the church. Instead, William Clayton, also a friend of Emma, was named acting trustee as a compromise. See Linda King Newell and Valeen Tippetts Avery, *Mormon Enigma: Emma Hale Smith* (Garden City, NY: Doubleday, 1984), 201-202.

47. John Taylor had been with Joseph Smith when Joseph was murdered on June 27, 1844. After the mob stormed Carthage Jail, Taylor was shot as he tried in vain to jump out a window and again as he crawled across the floor. Bullets struck him in the left thigh, hip, wrist, and knee.

6. eve[ning] council at Council Chamber to talk over business Church[.]

—Willard Richards, Diary.

5 o'clock went to council with the Quorum on the subject of appointing a Trustee in Trust. ... I [William Clayton] was late at the Council. The brethren had agreed not to appoint a Trustee untill the Twelve [Apostles] came home, and that I should act in the place of Trustee to receive property &c. untill one was appointed.

—William Clayton, Diary.

Wednesday, July 10, 1844
Council Chamber

Elder Willard Richards, Patriarch John Smith, Samuel H. Smith and W. W. Phelps met in council in the council chamber.

—"Manuscript History of Brigham Young," in *History of the Church,* 7:175.

Friday, July 12, 1844
Location unknown.

At 3 we went to meeting. Emma [Smith] was present and urged the necessity of appointing a Trustee immediately. But on investigation it was considered we could not lawfully do it. Another meeting was appointed for Sunday Eve. Dr. [Willard] Richards and [William W.] Phelps seem to take all the matters into their own hands and won't tell us anything what they intend or have thought to do.

—William Clayton, Diary.

A council was held at 3 p.m.; but as Dr. Willard Richards and Bishop [Newel K.] Whitney considered it premature, the council was adjourned till Sunday evening, the 14th.

—"Manuscript History of Brigham Young," in *History of the Church,* 7:183.

Sunday, July 14, 1844
Council Chamber

At 6 went to the Council. [William W.] Phelps and [Willard] Rich-

81

ards and P[arley] P. Pratt stated that they had concluded to appoint 4 Trustees when a majority of the Twelve [Apostles] returned. These three brethren seem to keep matters very close to themselves and I [William Clayton] and several others feel grieved at it. After meeting I informed Emma [Smith] of the proceedings. She thinks they don't use her right.

—William Clayton, Diary.

....

6 *p.m.* Several councilors came to the council chamber to investigate the subject of choosing trustees, but decided to wait until the Twelve [Apostles] arrived.

—"Manuscript History of Brigham Young," in *History of the Church,* 7:184.

Friday, July 19, 1844

Location unknown.

Elders Parley P. Pratt, Willard Richards, John Taylor, and W. W. Phelps spent afternoon in council.

—"Manuscript History of Brigham Young," in *History of the Church,* 7:200.

Wednesday, July 24, 1844

Location unknown.

[C]ouncil with Parl[e]y [Pratt]. [William W.] Phelps &c. and anointed Samuel H. Smith[.]

—Willard Richards, Diary.

....

Elders Parley P. Pratt, Willard Richards. W[illiam]. W. Phelps, George Miller and L[ucien]. Woodworth met in council. They anointed and administered to Elder Samuel H. Smith, who was very sick.

—"Manuscript History of Brigham Young," in *History of the Church,* 7:202.

Friday, August 9, 1844

Brigham Young House

Council at B[righam]. Young's — 1 P.M. B[righam]. Young, H[eber]. C. Kimball A[masa]. Lyman, G[eorge]. A. Smith, W[ilford] Woodruff

P[arley]. P. Pratt, O[rson] Pratt W[illard]. Richards. & 11 others[.]

Pres[iden]t. [Brigham] Young. proposed righting up the Quorums. giving every one his place &c. Joseph [Smith']s presence has superseded the necessity of carrying out a perfect operation of the organization of the several Quorums. — [To] The oldest Bishop of the Church belongs the general financial concerns of the Church — the several committees to be arranged — Mayor chosen — 70s organized &c.

P[arley]. P. Pratt thought the 12 [Apostles] would have enought to do — without attend[ing] to city councils &c. Temple Committee & affairs referred to. by Pres[iden]t. [Brigham] Young & [Reynolds] Cahoon[.]

H[eber]. C. Kimball motioned that the committee of the Nauvoo House [should have] gotten up their papers to settle up their assets & report to the 12.

L[yman]. Wight said Joseph [Smith] said let the Nauvoo House rest on my shoulders till the temple is done & I will put it up without hindrance. [Lyman] Wight — said he was ready to settle.

Geo[rge]. Miller said when he went to the pinery. put a good deal of property into the hands of the Trustee in trust.

W[illiam] W Phelps said that when he heard of Joseph [Smith']s Death — went to Winters [Hiram Winters?][48] got the key to shew a stranger the house and moved in —

[Newel K.] Whitney said Hiram Kimball[49] had Mortgage on Temple at Kirtland [Ohio] — & $4 or 5,000 as against the church.

H[eber]. C. Kimball moved that Bishop [Newel K.] W[h]itney assist W[illia]m Clayton to settle the trustee books — soon to be ready to enter on the duties of his office[.]

Moved that Bishops N[ewel]. K. Whitney and Geo[rge] Miller go forward to settle the property of the Trustee in Trust Joseph Smith — &

---

48. Perhaps Hiram Winters (1805-89), who converted to Mormonism in 1833 and moved to Kirtland, Ohio, that fall. He was a cook during Zion's Camp, the paramilitary campaign to defend Missouri Saints against hostile neighbors. He was also the first man ordained to the office of Seventy in the church and filled a mission to New York. He moved to Quincy, Illinois, in 1837, then to Nauvoo, and received his endowment in the temple in February 1846. His wife died on the trek west; Hiram continued on to Utah and settled there in 1852.

49. Hiram Kimball (1806-63) was a land owner in the Nauvoo area prior to the arrival of the Saints in 1839. He was married to Sarah Melissa Granger. In 1843 he was baptized a member of the LDS church. He died en route to a mission to the Sandwich Islands when a boiler on the steamer he had boarded in San Pedro, California, exploded.

be prepared to enter upon the duty of Trustees. voted that they [represent] the Church. of Jesus Christ of Latter day Saints in Hancock County [Illinois].

Quorum conversed about voted no ~~women~~ ^& men^ more to [be] admitted on Quorum till times will admit.

Voted that Uncle John Smith have the privilege of appointing another president at Macedonia [Illinois]. & come to Nauvoo at his option.

—Willard Richards, Diary.

....

I [Brigham Young] met in council with Elders Heber C. Kimball, Parley P. Pratt, Orson Pratt, Wilford Woodruff, Willard Richards, George A. Smith, Amasa M. Lyman and eleven others at my house.

On motion of Elder Heber C. Kimball, Bishop Newel K. Whitney and George Miller were appointed to settle the affairs of the late Trust-in-Trust, Joseph Smith, and to be prepared to enter upon their duties as Trustees of the Church of Jesus Christ of Latter-day Saints.

—"Manuscript History of Brigham Young,"
in *History of the Church,* 7:247.

Sunday, August 11, 1844
Brigham Young House

In the after noon we met in the Holly Order at B[righam]. Young. All well.
—Heber C. Kimball, Diary.

....

[I]n the afternoon I [Wilford Woodruff] met with the twelve [apostles] for prayer. Had a good time.
—Wilford Woodruff, Diary.

....

3 P.M. A few of the Quorum met at Bro[ther] [Brigham] Youngs — to pray for deliverance from the mob.[50]
—Willard Richards, Diary.

....

P.M. attended meeting for prayer with Elders B[righam] Young, G[eorge] Miller, H[eber] C. Kimball, A[masa] Lyman, W[illard] Richards,

---

50. "So concerned were they for the lives of the members of the [Anointed] Quorum," wrote Ehat ("Introduction of Temple Ordinances," 207), "that the whole Quorum did not meet again until ordinance work began in the Nauvoo Temple."

L[evi] Richards, J[ohn] P. Green, L[ucien] Woodworth, N[ewel] K. Whitney, and G[eorge] A. Smith and W[ilford] Woodruff.

—William Clayton, Diary.

At 3 p.m. a few of the authorities met at my [Brigham Young's] house to pray for deliverance from the mob.

—"Manuscript History of Brigham Young," in *History of the Church,* 7:248.

Thursday, August 15, 1844
Brigham Young House?

I [Wilford Woodruff] met with the quorum in the afternoon for Prayer, to Pray for the Sick. Mrs [Phoebe] Woodruff was with me. {Geo[rge] M[iller]} {Mrs [Mary] M[iller]} Br[other] [George] and Sister [Mary] Miller was Present.[51] Was Prayed for as Sister [Mary] Miller was quite out of health.

—Wilford Woodruff, Diary.

....

I [Brigham Young] met in a prayer circle with the Twelve [Apostles] and a few others in the afternoon and prayed for the sick.

—"Manuscript History of Brigham Young," in *History of the Church,* 7:249.

Wednesday, September 4, 1844
Brigham Young House

The Holly Preasthood met in the Ev[e]ning. ... We Praid as follows, to overcome the smit [suit] fore the [Nauvoo] Temple of the Church.

—Heber C. Kimball, Diary.

....

In the evening the Twelve [Apostles] and a few others of us met at Elder [Brigham] Youngs and offered up prayers for our preservation and the preservation of the church, and that the Lord would bind up the dissenters that they may not have power to injure the honest in heart. We had a good time and we believe the Lord will answer our prayers.

—William Clayton, Diary.

---

51. A second anointing.

The Twelve Apostles and a few others met at my [Brigham Young's] house in the evening and prayed for the preservation of the church and ourselves; and that the Lord might bind up the apostates and preserve the honest in heart.

—"Manuscript History of Brigham Young,"
in *History of the Church,* 7:267.

Thursday, September 5, 1844

Location unknown.

Br[other] [William] Marks came to see me [Brigham Young] about Pr[e]s[ident] [Sidney] Rigdon and his revelations[.] in the afternoon went to the prayer meeting and exposed the fals Prophets[.][52]

—Brigham Young, Diary.

Prair meeting in the after noon, the Twelve [Apostles] spoke of the wick[ed]ness of Elder [Sidney] Rigdon.

—Heber C. Kimball, Diary.

... Elder [Sidney] Rigdons course since he came here has been a continued course of deception and falsehood and that his object is to scatter the people and break up the foundation laid by our beloved prophet Joseph Smith. The people seem to feel indignant at Elder [Sidney] Rigdon for it [and] is now reduced to a certainty that he is conspiring with the apostates to bring a mob upon us.

—William Clayton, Diary.

Brother W[illia]m. Marks came to see me in relation to President [Sidney] Rigdon and his revelations. Afternoon, attended public [sic] prayer meeting[53] and exposed the false prophets.

—"Manuscript History of Brigham Young,"
in *History of the Church,* 7:267.

---

52. Sidney Rigdon, who had served as first counselor in the First Presidency, rejected the leadership of the Twelve Apostles and proclaimed himself church guardian. He was excommunicated three days after the above-mentioned meeting of the Anointed Quorum. William Marks's encounter with Brigham Young is important, as Marks was sympathetic to Rigdon and would defend him at his excommunication trial. Because of this, and his own lack of support for the Twelve, Marks was released from his position as president of the Nauvoo Stake on October 7, 1844.

53. As Quinn (*Origins,* 503) points out, the *History of the Church* "makes the misleading addition: 'public prayer meeting.'"

Saturday, September 14, 1844
Brigham Young House

[C]auld on Sister Hyram Smith Bro[ther] H[eber] C Kimball & G[eorge] A Smith was with me attended to offering up prayrs for A[masa] Lyman ... in the evening paid Bro[ther] Amasa Lymond a visit found him much better ½ past 8 o.c[lock]. P.M.
—Brigham Young, Diary.

Met with Elders [Brigham] Young and [Heber C.] Kimball and visited Elder Amasa M. Lyman, who is very sick.
—George A. Smith, Diary, LDS Archives.

Elder Amasa M. Lyman being very sick and reported to be dying, Brothers [Heber C.] Kimball, George A. [Smith] and I [Brigham Young] retired to my upper room and prayed for him: he was healed from that very hour.
—"Manuscript History of Brigham Young,"
in *History of the Church,* 7:271.

Thursday, September 26, 1844
Heber C. Kimball House?

Tended prair meeting in the after noon, had council at the [Nauvoo] Temple[.]
—Heber C. Kimball, Diary.

Tuesday, October 1, 1844
Heber C. Kimball House

Had a meeting at my [Heber C. Kimball's] hous in the ev[e]ning of the Holy Order. Praied fore the sick and fore the Governer [Thomas Ford[54] of Illinois].
—Heber C. Kimball, Diary.

---

54. Thomas Ford (1800-50) served as governor of Illinois from 1842 to 1846. He had earlier been a circuit court judge in northern Illinois (1835-37) and in the Galena district (1839). He was appointed to the state supreme court in 1841, but resigned to accept the Democratic nomination for governor. After serving his term, he authored *A History of Illinois: From Its Commencement as a State in 1818 to 1847* (Chicago: S.C. Griggs, 1854).

[M]et the 12 & others in A Prayer Meeting.

—George A. Smith, Diary, LDS Archives.

....

Met with the Twelve [apostles] and others at a prayer meeting.

—George A. Smith, "History of George Albert Smith."

....

Evening met the Twelve [apostles] at Brother [Heber C.] Kimballs and offered up prayer for the Governor [Thomas Ford of Illinois] and Emma [Smith] and sundry other things. We had a very interesting season of conversation. A man has a right to be baptized for his acquaintances who are not relatives and sealed to them only by the consent and authority of him who holds the keys.[55]

—William Clayton, Diary.

....

Evening, attended a meeting of the quorum for prayer: a very interesting session.

—"Manuscript History of Brigham Young," in *History of the Church,* 7:280.

Friday, October 11, 1844
Heber C. Kimball House

Evening at Heber C. K[imball]'s in company with President [Brigham] Young. H[eber]. C. K[imball] and G[eorge] A. S[mith] of the Twelve [Apostles], the two Trustees [Newel K. Whitney and George Miller] and Sisters [Vilate] Kimball and [Elizabeth Ann] Whitney. We offered up prayer for the sick and Sister Emma [Smith] &c. and also that the enemies may have no more power over us. We had much conversation respecting the [Nauvoo] Temple Committee.[56]

—William Clayton, Diary.

---

55. This may be an early reference to the Law of Adoption. Under this law, members of the church could be sealed to prominent church leaders. The practice began in Nauvoo and became common practice in Utah. It was discontinued in 1894. See Gordon Irving, "The Law of Adoption: One Phase of the Development of the Mormon Concept of Salvation, 1830-1900," *BYU Studies* 14 (Spring 1974): 291-314.

56. The Temple Committee was appointed in October 1840 and was headed by Alpheus Cutler, Reynolds Cahoon, and Elias Higbee. Their purpose was to oversee construction and secure building materials for the temple, which took over five years to complete. After Higbee died in 1843, Hyrum Smith took his place.

Evening, I [Brigham Young] attended prayer meeting at Elder [Heber C.] Kimball's.

> —"Manuscript History of Brigham Young,"
> in *History of the Church,* 7:310.

Monday, December 2, 1844
Willard Richards House

The brethren had a council at Dr [Willard] Richards but I [William Clayton] was not permitted to be there, probably they did not think worthwhile to tell me. I feel sorry and grieved at heart, but dont intend they shall know it.

> —William Clayton, Diary.

Sunday, December 22, 1844
Location unknown.

Met with the brethren of the first quorum to pray and counsel. My [William Clayton's] wife [Ruth] and O[rson] Pratts wife [Sarah], P[arley] P. Pratts wife [Mary] and A[masa] Lymans wife [Mary] was voted in. We have to use the greatest care and caution and dare not let it be known that we meet.[57]

> —William Clayton, Diary.

I [Brigham Young] met as usual with the Twelve Apostles and others for prayer.

> —"Manuscript History of Brigham Young,"
> n *History of the Church,* 7:327.

---

57. "Even at this time," writes Ehat ("Introduction of Temple Ordinances," 208), "six months after the Martyrdom, such precautions seemed so necessary that the persons Clayton mentioned were not admitted until over a month later. Meeting together in one place, the [Anointed] Quorum felt they increased the chances that the keys might be lost if a mob stormed their meeting and killed them. Yet if they did not meet, they could not offer the united prayers that they knew were their ultimate protection."

IV.

The Year

1845

COMPLETING THE TEMPLE

Sunday, January 12, 1845
Parley P. Pratt Store

[E]ve[ning] prayer Meeting over Trustees office ([Parley P.] Pratts store.) Joseph Young & wife [Jane] present.
—Willard Richards, Diary.

....

Evening met with the first quorum at Parley [P. Pratt]'s. Joseph Young and his wife [Jane] were annointed with the second ordinance.
—William Clayton, Diary.

....

Evening, attended prayer meeting.
—"Manuscript History of Brigham Young," in *History of the Church,* 7:32.

Friday, January 17, 1845
Brigham Young House

[I]n the evening Br[other]s [Heber C.] Kimball J[ohn]. Taylor & G[eorge] A Smith was at my [Brigham Young's] uperroom in the evening[.]
—Brigham Young, Diary.

Elder H[eber]. C. Kimball, John Taylor and George A. Smith met with me [Brigham Young] in my upper room: we counseled and prayed.

—"Manuscript History of Brigham Young,"
in *History of the Church,* 7:361.

Tuesday, January 21, 1845
Lucien Woodworth House

In the ev[e]ning spent at Br[other]. [Lucien] Wooderds [Woodworth's] in company with B[righam]. Young, G[eorge]. A. Smith, John Tailor [Taylor], W[illiam]. [W.] Phelps, and sevrel others, with our wives.

—Heber C. Kimball, Diary.

....

Met in council with the Twelve [apostles] and wrote letters of instruction to the Elders in the eastern cities.

—George A. Smith, "History of George Albert Smith."

Thursday, January 23, 1845
Location unknown.

I [Zina D. H. Jacobs] went to Prayer meeting[1] with sister [Roxena] Ripshier [Repshire].[2] Br[other] [Peter] Hause [Hawes?][3] took the Lead of the meeting. Had a good meeting.

—Zina D. H. Jacobs, Diary, in "'All Things Move in Order in
the City': The Nauvoo Diary of Zina Diantha Huntington
Jacobs," edited by Maureen Ursenbach Beecher,
BYU Studies 19 (Spring 1979): 285-320.

Friday, January 24, 1845
Brigham Young House

---

1. This may be a general meeting of prayer and instruction and not a meeting of the Quorum of the Anointed since Peter Hawes had apparently not yet been anointed.

2. Roxena Repshire was the plural wife of the deceased James Adams.

3. Peter Hawes (1795-1862), a member of the Nauvoo Agricultural and Manufacturing Association, helped to build the Nauvoo House and raised money for its construction. He was a member of the Nauvoo Stake High Council and of the Council of Fifty.

Br[other]s H[eber]. C. Kimball and N[ewel]. K. Whitney was at my [Brigham Young's] house[.] we washed an[d] anointed and Praid had a good time. I inquaired of the Lord whether we should stay here and finish the templ[e.] the ansure [answer] was we should.[4]

—Brigham Young, Diary.

....

N[ewel] K Whitney B[righam] Young and my self [Heber. C. Kimball] met at B[righam] Young. Spent the after noon in washing and inointing [anointing] our bodies, and fore prair. The Lord was with us.

—Heber C. Kimball, Diary.

Saturday, January 25, 1845
Location unknown.

In the Ev[e]ning fore [four] persons, females recieved thare Anointing Hellen Kimball.

—Heber C. Kimball, Diary.

Sunday, January 26, 1845
Parley P. Pratt Store

In the ev[e]ning the Holly Preast hood meet over Elder Parly P. Pratt store. Elder [John E.] Page Recieved his admitence in to the Holy Order.

—Heber C. Kimball, Diary.

....

In the evening met with the Twelve [apostles] in the High Quorum.

—John Taylor, Diary.

....

Had A Council in the Evening[.] Elder [John E.] Page was present & & &.

—George A. Smith, Diary, LDS Archives.

....

Held Council in the evening. Elder John E. Page was present.

—George A. Smith, "History of George Albert Smith."

....

[I]n the evening meet in the Quorum.

—Amasa Lyman, Diary, LDS Archives.

---

4. Here washing and anointing precede a prayer circle instead of an endowment. This apparently was not a regular meeting of the Quorum of the Anointed.

Evening met with the quorum. John E. Page & J[oseph]. C. Kingsbury were received[;] also Sara Ann Whitney, Hellen M. Kimball, Eliza R. Snow, [Mary] Page, [Mary Ann] Pratt, Olive G. Frost, Lucy [Decker] Seeley, Louisa Beaman.

—William Clayton, Diary.

....

I [Joseph C. Kingsbury] received my first Anointing and was received into the Quoram of the Priesthood & met with the quoram at times, offered up prayer & received instructions very beneficial ...

—"History of Joseph C. Kingsbury," entry dated January 1845, Special Collections, Western Americana, Marriott Library, University of Utah, Salt Lake City, Utah.

....

Evening, I [Brigham Young] attended prayer meeting.

—"Manuscript History of Brigham Young," in *History of the Church,* 7:365.

Wednesday, January 29, 1845
Location unknown.

Afternoon, attended council.[5]

—"Manuscript History of Brigham Young," in *History of the Church,* 7:368.

Thursday, January 30, 1845
Location unknown.

Went to prayer meting. Had a good meeting.[6]

—Zina D. H. Jacobs, Diary, in "'All Things Move in Order in the City': The Nauvoo Diary of Zina Diantha Huntington Jacobs," edited by Maureen Ursenbach Beecher, *BYU Studies* 19 (Spring 1979): 302.

---

5. This may or may not be a meeting of the Quorum of the Anointed.

6. As with the entry for January 23, 1845, this may or may not be a regular meeting of the Quorum of the Anointed. In any event, Quinn (*Origins,* 504) summarized his findings for this date as follows: "Thursday prayer circle meeting; anointing and endowment for Joseph B. Noble, Zina D. Huntington (Jacobs, Smith), and—probably also on this date—Mary Elizabeth Rollins (Lightner, Smith) ... Between 30 January and 20 March [1845], Sylvia P. Sessions (Lyon, Smith, Kimball), Harriet Page Wheeler (Decker), and Mary A. Be(a)man (Noble) were anointed and endowed" (source citations omitted).

Thursday, February 13, 1845
Heber C. Kimball House

Went to the [Nauvoo] Temple in the Ev[e]ning. B[righam]. Young, W[illard]. Richards, G[eorge]. A. Smith, Br[other]. [Lucien] Woodard [Woodworth?], Br[other]. Vance,[7] with thare wives come and spent the Ev[e]ning.[8] Had a good time.

—Heber C. Kimball, Diary.

[M]et with the twelve [apostles] in counsel & others.

—George A. Smith, Diary, LDS Archives.

Met in Council with the Twelve [apostles] and others.

—George A. Smith, "History of George Albert Smith."

I [Brigham Young] met in council with the Twelve [apostles] and others. With Elders Willard Richards, George A. Smith, and others, I spent the evening at Elder [Heber C.] Kimball's: had a good time.

—"Manuscript History of Brigham Young,"
in *History of the Church,* 7:373.

Friday, February 14, 1845
Location unknown.

In the evening the following brethren met together to pray and ask God to thwart the plans of the mob and deliver the brethren out of their hands viz. B[righam]. Young, H[eber]. C. Kimball, O[rson]. Pratt, G[eorge]. A. Smith, W[illar]d. Richards, N[ewel]. K. Whitney, Geo[rge]. Miller, A[lpheus]. Cutler, R[eynolds]. Cahoon, Isaac Morley, O[rson]. Spencer, Joseph Young and myself [William Clayton]. We have a very good time and the Lord blesses us and I believe we will have the desires of our hearts. After prayers it was voted that Father [Isaac] Morley move in to Nauvoo as soon as possible and that Solomon Hancock[9] be appointed to preside over

7. Perhaps William P. Vance (1822-1914), who was baptized in 1842, moved to Nauvoo, and for a time lived with Joseph Smith. He would become one of the original Utah pioneers and help Parley P. Pratt explore the regions south of the Salt Lake Valley. He would be one of the first settlers in Iron County and later serve as the first judge of Summit County.

8. Quinn (*Origins,* 504) suggests that "Heber C. Kimball apparently also listed unendowed people who attended an after-meeting social: 'Br[other]. Woodard, Br[other]. Vance,' and their wives."

9. Solomon Hancock (1794-1847) served as an LDS missionary to Jackson

the Lima [Illinois] Branch in his stead. It was also voted that Dr. [John M.] Bernhisel be appointed a traveling Bishop to visit the churches. We had also some conversation on the subject of sending six brethren with brother Lewis Dana[10] to the West, and especially to Texas.[11]

—William Clayton, Diary.

I [Brigham Young] met with the Twelve [apostles] and others and prayed for the deliverance of these brethren. Father [Isaac] Morley was counseled to remove his family to Nauvoo and Solomon Hancock was appointed to preside over that [Morley Settlement] branch. Dr. John M. Bernhisel was appointed a Traveling Bishop to visit the churches. Some conversation ensued on the subject of sending six brethren with Brother Lewis Dana to the west and especially to Texas.

—"Manuscript History of Brigham Young,"
in *History of the Church,* 7:374.

Sunday, February 16, 1845
Trustee's Office

[E]ve[ning], prayer meeting at Trustees office prayed that Father [Isaac] Morl[e]y might be delivered from his enemies. & that the 5 brethren who had been arrested at Morl[e]y Settlement might be set free. & the enemy stopped at that place.[12]

—Willard Richards, Diary.

County, Missouri, in 1831 and later was a member of the high councils in Far West and Clay County, Missouri. He was called in October 1844 to preside over a branch of the church in one of the congressional districts of the United States.

10. Lewis Dana, an Oneida Native American, converted to Mormonism and was called to preach to his brethren in April 1845 in company with Phinehas Young, Jonathan Dunham, Charles Shumway, and George S. Tindale.

11. This mission to the West to find a new home for the Saints eventually included eight men. Lewis Dana and four of the party left Nauvoo on April 24, 1845. One goal was to form friendships with Native American tribes along the way, especially in Council Bluffs, Iowa. Before returning at the end of the summer, the missionaries had secured permission to establish settlements in the middle Missouri River region and promises from local natives to assist them in exploring the regions to the west.

12. The Morley Settlement was located in Lima, Adams County, Illinois, twenty-five miles south of Nauvoo. Isaac Morley had moved there from Missouri, and several hundred Saints soon followed.

Evening, I [Brigham Young] attended prayer meeting at the Trustees' Office.

—"Manuscript History of Brigham Young,"
in *History of the Church,* 7:374.

Sunday, February 23, 1845
Brigham Young House

[I]n the Evening met with the Elders of A[nointed] Council at Elder B[righam] Youngs.

—George A. Smith, Diary, LDS Archives.

I [George A. Smith] met with the brethren of the Council.

—George A. Smith, "History of George Albert Smith."

Evening in Council with the Twelve [apostles] and others.

—William Clayton, Diary.

Evening, the Twelve Apostles and others met in council and for prayer.

—"Manuscript History of Brigham Young,"
in *History of the Church,* 7:375.

Thursday, February 27, 1845
John Smith House

[I]n the evening went to Fathers John Smiths to Pray for him[.] we drest and prayed and had a good meeting and he was blest.

—Brigham Young, Diary.

Evening, called on Father John Smith, who was still sick; united with the brethren and prayed for him: he felt blessed.

—"Manuscript History of Brigham Young,"
in *History of the Church,* 7:378.

Monday, March 9, 1845
Brigham Young House

Went to Elder B[righam] Youngs had A Council with Elders Young & H[eber]. C. Kimball John Taylor N[ewel]. W. [sic] Whitney Geo[rge].

97

Miller Sat with them for for [sic] most of the day.

—George A. Smith, Diary, LDS Archives.

....

I [Brigham Young] attended council with Elders Heber C. Kimball, John Taylor, George A. Smith, N[ewel]. K. Whitney and George Miller, most of the day.

—"Manuscript History of Brigham Young,"
in *History of the Church,* 7:380.

Thursday, March 20, 1845
Joseph Bates Noble House

The Holly Order met in the Ev[e]ning at B[rother]. [Joseph Bates] Nobles.

—Heber C. Kimball, Diary.

....

[W]ent to ... a council and prayer meeting.

—George A. Smith, "History of George Albert Smith."

....

[W]as in counsil at night.

—Amasa Lyman, Diary, LDS Archives.

....

Evening, attended prayer meeting at Brother Joseph B[ates]. Noble's.

—"Manuscript History of Brigham Young,"
in *History of the Church,* 7:387.

Friday, March 21, 1845
Joseph Bates Noble House

[I]n the Ev[e]ning met with the Holy Order [at] B[rother] [Joseph Bates] Nobles [blank] with me.

—Heber C. Kimball, Diary.

....

Went to council in the evening with the Twelve [apostles].

—George A. Smith, "History of George Albert Smith."

....

[S]pent the eve[ning] with. B[righam]. Y[oung]. A[masa]. L[yman]. —G[eorge]. A. S[mith]. —N[ewel]. K. W[hitney]. —H[eber]. C. Kimball. prayer meeting— Lucy [Decker][13] was present.

—Willard Richards, Diary.

---

13. Lucy Decker married Brigham Young as his plural wife on June 15, 1842.

[A]t counsil at night.

—Amasa Lyman, Diary, LDS Archives.

....

Evening, attended prayer meeting at Brother Joseph B[ates]. Noble's.

—"Manuscript History of Brigham Young,"
in *History of the Church*, 7:387.

Tuesday, March 25, 1845
Location unknown.

Went to prayer circle with the Twelve [apostles].

—George A. Smith, "History of George Albert Smith."

....

[E]ve[ning] at <anointed?> Prayer meeting. E. Brown E[?][14]

—Willard Richards, Diary.

....

I [Brigham Young] attended council with the Twelve [apostles] and prayer meeting in the evening.

—"Manuscript History of Brigham Young,"
in *History of the Church*, 7:388.

Saturday, March 29, 1845
Location unknown

On Saturday [March 29, 1845] Ruth [Moon Clayton] and Margaret [Moon Clayton] received their anointing for which I [William Clayton] feel thankful. Margaret had some good instructions and she feels satisfied and reconciled. She says she will never leave me on any consideration. ... I still feel determined to do all I can and be as faithful as I know how for that is the desire of my heart, but my greatest desire is to so live that I may secure for myself and mine the highest degree of exaltation and glory

---

She entered the Quorum of the Anointed on January 26, 1845, and apparently received the second anointing on this date.

14. Quinn (*Origins*, 504-505) interprets this entry to mean: "Prayer circle meeting in evening; anointing and endowment for 'E. B.' ... Could be Emmeline B. Woodward (plural wife of Newel Whitney), or Elizabeth Brotherton (plural wife of Parley P. Pratt who was in the eastern states at this time). William Clayton refers to 'E. B.' accepting Heber Kimball's polygamous 'instructions' on 20 Sept. 1845" (source citations omitted).

which is possible for me to obtain, and to be with my friend Joseph Smith in the eternal world.
—William Clayton, Diary, entry dated March 31, 1845.

Thursday, April 3, 1845
Willard Richards House

Last Ev[e]ning [April 3, 1845] the Holly Order met at W[illard]. Richards. We felt the power of God.
—Heber C. Kimball, Diary, entry dated April 4, 1845.

....

[P]roceeded to Dr. [Willard] Richards[.]
—George A. Smith, "History of George Albert Smith."

....

Prayer Meeting at my [Willard Richards's] office 8 oclock. that the mob might be disunited & contend among themselves & have no power over the Saints & that [Thomas] Sharp[15] & his co[mpany?][16] might be visited with judgments[.]
—Willard Richards, Diary, entry dated April 2, 1845.

....

Evening met with a few of the high quorum at Dr. [Willard] Richards house for prayer. There were present B[righam]. Young, H[eber]. C. Kimball, W[illard]. Richards, John Taylor, O[rson]. Pratt, G[eorge]. A. Smith, J[ohn]. E. Page, G[eorge]. Miller, Joseph Young and myself [William Clayton]. Our prayers were that the plans of the mob might be frustrated that they might have no influence nor power to disturb nor trouble us. That the leaders of the mob especially [Thomas] Sharp may be visited

---

15. Thomas C. Sharp (1818-94) was a lawyer-turned-newspaper editor living in Warsaw, Illinois. In 1840 he bought and began publishing *The Western World,* which he changed to the *Warsaw Signal* the next year. He was an active voice in opposing Joseph Smith and the Mormons and was one of the men indicted for Joseph's murder in 1844. He was subsequently elected justice of the peace in 1851, and two years later was the first mayor of Warsaw. In 1854 he returned to journalism and bought the *Warsaw Express.* Ten years later he was elected county judge. He subsequently returned to law, although he also later edited the *Carthage Gazette.*

16. This probably refers to those charged with the murder of Joseph Smith: Mark Aldrich, Jacob C. Davis, William N. Grover, Thomas Sharp, and Levi Williams. The trial began on May 19 and lasted until May 30. The jury found the defendants not guilty. See Dallin H. Oaks and Marvin S. Hill, *Carthage Conspiracy: The Trial of the Accused Assassins of Joseph Smith* (Urbana: University of Illinois Press, 1975).

with judgements, and that we may be preserved in peace to finish the houses and see the Elders endowed and fulfil all that the Lord commanded us in this place, also that Brother [Newel K.] Whitney, A[masa]. Lyman and Uncle John Smith may be healed of their sicknesses, and that our families may be blessed &c. We had a good time.

—William Clayton, Diary.

Evening, the brethren of the Twelve [apostles] and others met at Elder [Willard] Richards' office and prayed; we remembered our enemies and prayed that their designs against Zion might fail; we felt the power of God.

—"Manuscript History of Brigham Young," in *History of the Church,* 7:390.

Thursday, April 10, 1845
Willard Richards House

In the evening I [George A. Smith] went to a prayer meeting at Dr. [Willard] Richards.

—George A. Smith, "History of George Albert Smith."

[E]ve[ning] The same [i.e., Elders Hyde, Kimball, Lyman, Richards, Smith, Taylor, and Young] & Bishop[s] [George] Miller & [Newel K.] Whitney at prayer meeting at my office. prayed for rain. (it has been very dry for some time) abundant harvest, a curse on [Thomas] Sharp. [F]osters.[17] Laws[18] Higbees[19] &c — blessings on the saints & our protection from enemies[.]

—Willard Richards, Diary.

---

17. This refers to brothers Robert D. and Charles A. Foster, both excommunicated in 1844, who soon after assisted in the publication of the *Nauvoo Expositor.* Robert, a physician, had accompanied Joseph Smith to Washington, D.C., in 1839-40 to seek redress for persecutions in Missouri. He served as a regent of the University of Nauvoo, member of the Nauvoo Agricultural and Manufacturing Association, county magistrate of Hancock County, Illinois, and brigadier-general of the Nauvoo Legion.

18. This refers to brothers Wilson Law (1807-77) and William Law (1809-92), who were both excommunicated along with Robert D. Foster in April 1844.

19. Willard Richards, who was present at Carthage Jail when Joseph and Hyrum Smith were murdered, identified the brothers Francis M. (1820-?) and Chauncey L. Higbee (1821-84) among the mob. The brothers were former church members and officers in the Nauvoo Legion, sons of Nauvoo high councilman and church historian Elias Higbee (1795-1843).

Evening, the Twelve [apostles] and bishops met at the Historian's Office and prayed for rain; an abundant harvest; deliverance from our enemies and blessings on the saints.

—"Manuscript History of Brigham Young,"
in History of the Church, 7:395.

Tuesday, April 15, 1845
Willard Richards House

In the evening the Holy order at Willard Richards.

—Heber C. Kimball, Diary.

[M]et in council in the afternoon.

—Amasa Lyman, Diary, LDS Archives.

Thursday, April 17, 1845
Willard Richards House

Met with the Holy Order at W[illard]. Richards.

—Heber C. Kimball, Diary, entry dated April 15, 1845.

Prayer meeting we prayed for rain[.]

—Willard Richards, Diary.

[A]t night meet at br[other] W[illard]. Richards for pray[e]rs and councill.

—Amasa Lyman, Diary, LDS Archives.

Evening tarried at the office till 8 o'clock. Afterwards met at Dr. [Willard] Richards' to pray in company with B[righam]. Young, H[eber]. C. Kimball, W[illard]. Richards, J[ohn]. Taylor, G[eorge]. A. Smith, A[masa]. Lyman, O[rson]. Pratt, of the twelve [apostles]; N[ewel]. K. Whitney and George Miller the two church bishops, John Smith, Patriarch and Joseph Young. The particular subjects asked for was father [Samuel] Bents[20] mis-

---

20. Samuel Bent (1788-1846) had been a Congregationalist deacon before joining the LDS church in 1833. He helped to establish the church in Far West, Missouri, and served a mission to the eastern states in 1840. He was a colonel in the Nauvoo Legion, a member of the Council of Fifty, and later served as the presiding elder at Garden Grove, Iowa, in 1846 until his death that same year.

sion to L[yman] Wights company[21] and the deliverance of the church from their enemies. At my [William Clayton's] suggestion the hands who labor on the [Nauvoo] Temple were remembered to be preserved from accidents, inasmuch as they are in danger all the while. We had a very good time.

—William Clayton, Diary.

Evening, the Twelve [apostles] and presiding bishops met and prayed.

—"Manuscript History of Brigham Young," in *History of the Church,* 7:401.

Friday, April 18, 1845
John Smith House

In the Ev[e]ning the Holy Order met at John Smiths and gave A[masa]. Limon and his wife [Maria] thare Annonting.[22]

—Heber C. Kimball, Diary, entry dated April 17, 1845.

Thursday, April 24, 1845
Willard Richards House

Last night had thunder shower. I thank my Father in heaven ... it rains hard, thunders and litning.

—Heber C. Kimball, Diary.

At noon we met in council about the Nauvoo House affairs. We feel thankful for the shower as it was good for the crops.

—George A. Smith, "History of George Albert Smith."

Prayer Meeting. Geo[rge] A Smith Geo[rge] Miller A[masa] Lyman — John Taylor W[illard] Richards — at my office. Thanked the Lord for rain & disunion among our ene[mies].

—Willard Richards, Diary.

---

21. Bent had just departed for Lyman Wight's camp in Wisconsin to advise him, by way of a letter from the Twelve Apostles, not to proceed with his colonizing mission to Texas. Joseph Smith had commissioned Wight, but Brigham Young decided not to continue the project.

22. Amasa and Maria Lyman received the second anointing.

Evening, attended prayer meeting with the Twelve at Elder Richards.

—"Manuscript History of Brigham Young,"
in *History of the Church,* 7:401.

Sunday, April 27, 1845
Willard Richards House

In the evening nine met to Elder W[illard]. Richards fore prair. Cald on the Father to confuse our Enimes, and flustrate [frustrate] thare plans, and give us power as a people.

—Heber C. Kimball, Diary.

Went to prayer meeting and had a good time conversing on matters pertaining to the [Nauvoo] Temple.

—George A. Smith, "History of George Albert Smith."

Evening met at Dr. [Willard] Richards with the Dr. [and] President B[righam]. Young, H[eber]. C. Kimball, A[masa]. Lyman, G[eorge]. A. Smith, O[rson]. Hyde, J[oseph]. Young and John Smith. Our object was to offer up prayers for a number of subjects. The meeting broke up about 10½ o'clock with perfect peace and union.

—William Clayton, Diary.

B[righam]. Young, H[eber]. C. Kimball, W[illard] Richards, Orson Hyde G[eorge]. A. Smith & W[illia]m. Clayton present in office — evening a Sacred meeting.

—Historian's Office Journal.

Evening, the Twelve Apostles, Presidents John Smith and Joseph Young met for prayer.

—"Manuscript History of Brigham Young,"
in *History of the Church,* 7:405.

Thursday, May 1, 1845
Willard Richards House

In the Even[ing] the Holy Order met at W[illard]. Richards fore Prair.

—Heber C. Kimball, Diary.

Attended a prayer meeting in the evening.

—George A. Smith, "History of George Albert Smith."

Prayer meeting at my [Willard Richards's] house[.] prayed that no Sheriff or constable should have power to come in the city to serve writs on any of the brethren.[23] &c[.]

—Willard Richards, Diary.

Evening met for prayer at Dr. [Willard] Richards. There were present B[righam]. Young, H[eber]. C. Kimball, W[illard]. Richards, A[masa]. Lyman, O[rson]. Hyde, O[rson]. Pratt, G[eorge]. A. Smith, John Smith, I[saac]. Morley and Joseph Young and myself [William Clayton].

—William Clayton, Diary.

Evening, attended prayer meeting.

—"Manuscript History of Brigham Young," in *History of the Church,* 7:405.

Friday, May 2, 1845
Location unknown.

In the after noon I [Heber C. Kimball] cold [called] in to see Charl[e]s Hide [Hyde].[24] Was Anointed in the Ev[e]ning.

—Heber C. Kimball, Diary.

Wednesday, May 7, 1845
Willard Richards House

In the Ev[e]ning the Holly Order met fore prayer at the hous of Elder [Willard] Richards in the Eve[ning].

—Heber C. Kimball, Diary.

---

23. In 1840 the Nauvoo Charter had granted city courts the right to issue writs of habeas corpus for all cases falling within the purview of the city's ordinances. This provision repeatedly enabled Joseph Smith to avoid trial for charges he and others considered unjust. "There is nothing," Joseph said in mid-1843, "but what we have power over, except where restricted by the constitution of the United States" (*History of the Church,* 5:470). The charter was repealed in January 1845, leaving citizens and church leaders vulnerable to writs that would take them outside of the Nauvoo court system and into more hostile venues.

24. Charles Hyde (1814–91) converted to Mormonism in 1834. After immigrating to Utah, he was ordained a patriarch in April 1853 by Brigham Young, Heber C. Kimball, and Willard Richards. The second sentence in this entry is unclear, possibly meaning that Hyde entered the Anointed Quorum on this date or perhaps that Kimball was anointed for his health.

[W]ent to a prayer meeting.

—George A. Smith, "History of George Albert Smith."

....

[P]rayer meeting eve[ning.]

—Willard Richards, Diary.

....

Evening met with the following brethren at Dr. [Willard] Richards for prayer being clothed &c. viz. B[righam]. Young, J[ohn]. Taylor, W[illard]. Richards, G[eorge]. A. Smith, A[masa]. Lyman, N[ewel]. K. Whitney, L[evi]. Richards. Brother [Heber C.] Kimball came in at the close of the meeting. We had a very pleasant time. The chief subjects were to pray that the Lord would hedge up the way of the mob so that they may have no power over us during court. Also that the Lord would hedge up the way of John Greenhow[25] that he may not have power or influence to go to England and publish the book of Doctrine and Covenants. Petitions were also offered for Brother [George] Miller and others who are sick. It was also agreed to send a letter to Elder [Wilford] Woodruff in England and warn him to forestall [John] Greenhow and get out a copy right for the Doctrine and Covenants before him.[26]

—William Clayton, Diary.

....

Evening, attended prayer meeting with the Twelve [apostles], N[ewel]. K. Whitney, and Levi Richards.

—"Manuscript History of Brigham Young,"
in *History of the Church,* 7:407.

Thursday, May 8, 1845
Willard Richards House

In the Ev[e]ning the Holy Order met. fore prair at the hous of W[illard]. Richards. The Lord was with us.

—Heber C. Kimball, Diary.

---

25. John Greenhow, an English immigrant, was ordained an elder in 1840.

26. This letter, dated May 8, 1845, may be found in the *History of the Church,* 7:407-408. Greenhow hoped to print copies of the church's scripture in England, thus securing copyright to them, and then either prevent the church from publishing its own edition or selling the copyright to the church for a high price. Wilford Woodruff learned of his plans and was able to secure the British copyrights before Greenhow did.

Attended prayer meeting at the house of Dr. Willard Richards.

—George A. Smith, "History of George Albert Smith."

Evening met at Dr. [Willard] Richards for prayer in company with President B[righam] Young, H[eber] C. Kimball, W[illard] Richards, J[ohn] Taylor, G[eorge] A. Smith, A[masa] Lyman, O[rson] Pratt, J[ohn] E. Page, N[ewel] K. Whitney, L[evi] Richards, Joseph Young. We had a very interesting time.

—William Clayton, Diary.

Evening, met and prayed with the Twelve [apostles].

—"Manuscript History of Brigham Young," in *History of the Church,* 7:407.

Sunday, May 11, 1845
Willard Richards House

In the evening we met at the house of Elder Willard Richards for prayer.

—George A. Smith, "History of George Albert Smith."

[P]rayer meeting in my [Willard Richards's] office in the evening.

—Willard Richards, Diary.

Evening met with Dr. [Willard] Richards for prayer with B[righam]. Young, W[illard]. Richards, J[ohn]. Taylor, O[rson]. Pratt, G[eorge]. A. Smith, J[ohn]. E. Page, N[ewel]. K. Whitney and Levi Richards. President [Brigham] Young advised me [William Clayton] to keep closed up for a week or two inasmuch as the apostates, especially S[amuel] James[27] and G[eorge] W. Robinson[28] have entered into measures to take me with a

---

27. Samuel James (1814-76) served missions for the LDS church in Virginia (1837), Pennsylvania (1839-40), and Washington, D.C. He followed Sidney Rigdon after the death of Joseph Smith and became one of his counselors in April 1845.

28. George W. Robinson (1814-78) was elected General Church Recorder in September 1837 and sustained as such, as well as clerk to the First Presidency, in Far West, Missouri, the following year. He was imprisoned with Joseph Smith and other church leaders in Liberty Jail in 1838; became the first postmaster at Commerce (later Nauvoo), Illinois, in 1839; and helped to establish the Nauvoo Agricultural and Manufacturing Association in 1841. The following year, he left the church and Nauvoo (he was Sidney Rigdon's son-in-law), settling at Friendship, New York. There, in 1864, he founded the First National Bank.

writ to Carthage [Illinois].[29] The mob also want to get President [Brigham] Young, H[eber]. C. Kimball, J[ohn]. Taylor, W[illard]. Richards, O[rson]. Hyde and W[illiam]. W. Phelps and it is said they have taken out writs for them. They want twelve men out of Nauvoo but we are unable to learn who the others are.

—William Clayton, Diary.

....

Evening, attended prayer meeting.

—"Manuscript History of Brigham Young," in *History of the Church,* 7:408.

Thursday, May 15, 1845
Willard Richards House

Met with the Holly Order at W[illard]. Richards, went home.

—Heber C. Kimball, Diary.

....

Evening met at Dr. [Willard] Richards for prayer, in company with President [Brigham] Young, H[eber]. C. Kimball, G[eorge]. A. Smith, O[rson]. Pratt, N[ewel]. K. Whitney and L[evi]. Richards.

—William Clayton, Diary.

....

Evening, met at Brother [Willard] Richards' for prayer.

—"Manuscript History of Brigham Young," in *History of the Church,* 7:411.

Sunday, May 18, 1845
Willard Richards House

In the Ev[e]ning the Holy Order met at W[illard]. Richards fore prair, present B[righam]. Young, W[illard]. Richards, Bishops [Newel K.] Whitney, [George] Miller, G[eorge]. A. Smith, Joseph Young, and my self

---

29. On May 1, William Clayton learned that Sidney Rigdon and his followers were going to have him arrested on polygamy charges. He spent the next several days sequestered in his office. On September 24, he left Nauvoo and was arrested and held in Carthage until his trial for treason began later that day. He and eleven others were released that evening when the only witness against them confessed that his affidavit had been based on rumor. See James B. Allen, *No Toil Nor Labor Fear: The Story of William Clayton* (Provo, UT: Brigham Young University Press, 2002), 155.

[Heber C. Kimball]. Went home at 2 Oclock.

—Heber C. Kimball, Diary.

....

In the evening attended prayer meeting at Dr. Willard Richards.

—George A. Smith, "History of George Albert Smith."

....

Prayer Meeting at my [Willard Richards's] room as usual. for peace — dominion over our enemies. overule the court &c[.]

—Willard Richards, Diary.

....

I [William Clayton] went to meet with the brethren at Dr. [Willard] Richards but felt too unwell to remain.

—William Clayton, Diary.

....

Evening, attended council and prayer meeting with the Twelve [apostles] at Brother [Willard] Richards': adjourned at 2 a.m.

—"Manuscript History of Brigham Young,"
in *History of the Church,* 7:414.

Thursday, May 22, 1845
Willard Richards House

Last Ev[e]ning [May 22] met at the office of W[illard] Richards. fore prair. present B[righam]. Y[oung], W[illard]. R[ichards], J[ohn E.] Page, G[eorge]. A. S[mith], George Miller, Levi Richards, Joseph Young. Continude till 12 Oclock.

—Heber C. Kimball, Diary, entry dated May 23, 1845.

....

P.M. Attended Council and prayer meeting.

—George A. Smith, "History of George Albert Smith."

....

Evening, I [Brigham Young] attended council and prayer meeting.

—"Manuscript History of Brigham Young,"
in *History of the Church,* 7:417.

Saturday, May 24, 1845
Willard Richards House

A number of Elders met at Elder Willard Richard's and spent three hours in prayer for the sick. Sister [Jennetta] Richards and a number of others in particular.

—George A. Smith, "History of George Albert Smith."

I [Willard Richards] went home at dusk found Jennetta [Richards] very sick some of the brethren called and prayed for her 3 times.

—Willard Richards, Diary.

Sunday, May 25, 1845
Willard Richards House

In the Ev[e]ning met at the office of W[illard]. Richards for prair till 12 Oclock. The Lord was with us. Prais His holy name.

—Heber C. Kimball, Diary.

Attended a council and prayer meeting.

—George A. Smith, "History of George Albert Smith."

At a little after 8 Brother [Heber C.] Kimball called and I [William Clayton] went with him to Dr. [Willard] Richards to meet with the quorum for prayer. Present President B[righam]. Young, H[eber]. C. Kimball, W[illard]. Richards, G[eorge]. A. Smith, A[masa]. Lyman, John E. Page and O[rson]. Pratt of the Twelve [apostles]. N[ewel]. K. Whitney, and G[eorge] Miller, Trustees, and Levi Richards, Patriarch John Smith, Joseph Young and myself. We had a good time and felt that our prayers would be answered. We broke up about half past eleven.

—William Clayton, Diary.

Evening, the Twelve [apostles] and others met for prayer.

—"Manuscript History of Brigham Young,"
in *History of the Church,* 7:419.

Thursday, May 29, 1845
Willard Richards House

In the Ev[e]ning we met at W[illard]. Richards offic[e] in whare we met fore prair of the Holly Order. Called on the Lord for Rain for the Brethren on the Ilsland of Sea and those that has gon west, for the sick, and fore union. Great peas [peace] and union prevails[.] Brock up at half past 1 in the morning.

—Heber C. Kimball, Diary.

....

In the evening I attended prayer meeting and council and didn't get home until half past 1 o'clock the next morning.

—George A. Smith, "History of George Albert Smith."

....

[E]ve[ning] prayer meeting at my [Willard Richards's] house[.]

—Willard Richards, Diary.

....

Evening met at Dr. [Willard] Richards for prayer in company with President B[righam]. Young, H[eber]. C. Kimball, W[illard]. Richards, John Taylor, Amasa Lyman, G[eorge]. A. Smith, O[rson]. Pratt, and O[rson]. Hyde of the Twelve [apostles], N[ewel]. K. Whitney and George Miller, Trustees, Joseph Young and Levi Richards. The subjects prayed for were many, especially that the Lord would over-rule the movements of W[illia]m. Smith who is endeavoring to ride the Twelve [apostles] down,[30] and also that the Lord would over-rule the mob so that we may dwell in peace until the [Nauvoo] Temple is finished. The Council broke up at half past 12 o'clock.

—William Clayton, Diary.

---

30. Five days earlier, despite Brigham Young's reservations, William Smith had been ordained Patriarch to the Church, a position previously held by his brother Hyrum. However, on May 27, William told James Monroe that Brigham was "not a whit beyond himself or any other of the Twelve [apostles], that he is more president by courtesy, that he has no higher keys and that the whole twelve are presiding over the church, not Brigham Young and that he does not stand in Joseph's shoes." Three weeks later, the May 15 issue of the *Times and Season,* which had been delayed, published an article by William entitled "Patriarchal," which the Twelve Apostles viewed as a direct challenge to their authority. According to William's biographers, "The Twelve chose to read a message between the lines of William's article: he was now Patriarch over the whole church. He held the position of his late brother Hyrum, a man who would have succeeded Joseph as *president* had he lived. Hyrum had never been below or subject to the Quorum of the Twelve in either his capacity as the Patriarch or his position as associate president. William stood before the membership as one of the Twelve Apostles and at the same time held authority previously seen as superior to that of the Quorum of the Twelve. If William could persuade the people that Brigham Young's authority was limited to one-twelfth of the Quorum, then William could match that one-twelfth and add his churchwide authority through the historical, primal dimensions of the patriarchal calling" (Irene M. Bates and E. Gary Smith, *Lost Legacy: The Mormon Office of Presiding Patriarch* [Urbana: University of Illinois Press, 1996], 83).

Evening met at Brother [Willard] Richards' for prayer in company with Brothers Heber. C. Kimball, Orson Hyde, Orson Pratt, Willard Richards, John Taylor, Amasa M. Lyman, N[ewel] K. Whitney, George Miller, Joseph Young and Levi Richards. Prayed that the Lord would overrule the movements of W[illia]m. Smith who is endeavoring to ride the Twelve [apostles] down; also that the Lord would overrule the proceedings of the mob so that we may dwell in peace until the [Nauvoo] Temple is finished.

—"Manuscript History of Brigham Young," in *History of the Church,* 7:420.

Sunday, June 1, 1845
Willard Richards House

In the Evning the Holly Order met at Elder [Willard] Richards for prair Praid for Rain, had a good time. Brock up at half past one in the morning. The Lord be Praised.

—Heber C. Kimball, Diary.

In the evening attended a meeting of the priesthood.

—John Taylor, Diary.

Attended Council in the evening and did not get home until 1 o'clock the next morning.

—George A. Smith, "History of George Albert Smith."

[E]ve[ning] prayer meeting. may justice overtake the murders of Joseph [Smith] & may G[eorge]. J. Adams be stopped in his career of wickedness[.][31]

—Willard Richards, Diary.

Evening at Dr. [Willard] Richards with B[righam]. Young, H[eber]. C. Kimball, W[illard]. Richards, J[ohn]. Taylor, J[ohn]. E. Page, O[rson]. Pratt, G[eorge]. A. Smith, A[masa]. Lyman, John Smith, N[ewel]. K. Whit-

---

31. Adams had been excommunicated two months earlier on April 10 for preaching against the Twelve Apostles and advocating unauthorized polygamy. He was now championing Joseph Smith's son Joseph III as heir to the presidency. "[I] cant support the twelve as the first presidency," he wrote on June 14, 1845. "[I] cant do it when I know that it belongs to Josephs Son—Young Joseph who was ordained by his father before his Death" (qtd. in Quinn, *Origins,* 228).

ney, G[eorge]. Miller, L[evi]. Richards and Joseph Young. It was decided
that [Peter O.] Hanson[32] translate the Doctrine and Covenants and Book
of Mormon into the Norwegian language and that Elder O[rson]. Pratt
assist. Also decided that the Trustees give G[eorge] D. Watt[33] a quarter of
a Lot and build him a house and employ him as a reporter for the Church,
and let his labors go towards paying for his house and lot. I [William
Clayton] read a part of the record which I prepared for a deposite, but it
was not as full as President [Brigham] Young wanted and the council
concluded to deposit all the Times & Seasons,[34] to give a perfect history
of the church in Nauvoo. Separated at 12 o'clock.

—William Clayton, Diary.

Evening, I [Brigham Young] met for counsel and prayer with Elders
H[eber]. C. Kimball, Orson Pratt, Willard Richards, John E. Page, John
Taylor, George A. Smith, Amasa M. Lyman, John Smith, N[ewel]. K.
Whitney, George Miller, Levi Richards, Joseph Young, and W[illia]m.
Clayton. Voted that Brother Peter O. Hanson translate the *Doctrine and
Covenants* and *Book of Mormon* into the Danish Norwegian language and
that Elder Orson Pratt assist. Voted that the Trustees give George D. Watt
a quarter of a lot and build him a house and employ him as a reporter for
the church and let his labors go towards paying for his house and lot. We
prayed that justice might overtake the murderers of Joseph and Hyrum
[Smith] and that George J. Adams be stopped in his mad career.

—"Manuscript History of Brigham Young,"
in *History of the Church,* 7:424-25.

Monday, June 2, 1845
George Miller House

[At] Bishop [George] Millers, held council all of the Twelve present

---

32. Peter O. Hansen (1818-95) became the third Dane to join the LDS church
after immigrating to America in 1843. He also served as the first missionary to
Scandinavia and translator of the Book of Mormon into Danish.

33. George D. Watt (1812-81) was an English convert who immigrated to the
United States in 1842. He was skilled at Pitman shorthand and recorded many of
the conference sermons included in the *Journal of Discourses,* which he published
semi-monthly in England beginning in 1854. He also recorded the trial of the accused murderers of Joseph Smith and later was on the committee that created the
Deseret Alphabet.

34. The *Times and Seasons* was published in Nauvoo from 1839 to 1846 as the

... it rained a fine shower in answer to prair. we praised the Lord for his great goodness.

—Heber C. Kimball, Diary.

I [Brigham Young] met with the Twelve in council.

—"Manuscript History of Brigham Young,"
in *History of the Church,* 7:425.

Thursday, June 5, 1845
Willard Richards House

In the Eve[ning] the Holy Order met at W[illard] Richards. Cold [called] on the Lord that he would come out in Judmet [judgement] against Jade [Judge] [Richard M.] Young[35] and others.

—Heber C. Kimball, Diary.

In the evening at a meeting of the priesthood.

—John Taylor, Diary.

prayer Meeting. ~~prayed~~ that Judge [Richard M.] Young. might be afflicted for joining hands with murders[.]

—Willard Richards, Diary.

Evening met at Dr. [Willard] Richards for prayer in company with B[righam]. Young, H[eber]. C. Kimball, W[illard]. Richards, J[ohn]. Taylor, O[rson]. Pratt, A[masa]. Lyman, J[ohn]. E. Page, G[eorge]. A. Smith, N[ewel]. K. Whitney, G[eorge]. Miller and L[evi]. Richards. We separated at 12 o'clock.

—William Clayton, Diary.

I [Brigham Young] met for prayer with the Twelve [apostles] and other brethren.

—"Manuscript History of Brigham Young,"
in *History of the Church,* 7:425.

---

church's journalistic voice. It was at first a monthly publication but, after the first year, came to be issued semi-monthly. Throughout its six-year run, it was edited by Don Carlos Smith, Ebenezer Robinson, Joseph Smith, and John Taylor.

35. Richard Montgomery Young (1796-1853) was a lawyer who served in the second general assembly of Illinois (1820-22), twice as a circuit judge (1825-27, 1829-37), and as a U.S. Senator (1837-43), then as a justice of the Illinois Supreme Court—presiding at the trial of those accused in the Smith murders—but resigned in 1847 to become commissioner of the General Land Office in Washington, D.C., where he later died in an insane asylum.

Sunday, June 8, 1845
Willard Richards House

In the eve[ning] the Holy Order met at W[illard] Richards. We praid fore rain as the Earth was drie and [prayed] fore the sick.

—Heber C. Kimball, Diary.

In the afternoon at meeting of the Priesthood, at Bro[ther]. Willard Richards'.

—John Taylor, Diary.

Went to prayer meeting.

—George A. Smith, "History of George Albert Smith."

[P]rayer meeting 4. P.M. May the Judge & Jury be afflicted. Elder [John] Taylor [be] prospered in sending for press type & paper to print the History — & church have means to build the tabernacle.[36]

—Willard Richards, Diary.

At 4 met at Dr. [Willard] Richards with B[righam]. Young, H[eber]. C. Kimball, J[ohn]. Taylor, W[illard]. Richards, O[rson]. Hyde, O[rson]. Pratt, J[ohn]. E. Page, G[eorge]. A. Smith, A[masa]. Lyman, N[ewel]. K. Whitney, G[eorge]. Miller, L[evi]. Richards, and J[oseph]. C. Kingsbury. We had a very interesting time and separated about [9] o'clock.

—William Clayton, Diary.

At four p.m., I [Brigham Young] met with the Twelve [apostles] and others for counsel and prayer: we decided that Elder Orson Hyde go to the east and buy canvas for a Tabernacle [tent], and type to print the History of Joseph Smith.

—"Manuscript History of Brigham Young,"
in History of the Church, 7:426.

Thursday, June 12, 1845
Willard Richards House

At 4 o clock met at Dr [Willard] Richards with Pres[iden]t B[rig-

---

36. The Twelve Apostles, following Joseph Smith's lead, had decided to purchase some 4,000 yards of canvas which would be fashioned into an outbuilding, or tabernacle, in which public meetings could be held along the west side of the temple. By early September, the necessary funds had been raised and the canvas had been

ham]. Young, H[eber]. C. Kimball, W[illard]. Richards, G[eorge]. A. Smith, A[masa]. Lyman, O[rson]. Pratt, N[ewel]. K. Whitney, G[eorge]. Miller, and Levi Richards. We had a very interesting time and separated about half past 8 o clock.

—William Clayton, Diary.

....

I [Brigham Young] spent the afternoon with several of the Twelve [apostles].

—"Manuscript History of Brigham Young," in *History of the Church,* 7:427.

Sunday, June 15, 1845
Willard Richards House

At the office till 4 P.M. Afterwards at Dr [Willard] Richards with B[righam]. Young, H[eber]. C. Kimball, W[illard]. Richards, O[rson]. Pratt, G[eorge]. A. Smith, Amasa Lyman, N[ewel]. K. Whitney G[eorge]. Miller, L[evi]. Richards & J[oseph]. C. Kingsbury.

—William Clayton, Diary.

....

Evening, I [Brigham Young] met with the Twelve [apostles].

—"Manuscript History of Brigham Young," in *History of the Church,* 7:427.

Thursday, June 19, 1845
Willard Richards House

At fore in the after noon, we met at W[illard]. R[ichards]. for prair, may the Lord bless His people. Present to this meting of the twelve [apostles] B[righam]. Y[oung], G[eorge]. A. [Smith], J[ohn]. T[aylor], Orson Pratt, Bishop [George] Miller, W[illia]m. Cla[y]ton, W. R[ichards]. and my Self [Heber C. Kimball], Elder Levi Richards, A[masa]. Limon, O[rson]. Hide. We offerd prair [for] Br[other]. [Newel K.] Whitney as he had gon to St. Lewis [Missouri], that he might pro[s]per, also for Sister [Jennetta] Richards, and for my wife [Vilate] that they might recover, that

shipped to Nauvoo. In the interim, public meetings were already being conducted on the site selected for the tabernacle. By the time the canvas arrived in October, the Saints were preparing to leave Nauvoo and the need for a tabernacle had passed. The Saints brought the canvas with them to Utah.

Elder [Orson] Hide might prosper in the East, and that Jugment to come on Juge [Richard M.] Young, that our Enimes might be cursed.

—Heber C. Kimball, Diary.

In the afternoon attended meeting of the priesthood.

—John Taylor, Diary.

[P]rayer meeting at 3 o'clock.

—George A. Smith, "History of George Albert Smith."

Afterwards at Dr. [Willard] Richards ... Prayers were offered up for many things especially that the curse of God may fall upon Judge [Richard M.] Young and the Lawyers who have justified the murderers, and that they may not be able to hold court.

—William Clayton, Diary.

[A]t 4 meeting in office B[righam]. Young, H[eber]. C. Kimball W[illard]. Richards, G[eorge]. A. Smith, O[rson]. Hyde, O[rson] Pratt A[masa] Lyman, J[ohn]. Taylor, G[eorge]. Miller, L[evi]. Richards & W[illiam]. Clayton till ep [?] 7.

—Historian's Office Journal.

Evening, the Twelve [apostles] met for council and prayer.

—"Manuscript History of Brigham Young," in *History of the Church,* 7:428.

Sunday, June 22, 1845
Willard Richards House

[W]e went back to W[illard] Richards, as the Holy Order met for prair. 13 present. Had a good time.

—Heber C. Kimball, Diary.

In evening attended a meeting of the priesthood, where we have been in the habit every Sunday and Thursday afternoon of meeting together according to the holy order of God, to offer up our oblations, and prayer according to the divine pattern, for such things as the Church and ourselves stand in need of; and we know that God hears our prayers, and bestows upon us those things, that we ask at his hands, and therefore we have confidence and come to God as our chief source of comfort, blessings, security, and protection in all times of trouble; and our souls are

117

feasted on the good things of God, for we are one and God is with us.

—John Taylor, Diary.

....

Attended council at 4 o'clock. Administered to the sick and spent some time in prayer.

—George A. Smith, "History of George Albert Smith."

....

4 P.M. Quorum in my room[.] 5 prayed for & anointed Jennetta while 8 remained in the room & prayed for her. Sister [Mary Ann?] Young brought in J[ohn]. M. [sic] Willard [Young][37] & I [Willard Richards] blessed him before the Quorum. & her also.

—Willard Richards, Diary.

....

P.M. met at Dr. [Willard] Richards ... Sister [Jennetta] Richards is yet very sick and it was agreed that four of the company should go down with Elder [Willard] Richards to lay hands on her while the other remained to offer up prayers for her in the room. Elders J[ohn]. Taylor, O[rson]. Pratt, J[oseph]. C. Kingsbury, and myself [William Clayton] were appointed to go with the Doctor [Willard Richards]. He anointed his wife and we then laid hands on her. After we returned to the room prayers were offered up for sundry matters, especially that God would overrule the movements of our enemies &c.

—William Clayton, Diary.

....

Evening, I [Brigham Young] met with the Twelve [apostles] and others for prayer; Sister Jennetta Richards being very sick was administered to.

—"Manuscript History of Brigham Young," in *History of the Church,* 7:428.

Wednesday, June 25, 1845
Willard Richards House

At three we met at the same plase [i.e., Willard Richards's house] for prair. Nine present. Offerd up the Signs. and praid that the Lord would

---

37. John Willard Young (1844-1924) was born in Nauvoo to Brigham Young and Mary Ann Angell. He filled a mission to Europe from 1866-67 and later became an assistant counselor to his father. In 1876 he was called as first counselor in the First Presidency. After his father's death, he served for several years as a counselor to the Quorum of the Twelve Apostles.

bless [Miner] Demmen [Deming]³⁸ and deliver him from his enimes,³⁹ that our Enimes might be cursed.

—Heber C. Kimball, Diary.

[W]e appointed a meeting of the Quorum of the Priesthood at which however few but the Twelve [apostles] were present; we there prayed for William [Smith] that God would overrule every evil principle; that his violent spirit might be curbed by the spirit of God, and that we might be enabled to save him, that he might be an honor to his father's house, and a blessing to the Church; we also prayed for his Mother [Lucy Mack Smith], Sisters, and all his Father's family; we at the same time prayed for Gen[eral]. [Minor] Deming, that inasmuch as he had been our friend, and had rashly shot a man in self defence that things might be overruled for his good; and that his enemies might not be allowed to injure him.

—John Taylor, Diary.

Went with President Brigham Young to Dr. Willard Richards' house and read a letter from Brother William Smith stating that he was afraid of his life and made accusations against Brother [Elbridge] Tufts of the [Nauvoo] police. We agreed to call a council of the Twelve Apostles. We gave notice to everybody we met to attend meeting at 3 o'clock and prayed God to set the matter right.

—George A. Smith, "History of George Albert Smith."

3 P.M. Met had prayer. for Gen[eral] [Minor] Deming[.]

—Willard Richards, Diary.

W[illard]. Richards, G[eorge]. A. Smith, B[righam]. Young, J[ohn]. Taylor, O[rson]. Pratt, N[ewel]. K. Whitney in council in the office Also J[ohn]. E. Page.

—Historian's Office Journal.

---

38. Miner Rudd Deming (1810-45) was brigadier general of the Carthage Greys and later sheriff of Hancock County in 1844. Friendly to the Mormons, he issued a proclamation to the citizens of Hancock County the day following the murder of Joseph and Hyrum Smith, assuring them that the Mormons would not attack them in revenge. He died suddenly of consumptive fever on September 10, 1845, soon after resigning as sheriff.

39. The day before, Deming had shot and killed Samuel Marshall in self-defense. Marshall, a vocal anti-Mormon, was clerk of the Hancock County Commissioners Court. Deming was arrested for manslaughter and held in jail to protect him from Marshall's supporters.

> At three p.m., I [Brigham Young] met with the Quorum of the Twelve [apostles] for prayer; ...
>
> —"Manuscript History of Brigham Young,"
> in *History of the Church,* 7:428.

Thursday, June 26, 1845

Willard Richards House

At 4 Oclocks at W[illard]. Richards for prair. 12 Present. 6 of the Twelve [apostles] present, the two Bishops, Uncle John [Smith], Levi Richards, W[illia]m. Cla[y]ton, Joseph Young.

Clothed our selves and offerd up our praiers for the prosperity of the Saints and for distruction of our Enimes. A perfect union in corum [quorum]. Orson Pratt being Mouth. After we Got threw My [Heber C. Kimball's] Wife [Vilate] and Sister [Elizabeth Ann] Whitney with our litle Children of Promise [came in?].[40] We then offerd the Sings [signs]. B[righam] Young, W[illard] Richard[s] Laid hands on my Litle son Brigham Willard[, while held by] Heber C Kimball, and sealed the Blessing of Life and [that] health should rest on him and the holy Preast hood [which had] rested on him from his Mothers womb. then [a blessing] on Mary Jane Whiteny and simelor things [promised]. Then they left the room. Then we offered the signs, and con[se]crated three botels of Oil,[41] 2 for me and one fore John Smith, I being mouth. We then praid onece more B[righam] Young being mouth. We had a good time and the Lord was with us. He shall have the glory.

—Heber C. Kimball, Diary.

....

Spent the afternoon in council and prayer at Elder Willard Richards.

—George A. Smith, "History of George Albert Smith."

....

4. P.M. Prayer Meeting ~~after whi~~ in which I [Willard Richards] took

---

40. This refers to the youngest child of Heber C. and Vilate Kimball, Brigham Willard Kimball (b. January 29, 1845), and of Newel K. and Elizabeth Ann Whitney, Mary Jane Whitney (b. January 17, 1844). Both children were born after their parents had been sealed for eternity and thus born under the new and everlasting covenant. As indicated by William Clayton below, the daughter of Willard and Jennetta Richards, Rhoda Ann Jennetta Richards (b. September 15, 1843), was also blessed.

41. Olive oil was consecrated, or "made holy," through priesthood ordinance for use in blessing the sick. It was also employed for the first anointing, or initiatory stage, of the endowment, and for the second anointing.

Rhoda Ann [Richards] in. sick. & Pres[iden]t. [Brigham] Young blessed her. & Sister [Vilate] Kimball had Brigham Willard [Kimball] blessed by the Quorum & Sister [Elizabeth Ann] Whitney — had Mary Jane [Whitney] blessed by the Quorum — Prayed for the deliverance of Gen[eral] [Miner] Deming.—

—Willard Richards, Diary.

....

[A]fterwards at Elder [Willard] Richards with President B[righam]. Young, H[eber]. C. Kimball, W[illard]. Richards, G[eorge]. A. Smith, A[masa]. Lyman, O[rson]. Pratt, N[ewel]. K. Whitney, G[eorge]. Miller, J[oseph]. Young, L[evi]. Richards, and John Smith. Brother Richards [daughter] Rhoda Ann, Brother Kimball['s son,] Brigham Willard, and Brother Whitneys [daughter] Mary Jane were blessed each with great blessings. The afternoon was spent in conversation and prayer till 8 o'clock.

—William Clayton, Diary.

....

The Twelve [apostles] met for council and prayer: several children were blessed.

—"Manuscript History of Brigham Young," in *History of the Church,* 7:429-30.

Friday, June 27, 1845
Willard Richards House

Met in Council at W[illard]. Richards. One year ago Joseph and Hirum [Smith] was killed in Carthage Jail [Illinois]. So we met in cou[n]cil to pray that God would curs[e] those that had spilt thare [the martyrs'] B[l]ood and all those ^that^ percicute the Saints.[42] O Lord I [Heber C. Kimball] thank Thy holy name that Thou dost hear Thy servents and bring trouble on them [who do us harm]. Even now they are dum, and cannot do business and are all thrown in to confusion, in answer to the prairs of Thy servents, as we have felt to pleede with The[e] with uplifted hands in token of our regard to The[e]. I do thank The[e] O my Father, for Thou dost hear us in all things when we are agreed, and this

---

42. This marks the beginning of what would later be called the Oath of Vengeance or Retribution, a part of the endowment ritual until the 1920s, when it was dropped. Quinn (*Origins,* 508) suggests that "Willard Richards originate[d] the prayer of vengeance to curse enemies." What Saints viewed as a prayer for justice, critics interpreted as a blood-oath to avenge their prophets' deaths.

blessing Thou hast granted to Thy servents this day[, which] is set a part by Thy servents to fast and pray Thou woulst bless us with peas [peace] and prosperity, and that this blessing may rest on all of They saints, Even so Amen.

—Heber C. Kimball, Diary.

President [Brigham] Young, Elders Heber C. Kimball, John Taylor, William Clayton, George Miller, John E. Page, Newel K. Whitney, Amasa Lyman, Willard Richards and myself spent the day in prayer and council.

—George A. Smith, "History of George Albert Smith."

Anniversary of the death of Joseph & Hyrum [Smith]. B[righam]. Young, H[eber]. C. Kimball, O[rson] Pratt[,] A[masa]. Lyman, G[eorge]. A. Smith, W[illard]. Richards, John E. Page[,] George Miller, Joseph Young, John Taylor assembeled in the morning in my [Willard Richards's] room. & spent the day in fasting & Council.—till near 5. P.M. when they dressed [in the robes of the priesthood] & consecrated 9 bottles of oil. Thanked the Lord that they were not in Carthage Jail [Illinois].— that God would avenge the murders of Joseph & Hyrum [Smith]— &c &c &c.

—Willard Richards, Diary.

This was the anniversary of the day that Brothers Joseph and Hyrum [Smith] were killed and myself [John Taylor] shot. We met together (the Quorum of the Priesthood,) to pray, several of the Twelve [apostles] were present; ...

—John Taylor, Diary.

All things seem to go right according to our prayers ... At 9 met at Dr. [Willard] Richards with President B[righam]. Young, H[eber]. C. Kimball, W[illard]. Richards, J[ohn]. Taylor, A[masa]. Lyman, O[rson]. Pratt, G[eorge]. A. Smith, J[ohn]. E. Page, George Miller and Joseph Young. Most of the day was spent in conversation on various subjects, and towards the evening we clothed and consecrated [eight] bottles of oil and offered up prayers for general matters.

—William Clayton, Diary.

Elders Heber C. Kimball, Orson Pratt, Amasa M. Lyman, George A. Smith, Willard Richards, John E. Page, George Miller, Joseph Young and John Taylor met for fasting, prayer and counsel.

—"Manuscript History of Brigham Young,"
in *History of the Church*, 7:430.

Sunday, June 29, 1845
Willard Richards House

Attended prayer meeting at Dr. Willard Richards.

—George A. Smith, "History of George Albert Smith."

....

At 4 met at Dr. [Willard] Richards ... Prayers were offered for a variety of subjects. Sister [Jennetta] Richards is recovering.

—William Clayton, Diary.

....

Evening, I [Brigham Young] met with the Twelve [apostles] and others for prayer.

—"Manuscript History of Brigham Young,"
in *History of the Church,* 7:433.

Tuesday, July 1, 1845
Heber C. Kimball House

Our little Brigham[43] was verry sick. gave us much sorrow to see him in such paign [pain]. Bishop [Newel K.] Witney Joseph Young A[masa] Limon Willard Richards come in. to Join me [Heber C. Kimball] in prair. [I]n the Holly order to prair[,] Sister Jane Young, [and] Sister [Elizabeth Ann] Whitney. [were] present [and] the Lord was with us. I felt to prais his holy name for his kindess to me and family in giving us health.

—Heber C. Kimball, Diary.

Thursday, July 3, 1845
Willard Richards House

At 4 Oclock in the after noon[44] met for prair at the Hous of W[illard]. Richards. Present B[righam]. Young, W[illard]. Richards, O[rson]. Pratt, G[eorge]. A. Smith, J[ohn]. Tailor [Taylor], A[masa]. Limon [Lyman], Bishops [Newel K.] Whitney and [George] Miller, Levi Richards, W[il-

---

43. Brigham Kimball (1845-67), the five-month-old son of Heber C. and Vilate Murray Kimball mentioned above, would grow up to serve a mission to England beginning in 1864 but would be released early due to ill health and die on the journey home.

44. Quinn (*Origins,* 508) suggests that there was a general meeting of the Quorum of the Anointed at 3:00 p.m., to which John Taylor and Zina Jacobs refer, and a smaller meeting that continued beyond 4:00 p.m.

Heber C. Kimball's house, on the northeast corner of Munson Street and Partridge Street in Nauvoo, was erected in mid-1845, with an addition added later. The Quorum of the Anointed met here periodically in 1845. Photograph ca. 1885.

lia]m. Cla[y]ton Read a leter to Elder [Wilford] Woodruff to England.[45]
It was approved of by the council.

—Heber C. Kimball, Diary.

In afternoon at meeting of the Priesthood.

—John Taylor, Diary.

In the afternoon I attended ... a prayer meeting at Dr. Willard Richards', where we finished a letter to Elder Wilford Woodruff, and prayed for the sick.

—George A. Smith, "History of George Albert Smith."

At 4 met at Dr. [Willard] Richards with President [Brigham] Young, H[eber]. C. Kimball, W[illard]. Richards, J[ohn]. Taylor, A[masa]. Lyman, G[eorge]. A. Smith, O[rson]. Pratt, N[ewel]. K. Whitney, G[eorge]. Miller, L[evi]. Richards and J[oseph]. Young. We offered up our prayers for variety of subjects. I [William Clayton] read a letter which I wrote for President [Brigham] Young to Brother [Wilford] Woodruff in England, which was accepted. It was decided to employ Brother [Isaac] Morley to make 100 barrels of wine for sacrament. Also to purchase a raft of Lumber laying at the w[h]arf of 150,000 [board feet?].

—William Clayton, Diary.

At the Thursday Prayer meeting Father John Smith made some excelent remarks concerning the Priesthood, Prayer, Endewment, &c.

—Zina D. H. Jacobs, Diary, in "'All Things Move in Order in the City': The Nauvoo Diary of Zina Diantha Huntington Jacobs," edited by Maureen Ursenbach Beecher, *BYU Studies* 19 (Spring 1979): 285-320.

Saturday, July 5, 1845
Willard Richards House

At 4 P.M. met at Dr. [Willard] Richards ... We conversed till about 7 o'clock and then clothed and offered up prayers for general subjects. It was decided that the Trustees give to President [Brigham] Young a deed

---

45. This letter, from Brigham Young to Wilford Woodruff, dated June 27 and 29, 1845, is included in *History of the Church,* 7:430-32. It tells of the recent temple capstone ceremony, general progress of the construction of the temple and Nauvoo House, and growth of Nauvoo.

for the S.W. 25 7 N. 8 W and S.W. fr[om?] 10 7 N. 8 W. free of charge.

—William Clayton, Diary.

Sunday, July 6, 1845
Willard Richards House

[T]o W[illard]. Richards for prair and council. Present B[righam]. Young, W[illard]. Richards, Levi Richards, G[eorge]. A. Smith, Joseph Kingsbury, W[illia]m. Cla[y]ton, John Tailor [Taylor], Bishop [Newel K.] Whitney, George Miller, O[rson]. Pratt.

—Heber C. Kimball, Diary.

....

Attended prayer meeting at Dr. [Willard] Richards' office at 4 o'-clock.

—George A. Smith, "History of George Albert Smith."

....

4. P.M. Prayer Meeting. Quorum in my [Willard Richards's] room[.]

—Willard Richards, Diary.

Wednesday, July 9, 1845
Willard Richards House

W[illard] Richards sent fore me [Heber C. Kimball] to Lay hands on his wife [Jennetta]. She appeared as though she was diing. At about 10 in the Morning I went thare again to Clothe and pray for hur again. Present G[eorge]. A. Smith, Levi Richards, John Smith, J[ohn]. Tailor [Taylor]. We praied after the Holy Order and annointed her. She died in about half an hour after, this was in the fore part of the day.

—Heber C. Kimball, Diary.

....

Was called early to visit Sister Jeanette [Richards], wife of Dr. Willard Richards, who was in great pain. My father [John Smith] and Elders [Heber C.] Kimball and [John] Taylor administered to her, after which the pains left her and she fell asleep and breathed her last 15 minutes later.

—George A. Smith, "History of George Albert Smith."

....

[A]bout sun rise sent for Levi [Richards] [and at] about 6 sent for El-der H[eber]. C. Kimball, who come & laid on hand & prayed & she [Jennetta] revived also sent for father John Smith, John Taylor Geo[rge] A

Smith. Heber Kimball. John E. Page L[evi]. Richards & myself [Willard Richards] [who] dressed. prayed — went into her room [an]ointed. & prayed for her. — & felt encouraged —

—Willard Richards, Diary.

....

Sister [Jennetta] Richards died this morning at about ¼ after 10. She has suffered much for along time back. We have held her by faith alone, but she is gone to rest.

—William Clayton, Diary.

....

Sis[ter] [Jennetta] Richards much worse. T[homas] B[ullock] went for B[righam]. Young, J[ohn]. Taylor, G[eorge]. A. Smith, John Smith, H[eber]. C. Kimball being here — for prayer & supplication on her behalf. They came and after they departed — in about 20 minutes after (viz 14 past 10) she departed this temporal life ... I [Thomas Bullock] then went for Sisters B[righam]. Young, [John] Taylor & [Newel K.] Whitney to attend her.

—Historian's Office Journal.

Thursday, July 10, 1845
Willard Richards House

Met for prair[;] praid for rain after the Holly Order.

—Heber C. Kimball, Diary.

....

4 P.M. Quorum meeting at my [Willard Richards's] house[.]

—Willard Richards, Diary.

Sunday, July 13, 1845
Willard Richards House

At fore we met fore prair at W[illard]. Richards.

—Heber C. Kimball, Diary.

....

In evening attended meeting of the Priesthood. I [John Taylor] meet with many things in the world that have a tendency to depress me; but when I meet with my brethren, I feel well, for there is the spirit of God, the spirit of Peace, and the spirit of union.

—John Taylor, Diary.

....

At home till 4 P.M. then met at Dr. [Willard] Richards ... Prayers were offered for general matters.

—William Clayton, Diary.

Thursday, July 17, 1845
Willard Richards House

The Holy Order met at the usul place. The old company present.[46]

—Heber C. Kimball, Diary.

In the afternoon in Council and Quorum meeting with the Twelve [apostles].

—John Taylor, Diary.

I went to prayer meeting, which lasted about two hours.

—George A. Smith, "History of George Albert Smith."

[A]t 4. Prayer meeting at my [Willard Richards's] room — council agree John Pack[47] should buy the Masonic Hall & the Trustees hire the Mansion.[48] — that W[illard]. Richards & B[righam]. Young should have a barn built. present B[righam]. Young. W[illard] Richards O[rson]. Pratt. G[eorge]. A. Smith, A[masa] Lyman, John Smith, Bishops [Newel K.] Whitney & [George] Miller. L[evi]. Richards. Joseph Young, [and] J[ohn]. Taylor, W[illard] R[ichards]. was not present when the vote was taken on his barn[.] B[righam]. Young Prayed—

—Willard Richards, Diary.

At 4 P.M. met at Dr. [Willard] Richards ... It was decided in council that Dr. [Willard] Richards have a barn built by the Trustees, also that the Masonic Hall and Arsenal be prepared for store houses for grain, also that the Trustees purchase the New York store if it can be bought reasonable, also that Brother [John] Pack buy the Masonic Hall Tavern and that the Trustees rent or lease the Mansion for 3 or five years. Prayers were offered for the sick and a number of subjects and about 8 o'clock we separated.

—William Clayton, Diary.

---

46. Heber here refers to those who received the endowment under Joseph Smith. Five months later, he will make similar comments about a meeting of members of the Anointed Quorum held on December 7, 1945.

47. John Pack (1809-85) served many missions for the LDS church while living in Nauvoo. He led a pioneer company to the Salt Lake Valley in 1847 and then returned to Winter Quarters for his family. After settling in Salt Lake City, he helped to build Chase's Mill, at what would later become Liberty Park, and also built the first dance hall in Utah. He helped to settle Carson Valley, Utah Territory, in 1856.

48. Renting out the Masonic Hall and Mansion House (formerly the residence of Joseph Smith and his family) was an attempt by the church to raise needed money.

Sunday, July 20, 1845
Willard Richards House

In afternoon at Quorum meeting.

—John Taylor, Diary.

....

Attended council at 4 o'clock and prayer meeting at 6 o'clock.

—George A. Smith, "History of George Albert Smith."

....

4 P.M prayer Meeting at my [Willard Richards's] office at 4. P.M. no business in particular. H[eber] C. Kimball & B[righam]. Young prayed. Rhoda [A]nn [Richards] blessed for her health by the Quorum.

—Willard Richards, Diary.

....

[A]t 4 met at Dr. [Willard] Richards ... It was decided that the Trustees furnish Orson Pratt $33. for his expenses East. Prayers were offered for general matters especially that the Lord would turn away the sickness now prevailing amongst the children in the City.

—William Clayton, Diary.

Thursday, July 24, 1845
Willard Richards House

The Holly Order met at the usual place for prair.

—Heber C. Kimball, Diary.

....

At 4 o'clock I attended a council which lasted two hours. Several letters were read: among them was one from George P. Dykes relating to the window glass for the [Nauvoo] Temple. We spent two hours in prayer and administered to several sick persons.

—George A. Smith, "History of George Albert Smith."

....

4 P.M. prayer meeting—after which the Quorum agreed to take no more snuff & tobacco for 1 week —

—Willard Richards, Diary.

....

4 P.M. met at Dr. [Willard] Richards ... Quite a number of sick were prayed for myself amongst the number. I [William Clayton] felt immediate [relief?].

—William Clayton, Diary.

Sunday, July 27, 1845
Willard Richards House

[A]t 4 o'clock at Quorum meeting.

—John Taylor, Diary.

....

4 P.M. B[righam] Young. Geo[rge] Miller. W[illard]. Richards Geo[rge] A Smith John Taylor & Two more assembled in my [Willard Richards's] office for prayer — [Heber C.] Kimball & L[evi]. Richards come in after prayer.

—Willard Richards, Diary.

Thursday, July 31, 1845
Willard Richards House

At fore we held our prair meting.

—Heber C. Kimball, Diary.

....

In afternoon at 4 o'clock, at Quorum meeting.

—John Taylor, Diary.

....

I went with the Twelve [apostles] and others to Dr. Willard Richards' office and called up the affairs of the company. General Minor R. Deming was present. We conversed with him for some time, after which we spent an hour in prayer.

—George A. Smith, "History of George Albert Smith."

....

At 4 P.M. met at Dr. [Willard] Richards ... It was decided in council that the Nauvoo House committee get tithing teams to haul their wood, and grain from the country. Also that they have 2,000 feet of Lumber from the Trustees, also that they collect all the scaffolding poles and take them to the Nauvoo House. A letter was written to the [Nauvoo] Temple Committee rebuking them for abusing Brother Reese[49] and teaching them their duty.[50] During the conversation Brother [George] Miller in-

---

49. Probably Enoch Reese (1813-76), who was endowed in the Nauvoo temple in December 1845 and came to Utah in 1849, and whose sister was a plural wife of Heber C. Kimball. He presided over a branch of the church in Buffalo, New York, for a year, and served a mission to Europe. He built the first grist and saw mills in Carson Valley, Utah Territory, and owned an oil and lamp store. For several years he was a member of the Utah territorial legislature and the Salt Lake City Council.

50. It is not known how the Temple Committee had offended Reese, but this was not the first time the committee had elicited complaints. Three years earlier, on

sulted Brother [Newel K.] Whitney very meanly. Brother [Newel K.] Whitney felt angry but governed his feelings and merely said he felt above such insinuations. Prayers were offered for a number of the sick and for several other general subjects.

—William Clayton, Diary.

....

No prayer meeting to day.[51]

—Zina D. H. Jacobs, Diary, in "'All Things Move in Order in the City': The Nauvoo Diary of Zina Diantha Huntington Jacobs," edited by Maureen Ursenbach Beecher, *BYU Studies* 19 (Spring 1979): 316.

Sunday, August 3, 1845
Willard Richards House

In afternoon at 4 o'clock, at Quorum meeting.

—John Taylor, Diary.

....

I [George A. Smith] attended a prayer meeting and council in the evening.

—George A. Smith, "History of George Albert Smith."

....

4 P.M. the brethren assembled at my [Willard Richards's] office for prayer.— as usual.

—Willard Richards, Diary.

....

At 4 met at Dr. [Willard] Richards ... I [William Clayton] read a letter from Wilford Woodruff giving a very cheering history of the progress of the work in England. Prayers were offered up for a number of sick.

—William Clayton, Diary.

November 28, 1842, "Some charges having been instituted by the stone cutters against the Temple Committee, at president Josephs request the parties appeared at his house this day to have the difficulties settled. An investigation was entered in to before the prest & his council W[illiam]. Law. Pres[iden]t Hyrum [Smith] acted as council for defendents" (qtd. in Dean C. Jessee, ed., *The Papers of Joseph Smith* [Salt Lake City: Deseret Book, 1992], 2:494). According to Jessee, "The principle grievances brought against the committee were an unequal distribution of provisions to those who worked on the temple, and allowing [Reynolds] Cahoon's sons more iron and steel tools to work with than others" (ibid.).

51. Quinn (*Origins,* 509) implies that the female members of the Quorum of the Anointed were intentionally excluded from the quorum's meeting on this date.

Thursday, August 7, 1845

Willard Richards House

[A]t 4 in the after noon the Holy Order met for prair.
—Heber C. Kimball, Diary, entry dated August 8, 1845.

....

[A]t 4 Prayer Meeting by the Quorum as usual at my [Willard Richards's] office.
—Willard Richards, Diary.

....

At 4 P.M. met at Dr. [Willard] Richards ... It was decided to send John S. Fullmer[52] and H[enry] G. Sherwood[53] with James Emmett[54] to his [Emmett's] company, to council and instruct them. The subject of Brother [George] Millers abusing [them] sometime ago was talked over. Brother [George] Miller denies having done so, but his language is too fresh in my memory to forget it. It was decided to send out a number of the agents who went last spring to collect funds for the [Nauvoo] Temple and have them collect all the money and means they can so as to finish the [Nauvoo] Temple as speedily as possible.
—William Clayton, Diary.

Sunday, August 10, 1845

Willard Richards House

This morning went to Bro[ther] W[illard]. Richards office met with

---

52. John Solomon Fullmer (1807-83) served as a clerk to Joseph Smith in Nauvoo, and later worked on the committee to dispose of the Saints' properties there. (His sister, Desdemona, was one of Joseph Smith's plural wives.) After serving on the committee to close all church business in Nauvoo, he journeyed to the Salt Lake Valley with Willard Richards in 1848.

53. Henry Garlie Sherwood (1785-1862) was a member of the Kirtland Stake High Council (1837), clerk of the Nauvoo Stake High Council (1839-40) and high councilman (1839-46), and Nauvoo marshal (1841). Joseph Smith healed him of malaria in 1839. After settling in Utah, he became a member of the first high council there, in addition to being an agent for the Pony Express Company. He left Salt Lake City in 1852 to survey San Bernardino, California.

54. James Emmett (1803-52/3) labored as a missionary for the LDS church in several Midwestern states as well as in Kentucky. He was temporarily disfellowshipped in 1837. In August 1844, he led a company of a hundred immigrants out of Nauvoo to the French settlement of Fort Vermillion, South Dakota, contrary to the counsel of church leaders.

brothers W[illard] & L[evi] Richards H[eber]. C. Kimball G[eorge] A Smith A[masa]. Lyman N[ewel]. K. Whitney Geo[rge]. Miller W[illia]m Clayton Jos[eph]. Young I[saac]. Morley O[rson]. Spencer and E[van] M Greene.[55]

—Brigham Young, Diary.

....

Met in council at 9 o'clock and remained till 2 in the afternoon at Dr. Willard Richards.

—George A. Smith, "History of George Albert Smith."

....

[A]t 9. Orson Spencer. Amasa Lyman, Geo[rge] A Smith. W[illia]m Clayton, Geo[rge]. Miller. Isaac Morley Joseph Young. N[ewel]. K. Whitney. B[righam]. Young. H[eber]. C. Kimball L[evi]. Richards, come in. Pres[iden]t [Brigham] Young read letter from W[illia]m Smith — dated 9. Aug[ust]. (read by Evan Green) 2 store bills were presented for payment amounting to $74.24 — H[enry]. G. Sherwood & James Emmet came in. — Letter read from "Amos Fielding" ["]Alleghanny City, near Pittsburgh [Pennsylvania] Aug[ust] 25. 1845" to B[righam]. Young.— cable of Rigdonism is is [sic] if the shingles are all put on the Temple Rigdonism is done.— [Henry G.] Sherwood & [James] Emmet retired. — Wrote the Pres[iden]t. [Brigham Young] of the public meeting to have the Quorum meet at 2 P.M. — adjourn the meeting this P.M. have all the brethren vote for [Jacob] Backenstos[56] — &c — carried by father [Isaac] Morley[;] wrote answer to W[illia]m Smith — Prayed. — for Sick &c. —

Pres[iden]t [Brigham Young] Instructed to council the Quorums to bring 1/10 of their grain & all things raised & not attempt to pay their

---

55. Evan Milbourne Greene (1814-82) had earlier labored with John F. Boynton on a mission in Maine in 1833, baptizing over 130 converts between January and October. He was clerk of the elders quorum in Kirtland, Ohio (1836-37), and later postmaster in Kanesville, Iowa, and recorder and treasurer of Pottawattamie County (1848-52). Quinn (*Origins,* 509) writes: "This is the first evidence that Evan M. Greene had been endowed by this time unless he was an unendowed observer." As Willard Richards's and William Clayton's diaries suggest, however, Evan (like Henry Sherwood and James Emmett) probably left the meeting before the members of the quorum offered up prayers.

56. Jacob Backenstos (1811-57) served as clerk of the Hancock County, Illinois, circuit court from 1843 to 1845 and was elected to the Illinois legislature in 1844. He succeeded Miner Deming as Hancock County sheriff in 1845 after Deming's death. Like his predecessor, he befriended the Mormons in Nauvoo, having previously argued against repeal of the Nauvoo charter as a member of the legislature. After settling in Oregon in 1849, he died in the Willamette River in 1857.

tithing in team work &c and that agents be selected to go abroad to gather tithing.[57]

—Willard Richards, Diary.

....

At 9 A.M. met at Dr. [Willard] Richards ... a letter was read from Pittsburgh [Pennsylvania] from Amos Fielding dated July 25th, 1845 giving an account of W[illia]m. E. McLell[i]n[58] abusing him &c. Also that Sidney Rigdon has had a revelation requiring his followers to sell their property and give him the avails of it to purchase land in the East to build up the kingdom. This letter is [to be] published in the [Nauvoo] Neighbor [newspaper] of August 13th.

After reading the letter prayers were offered up.

—William Clayton, Diary.

Thursday, August 14, 1845
Willard Richards House

[T]he afternoon attended prayer meeting at Brother W[illard]. Richards.

—Brigham Young, Diary.

....

Also in quorum meeting, where we prayed for a good many that were sick.

—John Taylor, Diary.

....

Council met at 2 o'clock p.m. and convened all the afternoon.

—George A. Smith, "History of George Albert Smith."

....

1 P.M. the brethren began to assemble for prayer. read history an hour or two. had conversation on various subjects particularly about removing to a healthy climate after we have done the work appointed us in Nauvoo.

57. The previous January, Bishops Newel K. Whitney and George Miller had appointed forty-three agents to gather tithing. The present entry appears to document a renewal of those earlier efforts. See *History of the Church,* 7:369. Such agents were necessary as collecting tithing outside the immediate area of Nauvoo was difficult.

58. William E. McLellin (1806-83) was a school teacher who joined the LDS church in Missouri in 1831 and was ordained one of the original Twelve Apostles in 1835. He was disfellowshipped for a time that same year and excommunicated three years later for apostasy. He later affiliated with the break-off movements led by George Hinkle, Sidney Rigdon, James J. Strang, and David Whitmer.

& that Phinehas H. Young & Lorenzo Snow go immediately to Ohio. & gather up oxen & sheep & on tithing & drive to this place.

—Willard Richards, Diary.

Sacred Meeting at 3½ Closed at 6¾.

—Historian's Office Journal.

Sunday, August 17, 1845
Willard Richards House

[A]t 5 Quorum began to assemble. Bro[ther] [Benjamin F.] Johnson[59] from Ramus [Illinois] come in with Bro[ther] [Almon W.] Babbit to en-quire about the home he is building at Ramus. & taking the Mansion — council agreed to decide tomorrow 2 PM. at B[righam] Youngs — voted that Bish[op] [George] Miller furnish Bish[op] [Newel K.] Whitney with a p[ai]r of new Boots forthwith. Geo[rge] A Smith prayed. that the evils of the course W[illia]m Smith had pursued might fall on his own head.

—Willard Richards, Diary.

P.M. with D[iantha Farr Clayton][60] till 5 o'clock, afterwards at Dr. [Willard] Richards, with President B[righam]. Young, H[eber]. C. Kim-ball, W[illard]. Richards, J[ohn]. Taylor, G[eorge]. A. Smith, N[ewel]. K. Whitney, G[eorge]. Miller, O[rson]. Spencer, J[oseph]. Young, J[oseph]. C. Kingsbury and L[ucien]. Woodworth. A[lmon]. W. Babbitt and B[enja-min]. F. Johnson, called in to enquire whether it would be agreeable to the council [of Fifty] to let Brother [Benjamin F.] Johnson rent the Mansion. It was decided to call a council tomorrow at 2 o'clock to conclude on the matter inasmuch as Brother [Ezra T.] Benson[61] has been spoken to, to ei-

59. Benjamin Franklin Johnson (1818-1905) converted to Mormonism in 1831 and helped to build the Kirtland House of the Lord. Two of his sisters, Delcena and Almera, became plural wives of Joseph Smith. He was a member of the Council of Fifty. After Joseph's death, he managed the Nauvoo Mansion Hotel. In Utah, after arriving in 1848, he served in the legislature, spent time in prison for unlawful co-habitation, filled a mission to Hawaii from 1852 to 1855, and later moved to Mor-mon settlements in Mexico and Arizona.

60. Diantha Farr Clayton (1828-50) became a plural wife of William Clayton in Nauvoo on January 26, 1845.

61. Ezra Taft Benson (1811-69) was ordained an apostle in 1846 and was sent to preside over the Saints at Pottawattamie, Iowa, the following year. He served in the Provisional Government of the State of Deseret and the Utah Territorial Legislature

ther take the mansion or Masonic Hall. After the conversation ended [Almon W.] Babbitt and [Benjamin F.] Johnson withdrew, and we then offered up prayers as usual for general subjects. Last Tuesday Brother [Lucien] Woodworth was discharged from the work at the Nauvoo House as Architect by [George] A. Smith one of the Trustees on account of incompetency and an unwillingness to listen to Council. He foamed considerable at the time but feels tolerably well now.

—William Clayton, Diary.

Monday, August 18, 1845
Nauvoo House/Brigham Young House

Met the brethren of the council and committee at the Nauvoo House on the walls and there dedicated it up to the Lord and asked his blessing to attend the work[;] in the afternoon had a council at my house.

—Brigham Young, Diary.

Thursday, August 21, 1845
Willard Richards House

2 P.M. Present B[righam] Young W[illard] Richards. H[eber] C. Kimball Amasa Lyman, Geo[rge]. A. Smith. 2 Bishops, O[rson]. Spencer John Pack. Lucian Woodworth— Bro[ther] Benjamin F. John[son]. council at my [Willard Richards's] house[.] heard letter from Samuel Walker [Waldo][62] Post Master, Drewsville. N[ew]. H[ampshire]. July 21. — voted that Nelson Bates[63] be disfellowshipped & instructed to come home immediately & that a letter be sent to O[rson]. Pratt. Ohio — A letter from Samuel V. Searles.[64] for a licence, mailed at Salem [Massachusetts] Aug[ust] 3d. — voted that licence be sent. (voted that [John] Pack buy the Masonic Hall tavern if it has not already recorded) Letters written to

---

and completed several missions for the church, including an appointment as president of the British Mission in 1856.

62. Samuel Waldo (1794-1875) was born in Alstead, New Hampshire, and was postmaster in Drewsville, New Hampshire. He was the father of Asa Perry Waldo.

63. Nelson Bates (1813-85) was baptized in 1843 and received his endowment in the Nauvoo temple on December 23, 1845.

64. Samuel V. Searles was one of several witnesses sent to appear before attorney John S. Reid on behalf of Joseph Smith just prior to Joseph's murder in June 1844.

Orson Pratt. — Samuel W. Searles including licence — & notice for Times & Seasons. — voted that B[enjamin]. [F.] Johnson take the Mansion & John Pack the Masonic Hall. — prayed for the sick & every thing by Geo[rge] A Smith. Levi [Richards] came in after the prayer.

—Willard Richards, Diary.

P.M. met at Dr. [Willard] Richards ... A letter was read from Samuel Waldo of New Hampshire complaining of oppressive conduct and teaching doctrines calculated to break up the branch such as it being no harm for a man to sleep with a woman who was not his wife &c. in [the words of] Nelson Bates. The Council decided that fellowship be withdrawn from [Nelson] Bates and he be called home forthwith to give an account of his conduct. Elder W[illard]. Richards wrote a notice to the above effect for publication in the next Times & Seasons. He also wrote a letter to O[rson]. Pratt informing him of the same. A letter was then read from Samuel V. Searles requesting a license. It was voted to send him one and Elder W[illard]. Richards accordingly filled it out. The subject of the mansion and Masonic Hall again came up and it was decided that B[enjamin] F. Johnson take the Mansion and [John] Pack the Hall. These brethren then withdrew and the remainder clothed, offered up the signs of the Holy Priesthood and prayed for the usual subjects especially for the sick. There are a great many sick in the north part of town, so many that it is grievous to see their sufferings.

—William Clayton, Diary.

Sunday, August 24, 1845
Willard Richards House

[W]ent to Dr. [Willard] Richards office to our prayer meeting.

—Brigham Young, Diary.

In the evening, in council with the Twelve [apostles]; after which we had Quorum meeting and prayers; we remained until about eight o'clock.

—John Taylor, Diary.

[A]t 5. Quorum met in my room. prayed for about 22 sick — &c. voted to suspend stop the notice concerning Nelson Bates. in the Times & Seasons.

—Willard Richards, Diary.

137

Thursday, August 28, 1845
Willard Richards House

[T]hen to Dr. [Willard] Richards, to council where I [Brigham Young] spent the afternoon.

—Brigham Young, Diary, entry dated August 29, 1845.

In council with the Twelve [apostles], wherein we made arrangements, and voted for an expedition of a number of people to go to California in the ensuing spring. After which we had our Quorum meeting.

—John Taylor, Diary.

2. P.M Quorum met in my room. [Elder] Peter Shirts came in. he had started for the neighborhood of Quincy [Illinois] for grape juice. voted to send a co[mpany] of 3,000 to Calofornia next spring. & begin preparing immediately. prayed for the Sick. &c.

—Willard Richards, Diary.

P.M. met at Dr. [Willard] Richards ... It was voted to select three thousand men who are able to bear arms to prepare this winter to start to California next spring with their families. Prayers were offered up for the usual subjects.

—William Clayton, Diary.

At 4 [o'clock] B[righam] Young, Heber C. Kimball, P[arley]. P. Pratt, G[eorge]. A. Smith W[illard]. Richards, John Taylor, W[illia]m Clayton, Patriarch [Isaac] Morley, Joseph Young, Bishops [Newel K.] Whitney, and [George] Miller, Lucian Woodworth, Amasa Lyman met for council separated a little after 6.

—Historian's Office Journal.

Sunday, August 31, 1845
Willard Richards House

In afternoon at Quorum meeting.

—John Taylor, Diary.

In the evening I attended a council in company with a number of others.

—George A. Smith, "History of George Albert Smith."

[A]t 5 council at my [Willard Richards's] room prayed for many sick

(John Taylor Prayed. voted that Brigham Young be next Gov[ernor]. of Cala. [California] & Heber C. Kimball vice Gov[ernor].— Pres[iden]t. &c

—Willard Richards, Diary.

....

P.M. met at Dr. [Willard] Richards ... The subject of the Oregon expedition was again talked over and the Twelve [apostles] seem to think it important that they should go with the company to select a location and plant the standard. They would leave their families here and return when they had succeeded in finding a place. Prayers were offered up for quite a number of sick, amongst whom is Hugh Riding, one of our best carpenters now laying at the point of death. It is truly grievous to see the many sick in our midst especially in the north part of Town.

—William Clayton, Diary.

Thursday, September 4, 1845
Willard Richards House

I [John Taylor] was at Council with the Twelve [apostles] at Dr. [Willard] Richards'; after which had Quorum meeting.

—John Taylor, Diary.

....

Met in council.

—George A. Smith, "History of George Albert Smith."

....

2 P.M. council B[righam]. Young, [Heber C.] Kimball, [Parley P.] Pratt. A[masa]. Lyman, G[eorge]. A. Smith. [John] Taylor. W[illard] Richards. Bishops. [George] Miller, O[rson]. Spencer, L[evi]. Richards. J[oseph] Young.— at my [Willard Richards's] Room. Voted that the trustees let the Nauvoo House committee have 150 cords of sawed wood or enough to finish burning their brick. (Lent, them[.]) Pres[iden]t. [Brigham] Young proposed calling council of 50,000 [i.e., Council of Fifty]. on Tuesday next 2. P.M. — John Taylor Prayed. for the sick &c. — closed about sun set.

—Willard Richards, Diary.

....

I [William Clayton] had to tarry at the office instead of attending council.

—William Clayton, Diary.

....

[A]bout 2. B[righam]. Young, H[eber]. C. Kimball, W[illard] Richards, G[eorge]. A. Smith, P[arley]. P. Pratt, A[masa]. Lyman, J[ohn]. Taylor, Bish[op]. [Newel K.] Whitney & [George] Miller Fa[the]r. [Isaac] Morley, Joseph Young, Orson Spencer and 2 brethren who owned land in Texas met — the 2 latter left about 4.

—Historian's Office Journal, first entry under date.

....

At 2 B[righam]. Young. H[eber]. C. Kimball, W[illard] Richards. G[eorge]. A. Smith, P[arley]. P. Pratt, [Amasa] Lyman, J[ohn] Taylor, Bishops [Newel K.] Whitney & [George] Miller, Isaac Morley, Joseph Young O[rson] Spencer, and Br[other Jacob] Phelps from Boston [Massachusetts] and another with him the two latter on business about land in Texas came together for counsel.

—Historian's Office Journal, second entry under date.

....

2 p.m., met for counsel and prayer with the Twelve [apostles] and others.

—"Manuscript History of Brigham Young," in *History of the Church,* 7:437.

Sunday, September 7, 1845
Willard Richards House

In afternoon in council with Twelve [apostles]; after which at Quorum meeting.

—John Taylor, Diary.

....

I [George A. Smith] attended council at 5 o'clock. Bishop George Miller was directed to let the Nauvoo House committee have 50 white oak saw logs.

—George A. Smith, "History of George Albert Smith."

....

5. P.M council & prayer meeting at my [Willard Richards's] room as usual. voted that Bro[ther] McClary[65] be door keeper in the House of the

---

65. Possibly William McCleary (1793–?), second husband of Joseph Smith's sister, Sophronia (1803–76), a wagon maker and convert to Mormonism in Kirtland, Ohio. He was ordained an elder in May 1838 and was sealed to Sophronia in the Nauvoo temple on January 27, 1846. He built wagons for the Nauvoo exodus and died during that time, although the exact date is unknown.

Lord [i.e., Nauvoo temple] agreeable to his request. (when the house is completed.)

—Willard Richards, Diary.

At 5 met at Dr. [Willard] Richards with President B[righam]. Young, H[eber]. C. Kimball, W[illard]. Richards, A[masa]. Lyman, G[eorge]. A. Smith, J[ohn]. Taylor, P[arley]. P. Pratt, G[eorge]. Miller, L[evi]. Richards, I[saac]. Morley, and J[oseph]. C. Kingsbury. Prayers were offered up for the usual subjects. Notified the members of the Council of Fifty to meet next ...

—William Clayton, Diary.

Thursday, September 11, 1845
Willard Richards House

We (the Twelve [apostles]) held a council and thought it advisable as we were going West in the Spring to keep all things as quiet as possible and not resent anything.

—John Taylor, Diary.

B[righam]. Young. H[eber]. C. Kimball, J[ohn]. Taylor, A[masa]. Lyman, G[eorge]. A. Smith, W[illard]. Richards [Isaac] Morl[e]y, [George] Miller, Eleazer Miller. C[harles]. C. Rich come in my [Willard Richards's] office. Pres[iden]t [Brigham] Young related his dream Night before last, was chased by a mob. to a place like a barn. fully of corn, or grain, & dropped down into a low room. & one followed me so closely that he fell into the same room, & said I am come along & it was T[h]om[as] Ford [and I said] you are. about 2½ feel high — I took his wrists between my fingers & stepped to the door to the mob. & knocked down one after another when I discovered T[h]om[as] Ford was dead. 2 messengers have arrived, & stated that a mob of about 100 was collected at Lima [Illinois] yesterday & last night burned 1 or two houses. Edmund Durfee's house[.]

Gen[eral] [Charles C.] Rich[66] [to] send out 3 or 4 special messengers. Col[onel] [Stephen] Markham[67] [to] have his minute men in readiness[,] Gen[eral] Rich [to] be notified to have the Nauvoo Legion be in readi-

66. Charles Coulson Rich (1809-83) was baptized in 1832 and participated in Zion's Camp in 1834. In Nauvoo, he served on the high council, in the Nauvoo Legion, in the Council of Fifty, and in the Nauvoo Stake presidency. He was ordained an apostle in 1849 and later helped settle San Bernardino, California.

67. Stephen Markham (1800-78) served as a body guard to Joseph Smith and was a captain of the Nauvoo Legion. He entered the Salt Lake Valley in 1847 in

ness for any emergency, & he was notified accordingly by W[illard].
Richards[.] Names of council were selected to go to Oregon in Spring[.]
Letters was written by the Council to Solomon Hancock & sent by
bro[ther] Eells [i.e., Joseph Ells] & 3 others. to Morl[e]y Settlement. also
B[righam]. Young & Bro[ther] [Willard] Richards wrote to J[acob]. B.
Backenstos. Sheriff to quell the mob at Lima[.]

—Willard Richards, Diary.

....

P.M. met at Dr. [Willard] Richards ... It was decided to dispatch a
messenger to the Lima [Illinois] Branch and advise the brethren to propose to sell their possessions to the mob, and bring their families and grain
here. It was also decided to send a messenger to Michigan to advise the
brethren to sell their farms for Stock, wagons, sheep &c. Also to send a
messenger to Ottawa [Ontario, Canada] & advise the brethren to gather
all the hay they can. Prayers were offered up for the usual subjects and also
that the Lord would give us wisdom to manage affairs with the mob so as
to keep them off till we can accomplish what is required. Also to give us
wisdom to manage the affairs in regard to the Western emigration. A selection has been made by President [Brigham] Young of those of the
Council of Fifty who shall start west next spring. My [William Clayton's]
name is included in the list.

—William Clayton, Diary.

....

The Twelve [apostles] met in council; it was agreed to dispatch a messenger to the Lima [Illinois] Branch and counsel the brethren to propose
to sell their property to the mob and bring their families and grain here,
and to send a messenger to Michigan to advise the brethren to sell their
farms for stock, sheep, etc., also to Ottawa [Ontario, Canada] and recom-
mend the brethren to gather all the hay they can.

Prayers were offered up that the Lord would give us wisdom to manage affairs with the mob so as to keep them off till we can accomplish
what he requires at our hands in completing the [Nauvoo] Temple and
Nauvoo House, also to give us wisdom to manage the affairs in regard to
the Western emigration.

A selection was made of members of the council to start westward
next spring.

—"Manuscript History of Brigham Young,"
in *History of the Church,* 7:440.

Brigham Young's company and later served for many years as a bishop in Spanish
Fork, Utah.

Sunday, September 14, 1845
Willard Richards House

At 2 Oclock the quorum came together. At 5 we met for prair and council.

—Heber C. Kimball, Diary, under notes in rear of book.

....

At five o clock, met with the brethren in the quorum at Dr. [Willard] Richards, where after we attended to various matters of counsel[,] I [John Taylor] stated to the brethren that I had had thoughts of disposing of my house, stores, barn &c, providing I could get a purchaser, which I expected I could; and after using part of the means that I should need to liquidate some debts that I was owing turn in the remainder towards assisting in this expedition, under the direction of counsel. After some deliberation it was thought best to do so if practicable and as I supposed that probably five or six thousand dollars could be obtained for it, it might be of essential service in that way. I feel that I am the Lord's and that I and everything I have [are] at his disposal at all times. After which there were some general remark's made, pertaining to P[arley]. P. Pratt's property and others, whether it would be advisable to dispose of property that was eligibly situation in the City of Nauvoo, or not. Whereupon it was generally agreed to and a resolution passed that we would send an agent or agents, to Quincy [Illinois], St. Louis [Missouri], Cincinnatie [Ohio], and also to New York and other Eastern Cities, to propose to business men to sell out to them; for we considered that we had a perfect right so to do, that we had been driven from and despoiled of our property long enough, and that we should be justified in taking a course of that kind, that the City and [Nauvoo] Temple would be more likely to be preserved in safety by wealthy and influential men purchasing property and settling here, than by Apostates and half hearted Mormons having charge of affairs during our absence, and that if we should return we should again inherit our places, and if we do not inherit them in Time, we and our children will inherit them hereafter. ...

—John Taylor, Diary.

....

Council met in the afternoon at 5 o'clock.

—George A. Smith, "History of George Albert Smith."

....

5. P.M. President [Brigham] Young & Quorum present. Letter read

143

from Willard Snow.[68] 12" Aug[ust]. Boston. [Massachusetts] — Letter read from Samuel Brannon [Brannan][69] Aug[ust] 29.— read proclamation of J[acob] B Backenstos. — voted that Arthur Smith come into this council next thursday & tell us about water proofing clothing[.] Pres[iden]t [Brigham] Young prophesied on the stand this day that we would have a winter of peace in Nauvoo. Geo[rge]. A. Smith prayed [for] about 63 [who] were named as sick. decided to send a messenger to Quincy [Illinois] — St. Louis [Missouri] &c. to get rich men & merchants to b[u]y & rent our buildings so as to help us to Oregon. — & save our buildings after we are gone.

—Willard Richards, Diary.

Brother [George] Miller reported that he went to Carthage [Illinois] yesterday to attend to some business. While there he was arrested on a writ got up by the mob for the grave charge of Treason. He had a kind of trial and was admitted to parole bail till next Saturday. Col[onel]. [Levi] William[s] and [Thomas] Sharp were at Carthage with the mob. The writ is against President B[righam]. Young, H[eber]. C. Kimball, O[rson]. Hyde, O[rson]. Pratt, J[ohn]. E. Page, L[yman]. Wight and several others. The treason is for colleaguing with the Indians, building an arsenal, and making Cannon. The Higbees [Chauncey and Francis] are very active with the mob, and there seems to be a desperate effort to break us up. All the families have got up from Lima [Illinois] and there are a great number of teams gone to fetch up grain. The last report gives 44 buildings burned and considerable grain, furniture, clothing &c. belonging to the poor Brethren. The Sheriff J[acob]. B. Backenstos has issued his proclamation warning the mob to disperse and calling upon all the Law and order citizens to act as "posse commitatus" to preserve the peace.

---

68. Willard Trowbridge Snow (1811-52/53) would arrive in Utah in September 1847 with the Ira Eldredge Company and serve in the territorial legislature, the First Quorum of the Seventy, and on the Perpetual Emigration Fund Committee. A missionary to Scandinavia (1851-52), he would die en route to Britain and be buried at sea eighty miles from Hull, England.

69. Samuel Brannan (1819-89) migrated to Kirtland, Ohio, in 1833 and worked as a printer. He presided over the Saints in the eastern states (1845-46) and led a group from New York to San Francisco by ship (1846-47). He tried to persuade Brigham Young to settle in California rather than Utah, and failing in that attempt, he returned to the Bay Area. He was excommunicated in 1851. He became one of California's pioneer entrepreneurs and was the state's first millionaire. However, he had lost most of his property by the time of his death. He also published the first newspaper in San Francisco, the *California Star.*

It was decided in the council to offer some of our best property in the City for sale to respectable merchants in Cincinna[t]i [Ohio], Phi[l]adelphia [Pennsylvania] &c. judging it better for the safety of the property to sell out to such men than to leave it to the destruction of the mob. A great many sick were prayed for and we also prayed that the Lord would preserve us from the mob till the Elders can get their endowment. It was also agreed to turn more force of hands to the [Nauvoo] Temple even if it [will] have to hinder the Nauvoo House.

—William Clayton, Diary.

Thursday, September 18, 1845
Willard Richards House

Had prair and council.

—Heber C. Kimball, Diary.

....

[H]ome at 2. Quorum at my [Willard Richards's] office. Letter from A. B. [C]hambers — agreed to meet him in an hour — Pres[iden]t. [Brigham] Young prayed. — read a Letter from E[lijah]. Fordham[70] & others to the friends in New York &c. for 6 barrel pistols.

—Willard Richards, Diary.

Friday, September 19, 1845
George Miller House

The Twelve [apostles] ware in council most all day at Bishop [George] Miller.

—Heber C. Kimball, Diary.

....

At 5 evening met with some of the Twelve [apostles] and others at Bishop [George] Millers house ... Before council broke up President [Brigham] Young and the company kneeled down and he offered up prayers that the Lord would preserve his servants and deliver those who had been active in the mob that killed Joseph and Hyrum [Smith] into our hands that they might receive their deserts.

—William Clayton, Diary.

---

70. Elijah Fordham (1798–1879) was a lumber dealer and carpenter. He participated in Zion's Camp in 1834. He was the only church member in New York City in 1837 and assisted the first missionaries en route to Great Britain. He served on the Iowa Stake High Council in 1839 and migrated to Utah in 1850.

145

Sunday, September 21, 1845
Willard Richards House

[A]t 2 Oclock went to W[illard]. R[ichards]. for council and prair. Present the following persons B[righam] Y[oung]., H[eber]. C. K[imball]., G[eorge]. A. [Smith], A[masa]. L[yman]., P[arley]. [P.] P[ratt]., two Bishops [Newell K. Whitney and George Miller]. Two leters one from P. Pratt, 1 W[ilford]. Woodruff, good tidings.

—Heber C. Kimball, Diary, entry dated September 22, 1845.

....

[A]t 3. Quorum assembled at my [Willard Richards's] room. [Jacob] Backenstos was writing 4th proclamation.[71] [John] Taylor prayed — &c [Heber C.] Kimball prayed that the mob might have confusion in their midst.

—Willard Richards, Diary.

Wednesday, September 24, 1845
Willard Richards House?

½ past nine. the council adjourned the South room. except [Parley P.] Pratt, [William] Clayton [Almon W.] Babbit, & [Willard] Richards who wrote a communication for the council. with [Brigham] Young & [Heber C.] Kimball. at 12 W[illard]. Richards communication was accepted and sent to press.[72] After dedicating the same to Almighty God. by P[arley]. P.

---

71. Earlier, according to historian Marvin S. Hill, "Sheriff Backenstos issued a proclamation requesting all citizens to assist him in dispersing the mob operating in the southwestern part of the county. On 11 September a church council encouraged Backenstos now to 'quell' the mob but said nothing about using Mormon troops. William Clayton noted in his diary that the council was praying to 'manage affairs with the mob so as to keep them off till we can get ready to leave.' Letters were sent to outlying Mormon settlements advising them to sell out and gather to Nauvoo. Young told Solomon Hancock to move to Nauvoo but to be ready for a much longer move in the spring." On the date above, "Governor Ford had learned of Backenstos's drive to purge Carthage of insurgents and had dispatched a military force to the county under John J. Hardin to take Backenstos into custody. Ford said that anti-Mormons intended to kill him and that citizens from Adams, Brown, Marquette, McDonough, and Henderson counties had met and demanded his arrest. Ford warned the sheriff that the alternative to surrender was an immediate attack on Nauvoo" (Marvin S. Hill, *Quest for Refuge: The Mormon Flight from American Pluralism* [Salt Lake City: Signature Books, 1989], 173-75).

72. See B. H. Roberts, *A Comprehensive History of the Church of Jesus Christ of*

Pratt. Pres[iden]t Young prophesied [and] said the piece would have the desired effect. & prove a blessing to the Church.

—Willard Richards, Diary.

Thursday, September 25, 1845
Willard Richards House

At 2 Oclock had prair and council at W[illard]. Richards.

—Heber C. Kimball, Diary.

In the afternoon we met in council and received a proclamation purporting to be from the governor. The sheriff, J[acob]. B. Backenstos, pronounced it to be hoax. We spent some time in prayer.

—George A. Smith, "History of George Albert Smith."

2 P.M. Quorum at my [Willard Richards's] home. G[eorge]. A. Smith prayed.

—Willard Richards, Diary.

P.M. at Dr. [Willard] Richards with some of the Twelve [apostles] and others. We offered prayers for the sick &c. and especially that the Lord will preserve us in peace to finish the [Nauvoo] Temple and prepare to depart [for the] West in peace.

—William Clayton, Diary.

Friday, September 26, 1845
Willard Richards House

At 1 Oclock met for prair and council at W[illard] Richards.

—Heber C. Kimball, Diary.

Met again at the specified time [i.e., 1 o'clock] and spent an hour in prayer. I never have felt really free before now.

—George A. Smith, "History of George Albert Smith."

1. P.M. Quorum. Meeting at my [Willard Richards's] home. [Heber C.] Kimball prayed. for peace & that the mob might be overthrown.

—Willard Richards, Diary.

Latter-day Saints, Century I, 6 vols. (Provo, UT: Published by the Church and Brigham Young University Press, 1965), 2:508-10.

Saturday, September 27, 1845
Willard Richards House

[T]o W[illard] Richards for prair and council, five of the Twelve [apostles] and Bishop [George] Miller present. Got through at 3 Oclock.

—Heber C. Kimball, Diary.

Sunday, September 28, 1845
Willard Richards House

[W]ent to W[illard] Richards met in council.

—Heber C. Kimball, Diary.

....

1. P.M. Quorum at my [Willard Richards's] house E A Bedell[73] returned from the Gov[erno]r. [Thomas Ford]. [Bedell?] met [Heber C.] Kimball 35 mi[les] this side [and] returned with him. Gov[ernor] [Ford] had done all he [Bedell?] asked except discharging all the troops [but] had order[ed] Gen[eral] [John J.] Hardin[74] to discharge all the troops except 1 or 200 — Gov[ernor] [Thomas Ford] had issued the proclamations we supposed counterfeit. brought State Register. & Peoria papers. with Simpsons confession[.] P[arley] Pratt prayed. after which W[illia]m Clayton brought in a letter from W. G. Ferris.[75] Carthage. [Illinois] to [Jacob] Backenstos [?] [John J.] Hardins communication to Citizens of Hancock [County, Illinois] to discharge all troops. & not more than 4 armed men be seen at once[.]

—Willard Richards, Diary.

Monday, September 29, 1845
Willard Richards House

---

73. Edward A. Bedell (?-1854) was a postmaster of Warsaw, Illinois, quartermaster of the Warsaw militia, and a justice of the peace of Hancock County. He was friendly to the Mormons and was a witness at the trial of the accused murderers of Joseph and Hyrum Smith.

74. John J. Hardin (?-1847) was a lawyer who served as brigadier general in the Illinois Volunteers. He was instrumental in arresting Thomas Sharp and Levi Williams for the deaths of Joseph and Hyrum Smith. He was killed in the battle of Buena Vista during the Mexican War.

75. William Gano Ferris (1822-93) of Carthage, Illinois, was at the time the Hancock County deputy sheriff and later president of the Hancock County National Bank.

At 1 met at W[illard] Richards for prair and council. Adjourned at 4 in the after[noon].

—Heber C. Kimball, Diary.

....

1 P.M. Quorum at my [Willard Richards's] room. 2 P.M. committee of the California Co[mpany]. came in. — council gave an order on Trustees, for to pay $5.00 to a bro[ther] who had lent the Church some money[.] Gov[ernor] [Thomas] Fords proclamation printed at our office was brought in — Sam[ue]l Bent read 100 names he had selected for [an exploring expedition to] California[.] Letter from Ferris Carthage. [Illinois] to [Jacob] Backenstos or [Brigham] Young.

—Willard Richards, Diary.

Tuesday, September 30, 1845
Willard Richards House

The Twelve [apostles] and Bishops met at W[illard] Richards for prair and council. We asked the Lord to flustrat [frustrate] the designs of our Enimes, and to blind there Eis [eyes] and caus the trops to leave our City. Soon got through about 4 in the after noon.

—Heber C. Kimball, Diary.

....

[A]t 2 — Quorum met. [Almon W.] Babbit came in with a letter from Judge Ralston[76] telling of the doings of a meeting in Quincy & Adams County [Illinois].[77] requiring [Jacob] Backenstos & County commissioners to resign — &c Prayer by Pres[iden]t. [Brigham] Young.— Then the Council selected more than a hundred names to go west in their company & dispersed about sun set.

—Willard Richards, Diary.

---

76. James H. Ralston (1807-64), a lawyer in Quincy, Illinois, was elected to the state senate in 1841. He was employed as legal counsel to Joseph Smith in Nauvoo. After participating in the Mexican War, he moved to California, where he served in the first state senate there. He moved to Nevada in 1860.

77. The meeting, consisting of citizens of Quincy, was held on September 26, 1845, to deal with the Mormon question. Their list of twelve resolutions was published in the *Warsaw Signal Extra* on September 30, and in the *Quincy Whig* on October 1. Resolution number six stated: "*Resolved,* That in our opinion the peace of Hancock county cannot be so far restored as to allow the desired progress to be made in preparing the way for the removal of the Mormons while J. B. Backenstos remains sheriff of said county and that he ought to resign said office" (qtd. in *History of the Church,* 7:452).

Wednesday, October 1, 1845

Heber C. Kimball House

Had a meeting at my haus of the Holy order praid for the sick and the govern[ment.]

—Heber C. Kimball, Diary.

Thursday, October 2, 1845

Willard Richards House

[T]o W[illard] Richards for council and prair. Great union prevailled.

—Heber C. Kimball, Diary.

[C]ouncil B[righam] Young, H[eber]. C. Kimball, Isaac Morley at 3 o clock & N[ewel]. K. Whitney used the room Lucian Woodworth was also present.

—Historian's Office Journal.

Friday, October 3, 1845

Willard Richards House

Had council at W[illard] Richards for council and prair[.]

—Heber C. Kimball, Diary.

Quorum at my [Willard Richards's] room at 1. P.M. El[der] [Heber C.] Kimball prayed.

—Willard Richards, Diary.

[A]t 2 ¼ I [Franklin D. Richards] found Pres[ident] B[righam]. Young, P[arley]. P. Pratt G[eorge]. A. Smith, A[masa]. Lyman, in the office in council.

—Historian's Office Journal.

Saturday, October 4, 1845

Willard Richards House

[W]ent to W[illard] Richards for prair and council.

—Heber C. Kimball, Diary.

Quorum at my [Willard Richards's] room at 4. Geo[rge] A [Smith] prayed. — 6 present B[righam]. Young. H[eber]. C. Kimball. Geo[rge] A

[Smith] A[masa] Lyman W[illard] Richards. N[ewel] K Whitney.

—Willard Richards, Diary.

Sunday, October 5, 1845
John Taylor House/Willard Richards House

[T]he 12 [apostles] met with 3 or 4 others for prayer in the morning & in the evening at Elder John Taylor's to call on our Father in Heaven that he would save his servants from the hands of our enemies.

—Heber C. Kimball, Diary.

[A]t 7 the council Pres[ident] [Brigham] Young Geo[rge]. A. [Smith] [John] Taylor, [William] Clayton [Newel K.] Whitney. A[masa] Lyman met at my [Willard Richards's] room. Taylor prayed. tarried till 10½.

—Willard Richards, Diary.

Evening met at Dr. [Willard] Richards ... A letter from [Jacob] Backenstos covering a copy of a dispatch from [General John J.] Hardin to the mobocrats was read,[78] after which prayers were offered as usual.

—William Clayton, Diary.

Monday, October 6, 1845
Location unknown.

[T]he 12 [apostles] met in Council and for prayer morning and evening to our Heavenly Father to stay the wrath of our enemies & to overthrow all their designs. which he has done thus far, and we thank His Holy Name.

—Heber C. Kimball, Diary.

---

78. This refers to a broadside titled *To the Anti-Mormon Citizens of Hancock and the Surrounding Counties,* published October 4, 1845. This broadside contained two letters written to church leaders by the Anti-Mormon Committee, Brigham Young's response, and a cover letter to the Anti-Mormon Committee written by John J. Hardin, William B. Warren, Stephen A. Douglas, and James A. McDougal (members of the governor's committee). Hardin et al. told the anti-Mormon committee, comprised of citizens of nine counties, that the Mormons had promised "by word and in writing, to remove from the state ... The history of their church has shown that wherever the leaders go the members will follow. This is a part of their religious duties. When, therefore, this colony will have started for a home west of the Rocky Mountains, it will be the best possible evidence that all design removing, and will remove."

Tuesday, October 7, 1845
Willard Richards House/John Taylor House

In the morning the 12 [apostles] met for prayer in the usual place [i.e., Willard Richards's house]. ... in the eve[ning], the 12 [apostles], the bishops, & one or two others met for prayer at John Taylor's Upper Room.

—Heber C. Kimball, Diary.

Evening met at Dr. [Willard] Richards ... We offered up prayers as usual especially that the Lord in his providence would cause the Governors troops to leave this [Hancock] County, and preserve the saints from the ravages of the mob.

—William Clayton, Diary.

Wednesday, October 8, 1845
John Taylor House

[M]et for prayer in the morning ... in the evening the 12 [apostles], bishops, one or 2 others met in prayer at John Taylor's—their names are as follows. B[righam] Young, myself [Heber C. Kimball], P[arley] P Pratt, J[ohn] Taylor, G[eorge] A Smith, A[masa] Lyman, Bishops N[ewel] K Whitney, G[eorge] Miller, & W[illiam] W Phelps, Joseph Young, & occasionally Lucien Woodworth—this day was the close of the Conference, and all things went off in peace & union—not a dissenting voice in the congregation & a perfect union existing by the Saints to remove from the Country the coming Spring. all these things transpire in answer to the prayers of the Saints who meet together constantly after the Holy Order & the glory be to the Father & to the Son & to the Holy Ghost for his blessings upon Israel.

—Heber C. Kimball, Diary.

Thursday, October 9, 1845
Location unknown.

[I]n the morning met for prayer ... in the evening the usual Company met for prayer. the following things were prayed for—the prosperity of the Elders in the United States, the brethren on the South Pacific Islands & the brethren in the West among the Red Men of the Forest, that our enemies may be frustrated in all their designs, that confusion and disorder, and treachery might enter into their ranks—that the sick of the people

might be healed—union prevail, and that all of his servants be saved from
their enemies—& that they should not have power to serve their vexa-
tious writs—that the [Nauvoo] Temple & [baptismal] Font may be finished and dedicated & consecrated to the most high God—that his servants & handmaids may obtain their ordinances & sealing powers of the
Priesthood, and the way opened for his Saints to go to the West &c.

—Heber C. Kimball, Diary.

Friday, October 10, 1845
John Taylor House

Met for prayer in the morning— ... met for prayer as usual at Elder
John Taylor's.

—Heber C. Kimball, Diary.

P.M. met at E[lde]r [John] Taylors, with Prest B[righam]. Young
H[eber]. C. Kimball, John]. Taylor, P[arley]. P. Pratt, G[eorge]. A. Smith,
and Joseph Young. We councilled together on the best plan to be resorted
to in the present emergency. It appears [John J.] Hardin has pledged himself to the mob that he will come to Nauvoo [Illinois] with his troops and
either have O[rrin]. P[orter]. Rockwell, and some others of the brethren
or "he will unroof every house in Nauvoo." Three hundred of our enemies have volunteered to come with him from Quincey [Illinois] and
they expect to be joined by others on the way. There seems to be no disposition abroad but to massacre the whole body of this people, and nothing but the power of God can save us from the cruel ravages of the blood
thirsty mob. We concluded to plead with our heavenly father to preserve
his people and the lives of his servants that the saints may finish the
[Nauvoo] Temple and receive their endowment, and that the Lord will
soften the hearts of the Governor [Thomas Ford,] [General John J.]
Hardin, [W. B.] Warren[79] & others like he did the heart of Pharoah that we
may have peace this winter & depart in peace.

—William Clayton, Diary.

Saturday, October 11, 1845
John Taylor House

[M]et for prayer in the morning— ... prayer in the evening, we have

---

79. William B. Warren was a member of the Illinois Volunteers.

continued our Council & prayer in the evening until 10 or 11 at ~~the~~ night.

—Heber C. Kimball, Diary.

....

We had prayers in the forenoon and asked God to overrule the movements of the enemy and cause the Governor [Thomas Ford] to withdraw his troops from this county, and preserve us in peace untill we can depart in the spring.

After prayer we went to prepare a circular for the agents to take abroad with them. P.M. President [Brigham] Young did not attend, being completely worn down with fatigue. At 4 we adjourned till 7. I [William Clayton] went up to the office and attended to some little items of business. At 7 met again at Elder [John] Taylors with the brethren. We offered up our prayers for the same subjects, believing that the Lord will defeat our enemies and preserve his people. After prayer we finished an extract from the conference minutes for the circular. Also appointed additional captains of hundreds, making Captains for twenty five companies.

—William Clayton, Diary.

....

The council met at Elder [John] Taylor's. We joined in prayer, and wrote a circular for the agents to take abroad with them. ...

7 p.m., met for counsel and prayer. After prayer we finished an extract from the conference minutes for the circular. Also appointed additional captains of hundreds, making twenty-five companies, ...

—"Manuscript History of Brigham Young," in *History of the Church,* 7:481.

Sunday, October 12, 1845
John Taylor House

Met for prayer in the morning—Elder P[arley] P Pratt was appointed to attend the meeting—El[der] A[lmon W.] Babbitt preached in the morning the rest of us continued in council until 1 in the P.M. Much business was done in behalf of the Church. ... In the evening met for prayer.

—Heber C. Kimball, Diary.

....

At 7 met at Elder [John] Taylors with the brethren ... We had prayers again as usual.

—William Clayton, Diary.

Monday, October 13, 1845
John Taylor House

In the morning met in Council and for prayer ... we assembled at John Taylor's for prayer—Persons present B[righam] Young, myself [Heber C. Kimball], P[arley] P Pratt, G[eorge] A Smith, Amasa Lyman, John Taylor—Bish[op] [Newel K.] Whitney, Joseph Young, W[illiam] W Phelps.
—Heber C. Kimball, Diary.

Tuesday, October 14, 1845
John Taylor House

In the morning met in Council for prayer, also in the eve[ning] ... in the evening met in prayer as usual at John Taylor's.
—Heber C. Kimball, Diary.

[P.M.] We offered up prayers that they [i.e., Illinois state troops] might not be permitted to do any injury to any of the saints nor to interrupt our peace. They did not stay long, but returned accomplishing nothing, leaving us in peace.
—William Clayton, Diary.

The Twelve [apostles] &c in prayer in A.M.
—Historian's Office Journal.

The Twelve [apostles] met in morning and went to prayer.
—Thomas Bullock, Diary, in *Thomas Bullock Nauvoo Journal,* edited by Greg R. Knight (Orem, Utah: Grandin Book Company, 1994).

We prayed that they [Major Warren and a detachment of troops] might not be permitted to do any injury to any of the saints; nor to interrupt our peace; they stayed but a short time.
—"Manuscript History of Brigham Young," in *History of the Church,* 7:482.

Wednesday, October 15, 1845
John Taylor House

In the morning met in council for prayer & continued till about 2 in the evening ... in the evening we met in prayer—much business transacted.

—Heber C. Kimball, Diary.

Thursday, October 16, 1845

John Taylor House

We met in prayer in the morning & eve[ning] at bro[ther]. [John] Taylor's much business transacted ...

—Heber C. Kimball, Diary.

Friday, October 17, 1845

John Taylor House

[M]et in the morning & evening for council & prayer & in council thro' the day.

—Heber C. Kimball, Diary.

Evening met at Elder [John] Taylors with the Twelve [apostles] and others for prayer.

—William Clayton, Diary.

Saturday, October 18, 1845

John Taylor House?

In the morning met in council & for prayer, much rumors of war ... in the evening met in Council & for private.

—Heber C. Kimball, Diary.

Sunday, October 19, 1845

John Taylor House

[I]n the eve[ning] met for prayer & council at John Taylor's.

—Heber C. Kimball, Diary.

Monday, October 20, 1845

John Taylor House

Met for prayer in the morning—Gen[eral] [James] Arlington Bennet[t] came into this City—had an interview with him at Dr [Willard] Richards about an hour—I [Heber C. Kimball] solicited him [Bennett] to meet us at John Taylors in council this evening—he met according to agreement & continued with us until 10 oclock—after which we had prayer after the Holy Order.

—Heber C. Kimball, Diary.

General James Arlington Bennett from Arlington House[,] Flat Bush[,] Long Island arrived today and met the Twelve [apostles] and others at Elder [John] Taylors in the evening. I [William Clayton] was present part of the time. It appears he was opposed to our selling out to gratify the mob, and would rather we would fight them and maintain our ground, but when he was informed of our ultimate plans and matters to be accomplished, he seemed to feel very different. I should judge him to be a very ambitious and a[s]piring man. After the interview, we retired upstairs and had prayers as usual.

—William Clayton, Diary.

Evening, the Twelve [apostles] met in council at Elder [John] Taylor's. General James Arlington Bennett met with us, he expressed himself opposed to our selling out to gratify the mob, and would rather see us fight and maintain our ground.

—"Manuscript History of Brigham Young,"
in History of the Church, 7:483.

Tuesday, October 21, 1845
John Taylor House

[M]et for prayer in the morning ... in the evening met for prayer, continued till 11 o'clock—in matters of prayer &c wherein we have asked the Lord, he has answer[ed] us in every instance[.] I [Heber C. Kimball] therefore feel to praise & exalt his holy name, for his blessings & favors to his people Israel.

—Heber C. Kimball, Diary.

Evening met the brethren at Elder [John] Taylors and had prayers. The council wrote a letter to Judge [James] Ralston inviting him to come here. He says he thinks he can bring a hundred Catholic families to buy out some of our propertys.

—William Clayton, Diary.

Wednesday, October 22, 1845

John Taylor House

[I]n the eve[ning] met at John Taylor's for prayer.

—Heber C. Kimball, Diary.

....

[W]ent to Elder [John] Taylors to counsel with the Twelve [apostles] and others. Read a letter from R[euben] McBride[80] in Kirtland [Ohio] stating that the Rigdonites, S. B. Stoddard,[81] Jacob Bump,[82] R[obert] D. Foster, Hiram Kellog,[83] Leonard Rich[84] [and] Jewel Raney are the leaders of the rioters. They have broke into the House of the Lord and taken possessions of it and are trying to take possession of the Church Farm &c.

We also read a number of good articles from the New York Messenger relating to our troubles. After much conversation, we had prayers.

—William Clayton, Diary.

....

Evening, I [Brigham Young] met with the Twelve [apostles] at Elder [John] Taylor's. A letter was read from Reuben McBride, Kirtland, stating that the apostates were doing everything they could to injure the saints. S. B. Stoddard, Jacob Bump, Hiram Kellogg, Leonard Rich, and Jewel Raney are the leaders of the rioters; they have broken into the House of the Lord, and taken possession of it, and are trying to take possession of the church farm.

—"Manuscript History of Brigham Young," in *History of the Church,* 7:484.

---

80. Reuben McBride (1803-91) was a member of Zion's Camp in 1834 and remained behind after the Saints left Kirtland, Ohio, to take charge of the House of the Lord and other property. He would be the first man baptized for the dead in the Nauvoo temple. (His sister, Martha, was one of Joseph Smith's plural wives.) After settling in Utah in 1850, he served two missions to England.

81. Sylvester B. Stoddard (1823-?) was called in 1840 to serve in a bishopric in Quincy, Illinois, and in 1844 to preside over an outlying branch of the church. He later left the church and was accused of mob actions in Kirtland, Ohio.

82. Jacob Bump (1791-?) was a member of Zion's Camp in 1834, but left the LDS church four years later. He joined in the violence against the church.

83. Hiram Kellog (1793-1846) converted to Mormonism in 1836 and received his patriarchal blessing from Joseph Smith Sr. in ca. 1836, but left the church and joined in the violence against the Mormons.

84. Leonard Rich (1800-56) was one of the presidents of the Seventy from 1835 to 1837. He was also a participant in Zion's Camp in 1834. He left the church and remained behind in Kirtland, Ohio, after 1845.

Thursday, October 23, 1845
John Taylor House

We met in the morning at Brother [John] Taylors for Council & Prayer.
—Heber C. Kimball, Diary.

Friday, October 24, 1845
John Taylor House

We met at Brother John Taylors both Mo[rnin]g and even[in]g for Prayer, at this time matters look'd dark, and our enemies much enraged, but the Lord heard our prayers, and all things passed off in our favor.
—Heber C. Kimball, Diary.

....

Evening at Elder [John] Taylors. We then had prayers as usual, and all felt that the Lord will deliver [Nathan] B[igelow][85] out of their hands. After prayer, it was decided that Mary Smith and Emma [Smith] have all the wood they want off the church land. Also that we establish an agency over the river to receive and take care of tithing grain until spring so that when we move we can take it as we go. It was recommended that J[ohn] E. Page be appointed for that agency if he will do it. It was decided not to hire Pecks Mill, inasmuch as he wants $300 down for 6 months rent.

President [Brigham] Young seemed dissatisfied that Elder [John] Taylor did not take more interest in our councils. We had to sit without a fire.
—William Clayton, Diary.

....

Evening, council met at Elder [John] Taylor's.
—"Manuscript History of Brigham Young,"
in *History of the Church,* 7:485.

---

85. Nathan, or Nahum, Bigelow (1785-1851) would be endowed in the Nauvoo temple in January 1846 and come to Utah with William Snow's company. Two of his daughters (Lucy and Mary Jane) were plural wives of Brigham Young. In the incident referred to, Bigelow shot a soldier who had been sent to protect his house, mistakenly thinking he was one of the rabble who had recently threatened to evict him and burn his house down. The commanding officer, Major William B. Warren, faulted the soldier for not having identified himself. See *History of the Church,* 7:485-86.

Saturday, October 25, 1845

John Taylor House

[W]e met also for Prayer and Council at John Taylors both morning and evening.

—Heber C. Kimball, Diary.

Evening met the brethren at Elder [John] Taylors. Brother [Almon W.] Babbit related the circumstance of Father [Nathan] Bigelow [accidentally] shooting Lieutenant Edwards ... We talked the matter over ... and then offered up the signs and asked the Lord to overrule the matter and take it out of [Major] Warrens heart that he may not declare Martial law or otherwise let his hand be heavy upon him with judgment that he may not be able to bring trouble upon this people. President [Brigham] Young seems quite unwell.

—William Clayton, Diary.

Evening, I [Brigham Young] met with the council at Elder [John] Taylor's. We prayed that the Lord would overrule the matter and remove from [Major] Warren's heart the disposition to declare martial law or otherwise let his hand be heavy upon him with judgment that he may not be able to bring trouble upon the saints.

—"Manuscript History of Brigham Young,"
in *History of the Church,* 7:488.

Sunday, October 26, 1845

John Taylor House

We met for prayer at John Taylors as usual; the atmosphere appears more pleasant ...

—Heber C. Kimball, Diary.

Evening met again at Elder [John] Taylors, and had prayers as usual.

—William Clayton, Diary.

P.M. council met at Elder [John] Taylor's.

—"Manuscript History of Brigham Young,"
in *History of the Church,* 7:489.

Monday, October 27, 1845

John Taylor House

Council met at John Taylors for Prayer, much business done pertaining to the Church also in the even[in]g.

—Heber C. Kimball, Diary.

About 4 P.M. Elder [Almon W.] Babbit returned and the council were immediately summoned together ... The watchful care of our heavenly father in directing the matter last Saturday evening [October 25, 1845] was plainly visible ... We felt last night to return thanks to God for his kindness and ask him to overrule this matter also for the safety of his people and his servants.

—William Clayton, Diary.

The brethren in council expressed their feelings and all felt satisfied that the Lord would overrule this matter also for our good. The brethren of the Twelve [apostles] all concluded to leave their homes tonight, so that if the *posse* come in during the night there will be no danger.

—"Manuscript History of Brigham Young,"
in *History of the Church,* 7:492.

Tuesday, October 28, 1845
John Taylor House

[S]everal of the Quorum of the holy Order in our absence met a[t] John Taylor's mo[rnin]g and evening.

—Heber C. Kimball, Diary.

At 10 o'clock went to Elder [John] Taylors and met to pray with John Smith, N[ewel]. K. Whitney, W[illiam]. W. Phelps, J[oseph]. Young, O[rson]. Spencer, J[oseph]. C. Kingsbury, and L[ucien]. Woodworth. Afterwards at the office till 5½ and then met again at Elder Taylors. After we got through with our prayers President [Brigham] Young came in ...

—William Clayton, Diary.

Wednesday, October 29, 1845
John Taylor House

The Brethren of the Holy Order met at John Taylors Morning and evening for Prayer.

—Heber C. Kimball, Diary.

At 10 went to Elder [John] Taylors. Soon after we arrived, President

[Brigham] Young sent for Bishop [Newel K.] Whitney and myself [William Clayton] to go and see him as the Twelve [apostles] are still out of sight. We went to where he [Brigham Young] was at[,] A[lbert]. P. Rockwoods[,][86] and found him in company with H[enry] G. Sherwood and [Stephen] Markham, also George A. Smith and Amasa Lyman. Brother Sherwood and [David] Fullmer[87] returned from the West a few days ago. Brother [Henry G.] S[herwood] reported their mission [to South Dakota,] which was very satisfactory. He also gave us some very interesting information concerning our best route to the West which will be of service to us when we move.

There is a rumor that W[illia]m. Smith and others are trying to get up an influence with the president of the United States to prevent our going West and has already wrote to him on the subject, revealing the acts of the Council of Fifty &c. and representing the council guilty of treason &c.[88] ... Evening at Elder [John] Taylors with the Twelve [apostles] and others ... We had prayers as usual.

—William Clayton, Diary.

Evening, the Twelve [apostles] met at Elder [John] Taylor's. The following letter was read:[89] ...

---

86. Albert Perry Rockwood (1805-1879) converted to Mormonism in 1837. He was an officer in the Nauvoo Legion and a member of the First Council of Seventy from 1845 until his death. He would arrive in the Salt Lake Valley in 1847 and become warden of the state penitentiary, a member of the territorial legislature, and a director of the Deseret Agricultural and Manufacturing Society.

87. David Fulmer (1803-79) was baptized in 1839 and sat on the Nauvoo City Council. In Utah he would become a territorial legislator and treasurer of the University of Deseret. In the current entry, he and a small party of emissaries of the Twelve have just returned from visiting James Emmett's Mormon settlement in Vermillion, South Dakota.

88. William Smith had been excommunicated ten days earlier on October 19, 1845, and moved to St. Louis soon after. Whether the activities described above were rumor or not, his letters clearly show animosity toward the Twelve Apostles. On November 7, 1845, he said the Twelve were "mean enough to steel if they could get the chance eaven Christ's supper off his plate or seduce the Virgin Mary or Rob an orphan child of 25 c[en]ts and so damnable are their acts & conduct that old Judas ... would be a perfect genteelman to these men" (qtd. in Bates and Smith, *Lost Legacy,* 93).

89. The letter, entitled "Wild Schemes Proposed by 'Backwoodsman' of Palmyra, Missouri, for the Conjoint Occupancy of 'California' by the Latter-day Saints and Migrating Citizens from the United States, but to Live in Separate Communities—Founding of Independent Government–'The United States of the West,'" appears in the *History of the Church,* 7:499-502.

The above letter contains the lucubrations [i.e., pretentious writing] of some of Senator Benton's[90] mobocratic associations who, no doubt, desire to make us a barrier between them and the Mexican government. His falsehoods in relation to our social system, and interference with the rights and property of others, are too absurd to be noticed, but I [Brigham Young] copy the letter as a specimen of numerous others which I am constantly receiving and which show the vanity, folly and corruption to which the human heart has been prostituted.

We had prayers as usual.
—"Manuscript History of Brigham Young,"
in *History of the Church,* 7:502.

Thursday, October 30, 1845
John Taylor House

We met as usual with the brethren at John Taylors for Prayer Mo[rnin]g & Even[in]g.
—Heber C. Kimball, Diary.

Friday, October 31, 1845
John Taylor House

We met at the usual time and place for Prayer and Counsel.
—Heber C. Kimball, Diary.

Evening met the Twelve [apostles] and others at Elder [John] Taylors for prayer. The subject of the United States endeavoring to prevent our removal West by taking out U[nited]. S[tates]. writs for the Council of Fifty was talked over and plans devised to defeat them in case they undertake to do it.
—William Clayton, Diary.

P.M. council met at Elder [John] Taylor's. We wrote the following[91] to

90. Thomas Hart Benton (1782-1858), of Missouri, served in the U.S. Senate for thirty years beginning in 1821. Prior to his first election, he was editor of the *Missouri Enquirer* in St. Louis, where he established a successful law practice.

91. The letter, from Willard Richards to "Rev. Bishop Purcell, et al. Cincinnati," dated October 31, 1845, is found in *History of the Church,* 7:508-509.

Bishop John B. Purcell[92] of Cincinnati: — ...

—"Manuscript History of Brigham Young,"
in *History of the Church,* 7:508.

Saturday, November 1, 1845
John Taylor House

In the eve[ning] we met at Bro[ther] John Taylors for Council and prayer, President [Brigham] Young left before prayer[,] being sick.

—Heber C. Kimball, Diary.

Monday, November 3, 1845
John Taylor House

[I]n the Eve[ning] met for prair.

—Heber C. Kimball, Diary.

Evening met at E[lde]r [John] Taylor's with the Twelve [apostles] and others. [Henry G.] Sherwood, [David] Fulmer & [John L.] Butler[93] made a report of the country West. I [William Clayton] was sick and did not stay long.

—William Clayton, Diary.

Evening, council met at Elder John Taylor's. Brothers [Henry G.] Sherwood, [David] Fullmer and [John L.] Butler made a further report of the country west.

—"Manuscript History of Brigham Young,"
in *History of the Church,* 7:513.

Tuesday, November 4, 1845
Willard Richards House

At 4 in the after noon met for prair at W[illard] Richards.

—Heber C. Kimball, Diary.

---

92. John Baptist Purcell (1800-83) was born in Ireland and came to Emmitsburg, Maryland, to attend the Roman Catholic Mount St. Mary's Seminary in 1820. Seven years later he returned to the seminary as a professor. He was appointed bishop of Cincinnati in 1833 and archbishop in 1850.

93. John Lowe Butler (1808-61) served several LDS missions during the 1840s

4 [o'clock] — when the council who had absented themselves some weeks on account of my [Willard Richards's] health returned to my room, prayers at 5.

—Willard Richards, Diary.

....

At 5 p.m., council met for prayers at the Historian's Office. (Dr. [Willard] Richards').

—"Manuscript History of Brigham Young,"
in *History of the Church,* 7:514.

Wednesday, November 5, 1845
Willard Richards House

At Fore Oclock met at W[illard] Richards, for council and prair.

—Heber C. Kimball, Diary.

....

[A]t 4 Council in my [Willard Richards's] room & prayers as usual.

—Willard Richards, Diary.

....

[A]t 4 Pres[iden]t. [Brigham] Young, W[illia]m Clayton, W[illiam]. W. Phelps, Bishop [George] Miller, G[eorge]. A. Smith, O[rson]. Spencer, P[arley]. P. Pratt, H[eber]. C. Kimball, Bishop Isaac Morley, O[rson]. Hyde, br[other] [Lucien] Woodworth called to Council.

—Historian's Office Journal, first entry under date.

....

Council met at 4 PM — Pres[iden]t B[righam] Young H[eber] C Kimball J[ohn]. Taylor. — G[eorge]. A. Smith, Orson Hyde, Bishop [George] Miller, Orson Spencer, and another bro[ther] read several Letters on Emigration Council [and] continued to sit when I [Wilmer Benson] left at 6 PM.

—Historian's Office Journal, second entry under date.

....

Afternoon, in council at the Historian's Office.

—"Manuscript History of Brigham Young,"
in *History of the Church,* 7:514.

---

and scouted for Brigham Young in Iowa. He was also an officiator in the Nauvoo temple and later second bishop of Spanish Fork, Utah.

Thursday, November 6, 1845
Willard Richards House

The council met at W[illard] Richards Praid, after the Holly Order.

—Heber C. Kimball, Diary.

....

4 [o'clock] — when Council assembled. had prayers at 5.

—Willard Richards, Diary.

....

Evening attended council at Elder [Willard] Richards.

—William Clayton, Diary.

....

4 [o'clock] Pres[iden]t [Brigham] Young, W[illia]m Clayton W[illiam] W Phelps Bishop [George] Miller G[eorge] A Smith — O[rson] Spencer, P[arley] P Pratt, H[eber] C Kimball Bishop [Isaac] Morley O[rson] Hyde br[other] [Lucien] Woodworth called to council.

—Historian's Office Journal.

....

At ep [p.m.] 4 a council was held in the office.

—Thomas Bullock, Diary, in *Thomas Bullock Nauvoo Journal,* edited by Greg R. Knight (Orem, Utah: Grandin Book, 1994).

....

4 p.m., attended council and prayer meeting with the Twelve [apostles].

—"Manuscript History of Brigham Young," in *History of the Church,* 7:514.

Friday, November 7, 1845
Willard Richards House

[T]o Council at W[illard] Richards and prair. Brock up in the Eve[ning].

—Heber C. Kimball, Diary.

....

4 [o'clock] Council at my [Willard Richards's] room[.]

—Willard Richards, Diary.

....

Council met at 4 PM Present Pres[iden]t [Brigham] Young G[eorge] A Smith J[ohn] Taylor.

—Historian's Office Journal.

At 5 the council met in office.

> —Thomas Bullock, Diary, in *Thomas Bullock Nauvoo Journal,*
> edited by Greg R. Knight (Orem, Utah: Grandin Book, 1994).

....

4 p.m., attended council with the Twelve [apostles].

> —"Manuscript History of Brigham Young,"
> in *History of the Church,* 7:514.

Saturday, November 8, 1845
Willard Richards House

In the Eve[ning] met at W[illard] Richards for prair and council.

> —Heber C. Kimball, Diary.

....

Council at 4. Sheriff [Jacob] Backenstos came in the Council— brought two letter[s] from Gov[erno]r. [Thomas] Ford to George Miller & Orson Spencer, which were read[.]

> —Willard Richards, Diary.

....

Bro[ther] Jedediah Grant present Bro[ther] Brigham Young H[eber]. C. Kimball, G[eorge] A Smith, Dr [Willard] Richards Bishop [George] Miller and another also.

> —Historian's Office Journal.

....

[At 4 p.m.,] the Twelve [apostles] and others met for council and prayer.

> —"Manuscript History of Brigham Young,"
> in *History of the Church,* 7:514.

Sunday, November 9, 1845
Willard Richards House

At 4 in the after^noon^ the council met for prair at W[illard] Richards. Two leters from Governer [Thomas] Ford To J[acob] B Backenstos, he read them to us.

> —Heber C. Kimball, Diary.

....

[A]t 4 a Council in my [Willard Richards's] room[.] J[acob]. B. Backenstos came in Council read a letter from Gov[erno]r. [Thomas] Ford, another from Judge Caton[94] appointing a day for his [Backenstos's] trial.

—Willard Richards, Diary.

Evening met at Dr. [Willard] Richards with the Twelve [apostles].

—William Clayton, Diary.

Monday, November 10, 1845
Willard Richards House

[R]ead history till 4, when the Council come in, for prair. Brock up at dark.

—Heber C. Kimball, Diary.

....

Council &c at 4 P.M. as usual[.]

—Willard Richards, Diary.

....

The Council consulted on the subject of Purchasing the Copy right of her History (Mother Lucy [Mack] Smith) and also to settle with Bro[ther] [Howard] Corey [Coray] for his labor in compiling the same.

—Historian's Office Journal.

....

I [Brigham Young] spent the day with Elders Heber C. Kimball, Willard Richards and George A. Smith revising Church History; several of the Twelve and others called in the afternoon; we consulted on the subject of purchasing the copyright of Mother [Lucy Mack] Smith's History; and concluded to settle the matter with Brother Howard Coray for his labor in compiling the same.

—"Manuscript History of Brigham Young,"
in *History of the Church,* 7:519.

Tuesday, November 11, 1845
Willard Richards House

At fore the Brethen come in for council and prair[.]

—Heber C. Kimball, Diary.

---

94. John Dean Caton (1812-95) was born in New York and in 1833 came to Chicago, where he was an attorney; alderman (chosen in Chicago's first official city election in 1837); judge of the ninth judicial circuit, Ottawa, Illinois; and a state supreme court justice, appointed to office in 1842. He served as chief justice from 1855 to 1864. He was also president of the Illinois and Mississippi Telegraph Company.

Council in my [Willard Richards's] room as usual. El[der] P[arley]. P. Pratt read an Epistle to the Churches which he had been instructed to write[.][95]

—Willard Richards, Diary.

············

At 4 P.M. met at Dr. [Willard] Richards with the Twelve [apostles].

—William Clayton, Diary.

············

[I]n afternoon read History to Pres[iden]t [Brigham] Young G[eorge] A Smith H[eber] C Kimball & Dr [Willard] Richards Council commenced at 4 Cl[oc]k present the aforesaid, also P[arley] P Pratt, Orson Hyde John Taylor Orson Spencer W[illiam] W Phelps Bishop [George] Miller, Levi Richards, Reynold[s] Cahoon, William Clayton[,] bro[ther] [Joseph W.] Coolidge and bro[ther] [Cornelius P.] Lott.

—Historian's Office Journal.

············

Four p.m., the Twelve [apostles] met, Elder Parley P. Pratt read an epistle to the churches which he had been instructed to write.

—"Manuscript History of Brigham Young,"
in *History of the Church,* 7:520.

Wednesday, November 12, 1845
Willard Richards House

[A]t 4 PM met with the Council at Elder [Willard] Richards for prair, present G[eorge]. A. Smith, O[rson]. Hide [Hyde], P[arley]. Pratt, J[ohn]. Tailor [Taylor], Georg[e]. Miller, W[illiam]. Phelps, Or[son]. Spencer, Elder [Willard] Richards, and my Self [Heber C. Kimball]. Clo[t]hed our selvs and praid as follows that our Enimes be flustrated [frustrated], to sell our posessions, and so forth. Brock up at dark. Amasa Bonny [Amos Bonney][96] come to my hous in the Eve[ning] and Said his Brother Edwin Bonny [Edward Bonney][97] was sentance[d] to be hung. If so it is in answer to prair.[98]

—Heber C. Kimball, Diary.

---

95. This may refer to Parley P. Pratt's *Proclamation of the Twelve Apostles of the Church of Jesus Christ of Latter-day Saints to All the Kings of the World.* The proclamation was written on April 6, 1845, by assignment, and published in Liverpool, England, on October 22.

96. Amasa, or Amos, Bonney (?-1865) was the LDS brother of non-LDS Edward W. Bonney.

97. Edward W. Bonney (1807-64) was a non-Mormon aide-de-camp to Joseph

Council had prayers at 6.

—Willard Richards, Diary.

....

The Council assembled at the office at 4 PM.

—Historian's Office Journal.

....

Council met in the afternoon for prayer.

—"Manuscript History of Brigham Young,"
in *History of the Church,* 7:520.

Thursday, November 13, 1845
Willard Richards House

At 4 went to W[illard] Richards, met in council. Prese[nt] B[righam] Young, W[illard]. Richards, G[eorge]. A. Smith, P[arley]. Pratt, Georg[e] Miller, W[illiam]. Phelps, Ors[on] Spencer, L[ucien]. Woodworth, N[ewel]. K. Whitney. Brock up at dark.

—Heber C. Kimball, Diary.

....

4. in Council — ... Council decided that Mother [Lucy Mack] Smith should be furnished with Wood & flour — with food & clothing — Prayed as usual.

—Willard Richards, Diary.

Smith, although better known as a counterfeiter and Nauvoo city prosecutor during the trial of Joseph Smith after the destruction of the *Nauvoo Expositor.* The intent of the trial was to mollify a judge in Carthage, Illinois, whose arrest warrant for Joseph Smith had gone unfulfilled. In 1845 Bonney was involved in the arrest and conviction of the Hodge brothers of Nauvoo after they were charged with robbing and killing a non-Mormon family. Bonney was convicted of counterfeiting in 1846 but managed to avoid an apparent death sentence, later becoming famous for his best-selling novel, *The Banditti of the Prairies; or, the Murderer's Doom!! A Tale of Mississippi Valley and the Far West.* During the Civil War, he joined the Union army and was assigned to the secret service.

98. According to historian Stanley B. Kimball, "On one occasion, Brigham Young, John Taylor, Parley P. Pratt, Orson Hyde, and others, including the colorful non-Mormon, Edward Bonney, were indicted for counterfeiting. Later all charges were dropped except those against Bonney, who was sentenced to be hanged." After quoting Heber C. Kimball's comment above, he continued: "Heber, at least, was tired of his people being blamed for the wrongs of others. There is some evidence, however, that a few Mormons may very well have been involved in 'making bogus.' We learn from Heber that during the summer of 1845, two Mormons (or would-be Mormons) had been in jail in Quincy for counterfeiting and that 'Bishop Haywood [Joseph L. Heywood of Quincy] said they were guilty'" (Stanley B. Kimball, *Heber C. Kimball: Mormon Patriarch and Pioneer* [Urbana: University of Illinois Press, 1981], 120).

4 p.m., attended council with the Twelve [apostles]. It was decided that Mother Lucy Smith should be furnished with food, clothing, and wood for the winter.

We prayed as usual.

—"Manuscript History of Brigham Young,"
in *History of the Church*, 7:522.

Friday, November 14, 1845

Willard Richards House

At fore met for prair at El[der] [Willard] R[ichards]. Letter from Uriah Brown. Present. B[righam]. Y[oung], G[eorge]. A. [Smith], P[arley]. [P.] P[ratt], O[rson]. H[yde], W[illard]. R[ichards], H[eber]. C. K[imball], W[illia]m Cla[y]ton, Orson Spencer, W[illiam]. W Phelps, G[eorge]. Miller. Had a good time. I thank the Lord.

—Heber C. Kimball, Diary.

[M]et in council 5 P.M. B[righam]. Young, O[rson]. Hyde, P[arley]. P. Pratt G[eorge]. A. Smith, G[eorge]. Miller, O[rson]. Spencer, W[illiam]. W. Phelps, W[illard]. Richards. H[eber]. C. Kimball[.]

—Willard Richards, Diary.

Evening met with the Twelve [apostles] at Dr. [Willard] Richards.

—William Clayton, Diary.

Evening, the Twelve met at Dr. [Willard] Richards'.

—"Manuscript History of Brigham Young,"
in *History of the Church*, 7:522.

Saturday, November 15, 1845

Willard Richards House

At fore went to El[der] [Willard] Richards, for prair and council. All the saints buissey in Making Waggons for going west. Present G[eorge] A [Smith], W[illiam] W [Phelps], G[eorge] Miller, Cornelius [P.] Lott, P[arley P.] P[ratt]. After we praid, W[illard] Richards and B[righam] Young come, continued in council. J[acob] B Backenstos come in to our council. Just from Carthage [Illinois].

—Heber C. Kimball, Diary.

Council H[eber]. C. Kimball, P[arley]. P. Pratt G[eorge] A Smith.

G[eorge]. Miller. W[illiam]. W. Phelps[.]

—Willard Richards, Diary.

Evening, the Twelve [apostles] met for prayer.

—"Manuscript History of Brigham Young,"
in *History of the Church,* 7:523.

Sunday, November 16, 1845
Willard Richards House

[W]ent [to] W[illard] Richards for council and prair. Alford [Alfred] Corden[99] and James Grugark[100] come in to council. Edmond Durphy [Durfee Sr.][101] was just brought into our city dead. Chot [Shot] by the mob at Lima Last nite. Had a leter re[a]d from W[illia]m. Smith to Lewis Robins, it was filled with [w]rath against the Twelve [apostles]. I had a Leter from Samwell Brannen, one from the Moons.

J[acob]. B. Backenstos come in gave us the perticulers of the death of Durphy. Present B[righam]. Y[oung], G[eorge]. A. [Smith], O[rson]. Hide [Hyde], J[ohn]. Tailor [Taylor], W[illard]. Richards, P[arley]. [P.] P[ratt], Br. [Lucien] Woodworth, O[rson]. Spencer, Br[other]. [William] Magor[102] [Major?], G[eorge]. Miller.

—Heber C. Kimball, Diary.

Council assembled as usual. Sheriff [Jacob] Backenstos came and reported the murder of Edmund Durfee at Morley Settlement — Green

---

99. Alfred Cordon (1817-71) was a convert and emigrant from England. He returned to England twice on missions (1839-41, 1848-50) and also served a mission in Vermont (1844). He was later called as presiding bishop of Willard, Utah.

100. Perhaps James Grocott (1823-?), an English convert who immigrated to the United States in 1842. He was a seventy and would receive his endowments in the Nauvoo temple in January 1846.

101. Edmund Durfee (also Durphy) (1788-1845) was baptized in 1831 and served a mission to New York and later helped to lay the cornerstones for the House of the Lord in Kirtland, Ohio. He was shot and killed when he tried to stop mobsters who had set fire to his haystacks at his farm in the Morley Settlement south of Nauvoo. Oaks and Hill (*Carthage Conspiracy,* 203) note that "The *Quincy Whig* deplored the burnings and murder and maintained that it was the act of a drunk, but an anti-Mormon magistrate at Carthage would hear no Mormon witnesses, and charges were dismissed."

102. "It is not clear," observes Quinn (*Origins,* 512), "whether Mormon artist William Major had received his endowment, or like non-Mormon Jacob B. Backenstos attended this meeting after the prayer circle. Also see 29 Nov. 1845."

Plains precinct about midnight the evening previous — & Orson Hyde wrote a letter to Maj[or]. Warren concerning the same in behalf of the council[103] — C̶o̶u̶n̶c̶i̶l̶ a letter was read from W[illia]m. Smith to br[other]. Robins[.]

—Willard Richards, Diary.

Afternoon, council of the Twelve [apostles] assembled.

—"Manuscript History of Brigham Young,"
in *History of the Church,* 7:525.

Monday, November 17, 1845
Willard Richards House

Went to W[illard] Richards for cou[ncil] and prair. Present B[righam]. Y[oung], O[rson]. H[yde], P[arley]. [P.] P[ratt], G[eorge]. A. S[mith], W[illiam]. W. [Phelps], G[eorge]. Miller, [Lucien] Woodworth, J[ohn]. T[aylor], W[illiam]. Cla[y]ton, and H[eber]. C. Kimball, O[rson]. Spencer come in. Had prair G[eorge]. A. Smith being mouth. Some Rumer of trouble.

—Heber C. Kimball, Diary.

Council B[righam]. Young, G[eorge]. A. Smith, Bishop [George] Miller, Jos[eph]. Young O[rson]. Hyde, P[arley]. P. Pratt, W[illiam]. W. Phelps, L[ucien]. Woodwith, H[eber]. C. Kimball & self [Willard Richards] — John Taylor

—Willard Richards, Diary.

At 5 met the Twelve [apostles] at Dr. [Willard] Richards.

—William Clayton, Diary.

[I]n evening Council assembled as usual. Present B[righam]. Young, G[eorge]. A. Smith, O[rson]. Hyde, P[arley]. P. Pratt, H[eber]. C. Kimball, Bishop [George] Miller, Jos[eph]. Young, W[illiam]. W. Phelps, L[ucien]. Woodworth.

—Historian's Office Journal, first entry under date.

Council assembled at 4 PM Present Pres[iden]t Brigham Young, G[eorge] A Smith Pres[iden]t Joseph Young Bishop Y̶o̶u̶n̶g̶ [George

103. The letter from Orson Hyde to Major Warren, dated November 17, 1845, is found in the *History of the Church,* 7:525.

Miller] — Bro[ther] [George D.] Watt — Orson Hyde.

> —Historian's Office Journal, second entry under date.

....

I [Brigham Young] met in council at 4 p.m. with Elders Heber C. Kimball, Orson Hyde, Parley P. Pratt, John Taylor, George A. Smith, Joseph Young and Bishop George Miller.

> —"Manuscript History of Brigham Young,"
> in *History of the Church,* 7:527.

Tuesday, November 18, 1845
Willard Richards House

The Council met in council at 4 at W[illard]. Richards for priair. Present of the Twelve [apostles]: B[righam]. Y[oung], O[rson]. H[yde], P[arley]. [P.] P[ratt], H[eber]. C. K[imball], G[eorge]. A. Smith, J[ohn]. Tailor [Taylor], J[ohn]. Page, [Willard]. Richards, Bishops [Newel K.] Whitney and [George] Miller, L[ucien]. Woodworth, El[der] [William] Cla[y]ton. Sent Witnesses to Carthage [Illinois] [for the trial of Edmund Durfee's assailants]. S[tephen]. Marcum [Markham], [Albert P.] Rockwood to gether [as] witnesses. Got through priar Eigh[t] in the Eve. Bishop Joseph Heywood come in to give us some council about the Catholicks.

> —Heber C. Kimball, Diary.

....

Council. W[illard]. Richards, J[ohn]. E. Page, O[rson]. Spencer, B[righam]. Young, G[eorge]. A. Smith N[ewel]. K. Whitney, G[eorge]. Miller W[illiam]. W. Phelps, W[illiam]. Clayton, P[arley]. P. Pratt, John Taylor — O[rson] Hyde. L[ucien] Woodworth[.]

> —Willard Richards, Diary.

....

[A]t 4 Council met Pres[iden]t [Brigham] Young Heber C Kimball P[arley] P Pratt John Taylor, G[eorge] A Smith, Bishop [George] Miller, Orson Spencer, W[illiam]. W. Phelps, Bro[ther]. [Curtis E.] Bolton and [Robert] Campbell writing blessings.

> —Historian's Office Journal, first entry under date.

....

At the office ... [sometime after 3:15 while] I [Franklin D. Richards] went to copying Book C as aforetime C[urtis E.] B[olton] & R[obert] C[ampbell] copying W[illia]m Smith's Patriarchal Blessings[.] Howard

Coray, — [also] Wolfe [Samuel Rolfe?], David Candling, Orson Spencer, B[righam]. Young, Bishops [Newel K.] Whitney & [George] Miller, W[illiam]. W. Phelps, W[illiam] Clayton G[eorge]. A. Smith, John Taylor, P[arley]. P. Pratt, H[eber]. C. Kimball, [and] Lucien Woodworth went into council.
—Historian's Office Journal, second entry under date.

Council sat at 4 PM Present B[righam]. Young J[ohn]. Taylor, H[eber] C Kimball G[eorge]. A Smith P[arley] P Pratt also Howard Corey [?] Wolfe David Scalin Orson Spencer William Clayton W[illiam] W Phelps Bishops [Newel K.] Whitney [George] Miller & Lucien Woodworth.
—Historian's Office Journal, third entry under date.

The Twelve [apostles] met in council at Dr. [Willard] Richards'.

Mr. Brayman,[104] attorney for the state, wrote a letter to the council desiring witnesses against the murders of [Edmund] Durfee to be sent to Carthage [Illinois], also affidavits forwarded in relation to the burning of [William] Rice's house, and advising us of the arrest of George Backman,[105] Moss and Snyder, who were charged with the murder of Elder Edmund Durfee, Sen.

The council replied immediately and requested the witnesses to start in the morning for Carthage [Illinois] to perform their part in another judicial farce.
—"Manuscript History of Brigham Young,"
in *History of the Church*, 7:527.

Wednesday, November 19, 1845
Willard Richards House

[W]ent to W[illard]. Richards and met my [Heber C. Kimball's]

---

104. Mason Brayman (1813-95) was a printer and editor and later an attorney in Springfield, Illinois. In 1843 he was appointed by Governor Ford to investigate Mormon troubles in Nauvoo. In 1844-45 Brayman was selected to revise the statutes of the state. He also served as general solicitor of the Illinois Central Railroad, 1851-55. He became a major in the Twenty-ninth Illinois Volunteers in 1861, returned to Springfield to edit the *Illinois State Journal* from 1872 to 1873, and was appointed governor of Idaho from 1876 to 1880.

105. George Backman was a private in the Carthage Greys. The others mentioned were presumably fellow soldiers.

brethren in the Council. Present of Twelve [apostles] P[arley]. [P.] P[ratt], J[ohn]. Tailor [Taylor], Willard Richards, Levi Richards, O[rson]. Spencer, W[illiam]. W. Phelps, Geo[rge]. Miller, O[rson]. Hide [Hyde]. Elder Pratt read a sercular [circular] just come out to give the perticulers of the Death of Edmond Durphy and the burning of Rice haus.[106] Elder [Willard] Richards confined to his bed. B[righam]. Young came in just at dark. We Clothed our selves and offered up prair. I was mouth. Got threw at seven in the Eve. We conversed much on the California Mission and many other matters. P[hinehas]. Young come into our Council.

—Heber C. Kimball, Diary.

Thursday, November 20, 1845
Willard Richards House

I [Heber C. Kimball] met the council at W[illard]. Richards. Had priars. P[arley]. [P.] P[ratt] was mouth. Present: B[righam]. Y[oung], O[rson]. H[yde], G[eorge]. A. S[mith], H[eber]. C. K[imball], Bishop N[ewell]. K. [Whitney], G[eorge]. M[iller], Levi Richard[s], O[rson]. Spencer, W[illiam]. W. Phelps. We praid for the prosperity of Isreal. We talked much of the west. Chose men to go to England, as follows Franklin [D.][107] and Samwell [Samuel W.] Richards.[108] Elder W[illard] Richards sick abed.

---

106. Two days before the Durfee murder, thirty men arrived at the house of Samuel Hicks and demanded that William Rice be turned over, claiming to have a writ authorizing them to take him. After Hicks denied that Rice was there, the mob took Hicks outside and burned his house. They found Rice and burned his house as well.

107. Franklin D. Richards (1821-99) was baptized in 1838 and served four missions to England, three times as mission president, and helped to establish the Perpetual Emigrating Fund. He was ordained an apostle in 1849 and served as president of the Quorum of the Twelve Apostles from 1889 until his death ten years later. He also published the first edition of the Pearl of Great Price in 1851.

108. Samuel W. Richards (1824-1909) converted to Mormonism with his family in 1838. He served as a missionary in parts of New York, Connecticut, and Vermont, and he and his family moved to Nauvoo in 1842. He worked on the Nauvoo temple until its completion in 1846, then left to serve his first of four foreign missions, one as president of the European Mission, where he edited the *Latter-day Saints' Millennial Star*. He was a drill sergeant in the Nauvoo Legion and in Utah, where he furnished a company to suppress an Indian uprising in Sanpete County at his own expense. He was a member of the first city council in Salt Lake City, a member of the Utah Territorial Legislature, and U.S. Commissioner for Davis County. He was excommunicated in 1873 and reinstated in 1878.

Bishop [Newel K.] Whitney and Levi Rich[ards] quite porly.

—Heber C. Kimball, Diary.

Council — B[righam]. Young. W[illard]. Richards. P[arley] P. Pratt, G[eorge]. A. Smith, N[ewel]. K. Whitney, O[rson]. Spencer, W[illiam]. W. Phelps, Levi Richards, G[eorge]. Miller.

—Willard Richards, Diary.

Council assembled Pres[iden]t Brigham Young, Orson Spencer G[eorge] A Smith, P[arley] P Pratt. W[illiam] W Phelps, N[ewel] K Whitney, Geo[rge] Miller and Levi Richards. (this day had a private interview Pres[iden]t. Young)

—Historian's Office Journal, first entry under date.

[A]t 4 G[eorge]. A. Smith, W[illiam]. W. Phelps, N[ewel]. K. Whitney, B[righam]. Young, O[rson]. Spencer, P[arley]. P. Pratt, L[evi]. Richards, met in council.

—Historian's Office Journal, second entry under date.

Council of the Twelve [apostles] met in the afternoon.

—"Manuscript History of Brigham Young," in *History of the Church,* 7:530.

Friday, November 21, 1845
Willard Richards House

[W]ent to W[illard] Richards met the Brethren in council. Present B[righam] Y[oung], P[arley] P[ratt], O[rson] Hide, W[illard] R[ichards], H[eber] C K[imball] and others W[illiam W.] Phelps, G[eorge] Miller, G[eorge] A [Smith], J[ohn] T[aylor]. Br[other] [Lucien] Woodworth, David Yearsl[e]y[.][109] much said about the west mishon [mission.] A sherrif in to day, after Br[other]. Fellers.[110] The cherrif name was Stigall.[111] because Br[other] Fellers drove of[f] his own cattle[.] this is wonderfull.

109. Quinn (*Origins,* 513) writes: "David Yearsley may have been recently endowed, or may have been allowed as a non-endowed person to witness the prayer circle ceremony. Also see 29 Nov. 1845."

110. Possibly Albert Gallitin Fellows (1799-1880), baptized in 1839 and endowed in the Nauvoo temple in January 1846. He entered Utah in 1847 and later lived in Nephi and St. George, Utah.

111. George Stigall was the county coroner who served briefly as sheriff after Deming's death and before Backenstos's election.

At 7 in the Eve[ning] we got through prair, B[righam]. Young being mouth. After J[acob.] B. Backenstos come in he said Magaur [Major] Warren swore if the Anties [anti-Mormons] would not Help him bring those that killed [Edmund] Durphy he would Leave the County and [turn] Backensos on them with his forses. things seam to be in our favour. I thank the Lord our God — A Request from the old Jackson [Missouri] Brethren [who had lost property when they were expelled from Missouri] for to have the Twelve [apostles] me[e]t them at some place, to give them council. The Twelve [apostles] Agreed to meet them at the New York Store on [in] the trustees office at 2 OC[lock] in the after noon[.] Brock up at Eight[.]

—Heber C. Kimball, Diary.

....

Council. B[righam]. Young H[eber]. C. Kimball, G[eorge]. A. Smith, P[arley] P. Pratt, J[ohn]. Taylor — W[illard]. Richards, W[illiam]. W. Phelps, L[ucien]. Woodworth, D[avid]. Yearsley — Sheriff [Jacob B.] Backenstos came into Council about 7. said that he had watched Major Warren very closely for the last four days, & thought he had turned Jack Mormon,[112] that he had been very busy and energetic in arresting the murderers of [Edmund] Durfee & the burners of Royce [William Rice]'s house, that he had several of them under guard at Carthage [Illinois] & was in pursuit of more, that he had chased one of them into Missouri and forced him back at the point of a pistol, without any requisition from the Governor [Thomas Ford]. Maj[or]. Warren had made several very sharp speeches to the Anti Mormons & told them if they did not help to bring those murderers to Justice he would withdraw his troops from the County, and leave them in the hands of [Jacob B.] Backenstos. he had also intimated that if he could not bring them to justice without, he would es-tablish Martial law for a little season to try them by Court martial, and have them shot. Stephens[113] of Green Plains issued his Warrant for the ap-prehension of the murderers — & came to Carthage [Illinois] on the day of examination and claimed his privilege of trying his own Writs — War-ren knowing him to be [a] mobocrat caused Mr. Bartlett to issue new Writs [and,] while Stephens was contending for his rights, squashed Ste-

---

112. At some point, the meaning of "Jack Mormon" changed to designate a non-practicing Mormon, but in the 1840s it referred to a Mormon sympathizer.

113. Possibly Henry Stephens, a lawyer living in Warsaw, Illinois, who, according to Backenstos, was one of the leaders of the mob in Carthage "who took an active part in the massacre of Joseph and Hyrum Smith" (*History of the Church,* 7:143).

phen's writs, & took them the prisoners out of his hands. the Sheriff also stated, the Clerk of the Commissioner's Court had had an injunction served on him, and had refused to issue the orders granted by the last Comissioners Court for the payment of the Sheriff's posse in quelling the rioters & house burners — that he [i.e., the sheriff] had caused the instigators thereof to be arrested under 10,000 dollars bonds, that he had also planted five other suits in the premises of 5,000 doll: each.

—Willard Richards, Diary.

Evening met the Twelve [apostles] at Dr. [Willard] Richards and had prayers. [Jacob B.] Backenstos came in and stated that [Major] Warren has sworn he will have the men who murdered [Edmund] Durfee brought to justice.

—William Clayton, Diary.

[A]t 4 W[illiam]. W. Phelps, G[eorge]. A. Smith, B[righam]. Young, H[eber]. C. Kimball, D[avid]. Yearsley, John Taylor, Lucian Woodworth, P[arley]. P. Pratt, Geo[rge]. Miller, O[rson]. Hyde, Orson Spencer, Doctor [Willard Richards.] [I]n bed most of the day.

—Historian's Office Journal, first entry under date.

At 4 Council met comprising B[righam] Young — G[eorge] A Smith H[eber] C Kimball John Taylor P[arley] P Pratt, O[rson] Hyde D[avid] Yearsley Lucian Woodworth Geo[rge] Miller Orson Spencer.

—Historian's Office Journal, second entry under date.

The Twelve [apostles] met and prayed.

—"Manuscript History of Brigham Young,"
in *History of the Church,* 7:530.

Saturday, November 22, 1845
Willard Richards House

[T]he Twelve [apostles] went to Elder [Willard] Richards whare we had had prair. 9 present had some council on the weston [western] mission then went [home?].

—Heber C. Kimball, Diary.

Council W[illard]. Richards. O[rson] Spencer. P[arley]. P. Pratt and others. had some council on the Western Mission[.]

—Willard Richards, Diary.

Sunday, November 23, 1845

Willard Richards House

[W]ent to Council at El[der] [Willard] Richards. Sevrel [several] Leters read, 2 from Br[other]. [Theodore] Turl[e]y,[114] one from Roswell Fitch, 1 Ruben Miller[.][115] Edward Hunter come in. much rumer of threats by our Enimes. Had prair at about dark the usu[a]l Brethren present.

—Heber C. Kimball, Diary.

Council generally present — several letters read — Two from Bro[ther] [Theodore] Turley — One from Roswell Fitch — One from Reuben Miller — Edward Hunter came in — much rumor of threats by our enemies[.]

—Willard Richards, Diary.

Afterwards I [William Clayton] went to council.

—William Clayton, Diary.

Afternoon, the Council of the Twelve [apostles] met. Several letters were read. Many threats by our enemies were afloat.

—"Manuscript History of Brigham Young," in *History of the Church,* 7:532.

Monday, November 24, 1845

Willard Richards House

[W]e went to W[illard] Richards and met in Council[.] present B[righam] Y[oung], W[illard] R[ichards], G[eorge] A S[mith], P[arley] P P[ratt] Bishop [George] Miller L[ucien] Woodworth W[illiam W.] Phelps.

---

114. Theodore Turley (1801-71) converted to Mormonism in 1837 and traveled with members of the Quorum of the Twelve Apostles to England on their 1839-40 mission. While there, he spent time in prison for preaching. Earlier, he had participated in laying the corner stones for the Far West, Missouri, temple and was on a committee to relocate the Saints from Missouri. He settled in Utah in 1849.

115. Reuben G. Miller (1811-82) was baptized in 1844. In 1849 he immigrated to Utah and became bishop of the Mill Creek Ward in 1850. He was elected county commissioner that same year and held the post for over three decades.

The Docter [Willard Richards] still on well [unwell.] much Council on the west[.] O[rson] Spencer come in[.] O[rson] Hide [Hyde] come in and read a letter from Silas Hate [Haight].[116] He wishing to see the Head of the Church. J[ohn] Tailor [Taylor], L[evi] Richards come. got through Just at dark J[ohn] Tailor mouth in prair.

—Heber C. Kimball, Diary.

Council — B[righam]. Young. H[eber]. C. Kimball, W[illard]. Richards, G[eorge]. A. Smith, G[eorge]. Miller, L[ucien]. Woodworth, W[illiam]. W. Phelps, O[rson]. Spencer — P[arley]. P. Pratt. O[rson]. Hyde[.]

—Willard Richards, Diary.

[A]t 4 Council began to assemble and council.

—Historian's Office Journal, first entry under date.

[S]oon after Pres[iden]t B[righam]. Young, H[eber]. C. Kimball, Lucian Woodworth, P[arley] P. Pratt O[rson] Spencer, entered for Counsil and were present when we left ...

—Historian's Office Journal, second entry under date.

Afternoon, council met for prayers.

—"Manuscript History of Brigham Young," in *History of the Church*, 7:532.

Tuesday, November 25, 1845
Willard Richards House

[I]n the Eve[ning] we met at W[illard] Richards for council and prair. B[rother] [William W.] Phelps was Mouth. peas [peace] and union is constant with us. we spent some time in the Temple.

—Heber C. Kimball, Diary.

Council — W[illard]. Richards, O[rson]. Spencer, Jos[eph]. Young, P[arley]. P. Pratt & others.

—Willard Richards, Diary.

[A]bout 5 the Council began to assemble.

—Historian's Office Journal.

---

116. Silas Haight was deputy marshal of Iowa, who in October 1845 came to Carthage, Illinois, with writs for the Twelve Apostles.

Wednesday, November 26, 1845

Willard Richards House/John D. Lee House

In the Eve[ning] Cou[ncil] met At W[illard] Richards for prair and council. The us[u]al persons present. O[rson] Hide was mouth[.] great union prevailed. J[acob] B Backenstos come in after prair for council. all maters go on well. Bless the Lord[.]

—Heber C. Kimball, Diary.

Council G[eorge]. A. Smith, W[illard]. Richards, L[evi]. Richards, W[illiam]. W. Phelps, ~~bro Butler~~ John Taylor, P[arley]. P. Pratt, O[rson]. Hyde. Sheriff [Jacob B.] Backenstos called for Council — all matters go on well[.]

—Willard Richards, Diary.

At candle light the Presidents of the diffrint Quorums of the Seventies convened in the 2nd Story of Elder J[ohn]. D. Lee's dwelling house on the Flatt. A Hymn was sung by the Quorum & Prayer was offered by Pres[ident] Jos[eph] Young who observed that [he] had called a Meeting of the Presidents [of Seventies] ^& chief clerk^ for the purpose of seeing them togeather — And Also to have them get acquainted. — I will speak for the first time concerning the wine & oil notwithstanding the frequent inquireys that has been made of me by the Sevits [Seventies] you have (the greater part at least) the wine and oil that will be nessary for your Endowments — this is all right. Still there has been no council to that effect — I suppose the oil &c. will be furnished and consecrated for that purpose & if you had not have provided your own you certainly would had to have bowin [borrowed?] your part — So you see it is just as well. To day I learned from Br[other]. Brigham [Young] that there was two Rooms ready for the Seventies in the upper story of the Temple[117] — the rooms must be furnished with carpet 2 settees A stand Tables chairs Stoves & 2 lookingglass[es] all of which must be furnished [Jedediah?] M. Grant. has purchased carpet sufficient for both Rooms $4.00 of which is to be paid in cash — the remainder can be answered in Tithing — the whole will be but a trifle among the seventies & Knowing it will meet their feeling has [been] apart [apportioned and] we will take a collection to that effect on next Sunday — with regard to the garments that you will wear in the House of the Lord there has no special commandment ~~has~~ been given yet

---

117. The seventies were given Room 9 next to the Male Initiatory Room, near the southwest corner of the temple's attic story.

I Supose it would be well to procure bleach muslin & have it in readiness & wait for further order before you make them up — I have no disposition to speak long Br[other] Grant is presant & I should like hear him Speak — 2nd Br[other] J[edediah]. M. Grant then deliverd a brief narative of the Faith & Standing of himself & others in the Seventies since the commencement. After which Permission was given for question[s] to be asked — during which time 20 odd bushels of corn & some wheat was contributed to Br[other]. Grant for his Support — Some thing over $10.00 was made up to relieve Br[other] Grant from the embarrassment of the carpet that he has bought. Elder J[ohn]. D. Lee contributed $5.45 c[en]ts & 6 Chairs — Sat down [?] $5.00 After which meeting closed.

—"General Record of the Seventies, Book B," John D. Lee, principal scribe, photocopy in editors' possession, original in LDS Archives.

Thursday, November 27, 1845
Willard Richards House

[W]ent to W[illard] Richards found the Breth[ren] in council. Present B[righam] Young O[rson] Hide [Hyde] P[arley] P Pratt G[eorge] A Smith, W[illiam W.] Phelps G[eorge] Miller L[evi] Richards J[oseph] Young.

Silus Hate [Silas Haight] and Haskins Tailor come in to our city to Hunt after Bogus [counterfeit] Presses, and to take some of the Brethren, he being Orthorised by the United Stat[e]s.[118] We had prair Elder W[illiam W.] Phelps being mouth[.] we praid fore the prosperity of Zion that our Enimes might be keep Back till we can finished the [Nauvoo] Temple and get all things Ready for going west, and that fear should come on our Enimes. Brock up at About Eight in the Eve[ning]. Great union in our council and the Lord hears His servents his Name shall have all the *Praise*.

—Heber C. Kimball, Diary.

Friday, November 28, 1845
Willard Richards House

[W]ent to W[illard] Richards. met the Brethren in council, as fol-

---

118. In October 1845, an Iowa farmer accused the Twelve Apostles of counter-

lows, President B[righam] Young O[rson] Hide [Hyde] P[arley] P Pratt J[ohn] Tailor [Taylor] G[eorge] A Smith O[rson] Spencer W[illiam] W Phelps Livi [Levi] Richards G[eorge] Miller J[oseph] Young. [Silas] Hate [Haight] and Hakings left the Citty in answer to prair. Thank the Lord our God. J[oseph] Young did not dress as his hand was lame. The Br[ethren] all feel well. the Doctor [Willard Richards] in beed [bed] porly[.] It was moved and secconed that Benjamin L Clapp[119] A[lbert] P Rockwood, and Jeddediah Grant[120] Should form three of the first Pre[s]idents of the first Seventies. It was proposed that Br[other]. [John] Pulsifer[121] should go in to the High Preas Chorum [Quorum]. this was carrid[.] had prair[.] O[rson] Hide was mouth[.] the Lord was with us and His name shall have all the praise[.]

—Heber C. Kimball, Diary.

Council P[arley]. P. Pratt, G[eorge]. A. Smith, G[eorge]. Miller, W[illiam]. W. Phelps W[illard]. Richards H[eber]. C. Kimball[.]

—Willard Richards, Diary.

I [John D. Lee] was called upon to assist fitting up the rooms for the endowment in the house of the Lord — 10 days & I might as well say nights I was engaged in preparing the rooms referred to[.]

—John D. Lee, Diary, LDS Archives.

---

feiting. This led to a search for evidence and finally an indictment of several of the Twelve in December 1845 for counterfeiting American and Mexican money. The defendants denied the allegations and went into hiding to escape arrest.

119. Benjamin L. Clapp (1814-60) fought at the Battle of Crooked River in 1838 and later, from 1845 to 1859, was one of the first Seven Presidents of Seventy. He was excommunicated in Ephraim, Utah, in 1859 over differences with Bishop Warren S. Snow.

120. Jedediah Morgan Grant (1816-56) was a member of Zion's Camp in 1834 and a missionary to the southern states in 1839. He was called to preside over the LDS church in Philadelphia in 1842, as one of the Seven Presidents of Seventy in 1845 and became an apostle in 1854—simultaneously becoming second counselor to Brigham Young in the First Presidency. His wife and daughter both died as the family trekked west to the Salt Lake Valley in 1847. In 1851 he was elected first mayor of Salt Lake City.

121. John Pulsipher (1827-91) was baptized in 1835 and endowed in the Nauvoo temple in January 1846. He migrated west with his father's company, arriving in Salt Lake City in 1848. There he was called with thirty-nine others to form a police force. He also helped construct the Territorial State House in Fillmore, Utah, in 1852 and served a mission to the Indians from 1855 to 1857, learning the Shoshone language in the process. He then moved to southern Utah and was in a bishopric in Hebron.

Saturday, November 29, 1845
Nauvoo Temple

[A]fter dark the following persons went in to the Room of B[rig-ham] Young, which is the south East Cornor, and Bowed our selves before the Lord and gave Him thanks for his goodness to us in sparing our lives to finish this hous thus far, and menny other things. B[righam] Young being mouth Present H[eber] C Kimball. O[rson] Hide P[arley P.] Pratt G[eorge] A Smith O[rson] Spencer L[ucien] Woodworth G[eorge] Miller W[illiam] Phelps L[evi]. Richards A[lbert] P Rockwood. we did not Clothe ourselves, as others wished to be with us the first time in the Lords Hous when we should offer up the sign of the Holy Preasthood.[122]

—Heber C. Kimball, Diary.

Council met in the [Nauvoo] Temple for the first time this evening.

—Willard Richards, Diary.

During the day the Twelve [apostles], Bishops [Newel K.] Whitney and [George] Miller and some others met in the [Nauvoo] Temple and laid the carpet on the main floor of the attic story, and also on several of the small rooms ready for the first quorum to meet in.

—William Clayton, Diary.

I [Brigham Young] met with the Twelve [apostles], Bishops [Newel K.] Whitney and [George] Miller and a few others in the [Nauvoo] Temple and laid the carpet on the main floor of the attic story, and also on several of the small rooms ready for the First Quorum [of the Seventy[123]] to meet in.

—"Manuscript History of Brigham Young," in *History of the Church,* 7:533.

Sunday, November 30, 1845
Nauvoo Temple

[W]ent to the [Nauvoo] Temple at 10 in the Morning. Stopt at

---

122. This marks the quorum's first meeting in the Nauvoo temple. "Brigham Young allowed an unendowed person to see them performing signs of the priesthood," writes Quinn (p. 514), "but not to see them dressed in their endowment robes."

123. This editorial insertion—from B. H. Roberts's edition of the *History of the*

J[oseph]. [C.] Kingsbury[.][124] all well[.] when I got in to the Hous of the *Lord* most of the Brethren Present. No ones admitted only those that had recieved the Preasthood.[125] Those present are as follows, President B[righam] Young, H[eber]. C. Kimball O[rson] Hide [Hyde] P[arley] P Pratt, J[ohn] Tailor [Taylor] G[eorge] A Smith W[illard] Richards A[masa] Limon [Lyman], Others, Bishops [Newel K.] Whitney and [George] Miller, A[lpheus] Cutler R[eynolds] Cahoon, W[illiam W.] Phelps W[illia]m Cla[y]ton John Smith, C[ornelius P.] Lott O[rson] Spencer I[saac] Morly L[ucien] Woodworth J[oseph] Young[.] Evry thing seams to go on in peas [peace.] at about 12 Oclock we clothed our selves [in priesthood robes] for prair and council[.] Levi Richards come in at About Half past on[e] in the after noon. we offered up the Signs of the Holy Presthood. Joseph Kingsbury, B[righam] Young being Mouth offered up the dedacation of the Hall and small rooms. [Removed our robes and] Set [sat] a chort [short] time then H[eber]. C. Kimball was mouth then praid once more Joseph Young was mouth. we then clothed our selvs [in robes]. the Twelve [apostles] war [were] called to gether By the President in his room. P[arley] P Pratt had maters to lay before the Twelve [apostles]. Docter [Willard] Richards and A[masa] Limon quite sick they ware praid for and ware beter[.] We onclothed [unclothed] our selves ~~our selves~~[.] About 4 Oclock most of the Brethren left.

—Heber C. Kimball, Diary.

....

I [John Taylor] met with the brethren of ^the^ Quorum, not only of the Twelve [apostles] but others who had received an endowment during the life-time of Joseph Smith, in the upper room of the [Nauvoo] Temple for the purpose of dedicating it preparatory to receiving or giving the endowments. The large Room for giving the endowments in is 100 one hundred ^ninety^ feet long and eighty ^28^ feet wide—it was well fitted up and carpeted all over. The brethren had sent in their carpets from all part[s] the day before. There were also twelve rooms six on each side for that were well fitted up carpeted and furnished for the purposes of the priesthood[.]

[T]hose rooms were all of a [similar] size & were fourteen feet by

---

Church—should refer, not to the First Quorum of the Seventy, but to the Quorum of the Anointed.

124. Kimball was visiting his plural wife, Sarah Ann Whitney, Joseph Kingsbury's legal wife. (Appreciation to D. Michael Quinn for pointing this out.)

125. Meaning initiation into the Quorum of the Anointed.

fourteen feet five inches. The Room on the south East corner was the one occupied by President Brigham Young—the next room next west Br[other]. Heber C. Kimball & President [Brigham] Young ^together H[eber]. C. Kimball & Willard Richards. Willard Richards is Historian which necessarily throws him into that position^ the first one being intended partly for an office[.]

The third room from the East corner was occupied by Orson Hyde & Parley P. Pratt the fourth by ^John E. Page^ John Taylor & George A. Smith & Amasa Lyman—The fifth room by Joseph Young the President of the whole seventies & his council. The sixth room is for a preparation rooms to wash & annoint preparatory to the annointing. All of these rooms were on the south side of the building.

The first room on the north east corner was appropriated to Bishop ^Newel K.^ Whitney & [George] ^Miller^ [and] his coun[selors] their Council being intended for the bishopric. the second for the President of the Stake, & the High Priesthood & their Quorum. A number of those [officers] were present at the dedication who had heretofore received their endowment. The fifth room was appropriated for the president of the Elders & his Council. the sixth for a preparation Room[.]

The order of the rooms so far as the two east corners is concerned is according to the order of the priesthood in buildings & Temples. It is the order that the first ^or south East^ corner stone ^viz the south east^ that [will] be laid in a Temple should be laid by the president of the ^whole^ Church if present or (see revelation)—

The following persons were present Brigham Young—Isaac Morley —Heber C. Kimball—Alpheus Cutler—Orson Hyde—Reynolds Cahoon—Parley P. Pratt—W[illiam] W Phelps—Willard Richards—W[illia]m Clayton—John Taylor—Cornelius ^P^ Lot—George A. Smith— Orson Spencer—Amasa Lyman—Joseph Young—Newel K. Whitney —Lucian Woodworth—George Miller—Levi Richards—John Smith —Joseph [C.] Kingsbury—

> —John Taylor, "Nov[ember]. 30, 1845 Meeting of the Twelve [apostles] and others. Dedication of Upper Room of [Nauvoo] Temple. Some Journalizing," photocopy in editors' possession, original in LDS Archives.

Eight of the Twelve [apostles], to-wit: Brigham Young, Heber C. Kimball, Orson Hyde, Parley P. Pratt, Willard Richards, John Taylor, Amasa Lyman, John Smith and myself [George A. Smith], the two

Bishops, [Newel K.] Whitney and [George] Miller, Joseph Young and a number of High Priests belonging to the Priests quorum, numbering in all 22, met together in the attic story of the [Nauvoo] Temple and proceeded to dedicate the upper rooms. The dedication prayers were offered by Brigham Young, Heber C. Kimball and Joseph Young, and reported by William Clayton.

—George A. Smith, "History of George Albert Smith."

At 10 A.M. met in the attic story of the [Nauvoo] Temple with President B[righam]. Young, H[eber]. C. Kimball, W[illard]. Richards, P[arley]. P. Pratt, John Taylor, Orson Hyde, George A. Smith, and Amasa Lyman of the Quorum of the Twelve [apostles]. Also N[ewel]. K. Whitney and George Miller presiding Bishops, John Smith Patriarch and President of the Stake. Joseph Young president of the Seventies. Alpheus Cutler, and [Reynolds] Cahoon [Nauvoo] Temple committee. Cornelius P. Lott, Levi Richards, Jos[eph]. C. Kingsbury, Orson Spencer, W[illia]m. W. Phelps, Isaac Morley, L[ucien]. Woodworth. Composed some verses to the tune "Here's a health to all good lasses" before the brethren assembled. At about 12 o'clock we clothed and sung "Come all ye sons of Zion &c." We then offered up the signs of the Holy Priesthood and repeated them to get them more perfect. I [William Clayton] was requested to keep minutes. President [Brigham Young] offered up prayers and dedicated the Attic story, the male room and ourselves to God, and prayed that God would sustain and deliver from the hands of our enemies, his servants untill they have accomplished his will in this house. Elder [John] Taylor then sang "A poor wayfaring man of grief &c."[126] after which we again offered up the signs and Elder [Heber C.] Kimball prayed that the Lord would hear and answer the prayers of his servant Brigham [Young], break off the yoke of our enemies and inasmuch as they lay traps for the feet of his servants, that they may fall into them themselves and be destroyed, that God would bless his servant Joseph Young, heal his wife and bless his family, that God would bless and heal Elder [Heber C.] Kimballs family and put the same blessings on all our families which he had asked for Joseph Young and himself.

Hans C. Hanson[127] the door keeper reported that there were two of-

---

126. Taylor had earlier sung this hymn, originally titled "The Stranger and His Friend," at Carthage Jail just before Joseph and Hyrum Smith were murdered.

127. Hans C. Hanson (1813-90) was the second Danish convert to Mormonism and brother of Peter O. Hanson.

ficers waiting at the foot of the stairs for President [Brigham] Young. The President concluded that he could bear to tarry up in the warm as long as they could stay in the cold waiting for him. Brother Amasa Lyman requested hands to be laid on him that he may be healed. Five of the brethren laid hands on him.

We again offered up the signs and Joseph Young prayed that our enemies may have no power over our leaders. He prayed for our brethren in England, on the Islands, Brothers [Almon W.] Babbit, [Theodore] Turley and [Jackson] Reddins,[128] also that the Trustees may have means to liquidate all the debts.

At 3 o'clock we undressed.

—William Clayton, Diary.

....

At ten a.m. I [Brigham Young] went to the attic story of the [Nauvoo] Temple with Elders Heber. C. Kimball, Willard Richards, Parley P. Pratt, John Taylor, Orson Hyde, George A. Smith, and Amasa Lyman, of the Quorum of the Twelve [apostles]; also Newel K. Whitney and George Miller, Presiding Bishops; John Smith, Patriarch and President of the Stake, Joseph Young, President of the Seventies, Alpheus Cutler, and R[eynolds]. Cahoon, [Nauvoo] Temple Committee, Cornelius P. Lott, Levi Richards, Joseph C. Kingsbury, Orson Spencer, W[illia]m. W. Phelps, Isaac Morley, Lucien Woodworth. At about 12 o'clock, sung "Come All Ye Sons of Zion".

I requested W[illia]m. Clayton to keep minutes. I then offered up prayer and dedicated the attic story of the [Nauvoo] Temple and ourselves to God, and prayed that God would sustain and deliver us his servants from the hands of our enemies, untill we have accomplished his will in this house. Elder [John] Taylor then sang "A Poor Wayfaring Man of Grief", after which Elder Heber C. Kimball prayed, that the Lord would hear and answer the prayers of his servant Brigham [Young], and break off the yoke of our enemies and inasmuch as they lay traps for the feet of his servants that they may fall into them themselves and be destroyed—that God would bless his servant Joseph Young, heal his wife, and bless his family—that God would bless and heal his own [Heber C. Kimball's] fam-

---

128. R. Jackson Redden (a.k.a. Redding, 1817-90) served as a bodyguard to Joseph Smith. He would receive his endowment in the Nauvoo temple in December 1845. One of the original pioneers of Utah, he returned to Winter Quarters with Brigham Young and then repeated the trip to the Salt Lake Valley, this time bringing his family with him. He served as a justice of the peace in both Tooele and Summit Counties.

ily and asked for the same blessings on all our families which he had asked for Joseph Young and himself.

Hans C. Hanson, the door keeper reported that there were two officers waiting at the foot of the stairs for me. I told the brethren that I could bear to tarry here where it was warm as long as they could stay in the cold waiting for me. Brother Amasa Lyman requested hands to be laid on him that he might be healed; five of the brethren laid hands on him.

Joseph Young prayed that our enemies might have no power over our leaders, he prayed for our brethren in England, on the Islands of the Sea; Brothers [Almon] Babbit, [Theodore] Turley and the Reddens—also that the Trustees might have means to liquidate all the debts.

—"Manuscript History of Brigham Young,"
in *History of the Church*, 7:534-35.

Monday, December 1, 1845
Nauvoo Temple/Red Brick Store

[W]ent to The [Nauvoo] Temple, in company with the Twelve [apostles] Except J[ohn] Tailor [Taylor] John Page and Orson Pratt[.] about 4 in the after noon John Tailor come in with his wife [Leonora and] Sister Haywood[129] and hur sister. John M Bernhisel come in come in for the first time. we had praire in Presidents [Brigham] Young['s] Room about five Oclock then closed and went home.

—Heber C. Kimball, Diary.

E[lde]r [Almon W.] Babbit returned and a council was called and assembled in the council room over the store. Pres[iden]t. [Brigham] Young, H[eber]. C. Kimball, P[arley]. Pratt O[rson]. Hyde G[eorge]. A. Smith, N[ewel]. K. Whitney, G[eorge]. Miller A[lpheus]. Cutler, R[eynolds]. Cahoon, I[saac]. Morley and A[lbert]. P. Rockwood & E[lde]r Babbit present.

—William Clayton, Diary.

I [Brigham Young] met with several of the Twelve [apostles], the [Nauvoo] Temple Committee, and Trustees in the council chamber over the store.

—"Manuscript History of Brigham Young,"
in *History of the Church*, 7:537.

---

129. Probably Sarepta Maria Blodgett Heywood (1822-?), wife of Joseph L. Heywood.

Tuesday, December 2, 1845
Nauvoo Temple

We clothed our selvs just at dark. present in prair of the Twelve [apostles] B[righam] Young H[eber] C Kimball O[rson] Hide P[arley P.] Pratt G[eorge] A Smith, High Preas. John Smith ^P[arley] P Pratt was mouth^ George Miller Isa[a]c Morly. W[illiam W.] Phelps. after which Brothers A[lbert] P Rockwood, Bengamin L Clapp and J[edediah] Grant come in and we five fore mentioned ordained them to be three of the First Presidency of the Seventies. the three oldest of the Twelve [apostles] being mouth[.] then we come to a close soon after dark[.]

—Heber C. Kimball, Diary.

In the evening Albert P. Rockwood, Benjamin L. Clapp and J[edediah]. M. Grant were ordained to preside over the first quorum of Seventies filling vacancies caused by the death of Daniel S. Mills [Miles];[130] apostasy of Josiah Butterfield,[131] and the neglect of Roger Orton,[132] under the hands of Brigham Young, Heber C. Kimball, Orson Hyde, Parley P. Pratt and myself [George A. Smith]. Spent an hour in prayer.

—George A. Smith, "History of George Albert Smith."

Evening, Elders Heber C. Kimball, Orson Hyde, Parley P. Pratt, George A. Smith and I [Brigham Young] ordained Albert P. Rockwood, Benjamin L. Clapp and Jedediah M. Grant Presidents over the First Quorum of Seventies, filling vacancies which had been occasioned by the death of Daniel S. Miles, the apostasy of Josiah Butterfield, and the neglect of Roger Orton.

Spent an hour in prayer.

—"Manuscript History of Brigham Young," in *History of the Church,* 7:538.

130. Daniel Sanborn Miles (1772-1845) was one of the first Seven Presidents of the Seventy from 1837 to 1845, and one of the earliest settlers in Commerce (later Nauvoo), Illinois. He died before the Saints left Illinois.

131. Josiah Butterfield (1795-1871) was one of the Seven Presidents of Seventy from 1837 to 1844 and a missionary to Maine (1844). He had earlier been jailed in Mansfield, Ohio, for his connection to the Kirtland Safety Society, and was excommunicated in April 1844 for "neglect of duty."

132. Roger Orton (1799-1851) marched in Zion's Camp in 1834, then accompanied Joseph Smith to Michigan in October that same year. He served on the Kirtland Stake High Council in 1835; in 1845 he became one of the Seven Presidents of the Seventy.

Wednesday, December 3, 1845
Nauvoo Temple

Those of the Twelve [apostles] present this Eve[ning]. B[righam] Young H[eber]. C Kimball O[rson] Hide [Hyde] P[arley P.] Pratt G[eorge] A Smith John Tailor [Taylor] George Miller. R[eynolds] Cahoon A[lpheus] Cutler W[illia]m Cla[y]ton Isack Morly, [and] J[edediah] M Grant[, who] spent a chort [short] time, he has not Recieved his washings[.] Some part of petitions finished. the News come to us that W[illia]m Smith and George Adams was giving thare Affidavits against the Twelve [apostles]. as being Treaseners [treasonous] &c Br[other Hans] Criestion [Christian] Hanson a Dane is our Dore Keeper and fire Maker. His Brother is Translating the Book of Mormon. his [the door keeper's] Name is Hanes Christian Hanson. the other [is Hans] Peter Olsen Hanson two Brothers. they both from Denmark B[righam] Young. H[eber] C K[imball]. O[rson] Hide P[arley P.] Pratt G[eorge] A Smith John Tailor. met in the 2 Room. Clothed and praid[,] Elder O[rson] Hide being Mouth[.] Asked the Lord to bless his people and to open our way to go west. and to over come our enemies and let them fall in to the snar[e]s they lay for his servents[.]

—Heber C. Kimball, Diary.

Thursday, December 4, 1845
Nauvoo Temple

Present this Ev[e]ning B[righam] Young, H[eber] C. Kimball O[rson] Hide [Hyde] P[arley P.] Pratt G[eorge] A Smith John Tailor [Taylor] A[masa] Limon [Lyman.]

High Preas Present John Smith Isack Morly. Georg Miller R[eynolds] Cahoon Bishop [Newel K.] Whitney O[rson] Spencer L[ucien] Woodworth Joseph [C.] Kingsbury one of the Seventies, Present J[oseph] Young. Two nits [nights] that are past the Twelve [apostles] have praid by them selves, and the High Preas by them selvs. This order will continue fore the present[.] Hanes Cristien Hanson. is our fire man and dore keeper. his Brother['s] name [is] Hanes Peter Hanson. he is trans[la]ting the Book of Mormon two thirds through, they [are] Natives of Denmark. W[illia]m Cla[y]ton High Preast Levi Richards.

Prosperity seames to be prevlent in our City the Lord be praised for his goodness in preserving his people from time to time. we Clothed our selvs half past 7. The Twelve [apostles] and High Preas come to gether and

sung two hymns. being 19 present. Br[other] B[righam] Young praid —
we all knelt before the Lord then offered up the sign[s] Isack Morly was
mouth. had a good time. ... praid again. P[arley] P Pratt being mouth. we
had a glorious time. The Brethren felt to prais the Lord for His goodness
and great mercy, that we had got a place to worship and begin to give
Endewments[.]

The meeting Closed at Eight.

—Heber C. Kimball, Diary.

....

Evening met with the first quorum in the Attic story of the [Nauvoo]
Temple for prayer.

—William Clayton, Diary.

....

Evening, the council met for prayer in the [Nauvoo] Temple.

—"Manuscript History of Brigham Young,"
in *History of the Church*, 7:538.

Friday, December 5, 1845
Nauvoo Temple

Present of the Twelve [apostles], B[righam] Young H[eber]. C Kimball
O[rson] Hide P[arley] P Pratt G[eorge] A Smith J[ohn]. Tailor, High Preas
John Smith I[saac] Morly W[illiam W.] Phelps O[rson] Spencer Joseph
Kingsbury, Joseph Fielding L[ucien] Woodworth R[eynolds] Cahoon
George Miller. Clo[t]hed and praid. O[rson] Spencer being mouth then
Clothed and went home about 7[.] when we left the room we asked the
Lord to bless Isreal and hold us in safty till we could give some of his
faithfull Elders thare Endowment, and to liberate Cherriff [Sherrif] [Jacob]
Backenstos [being tried for the murder of Frank Worrell,[133] one of the
anti-Mormon vigilantes, and]. Theradore Turl[e]y from thare bonds[.][134]

—Heber C. Kimball, Diary.

....

[O]n the 6 5[th of December 1845] I [Joseph Fielding] entered it [the

---

133. Frank Worrell (?-1845) supervised the guards at Carthage Jail and evidently
allowed the mob to murder Joseph and Hyrum Smith. Worrell was himself shot and
killed by Orrin Porter Rockwell in 1845 as the latter defended the county sherrif,
Jacob Backenstos, who was being pursued by Worrell.

134. Theodore Turley had been arrested in Alton, Illinois, on charges of counterfeiting and was jailed in Quincy. He was released on a $250 bail in mid-December.

Nauvoo temple] for the first [time] and I truly felt as though I had gotten out of the World[.]

—Joseph Fielding, Diary, LDS Archives.

Saturday, December 6, 1845
Nauvoo Temple

Of the Twelve [apostles] Present President B[righam] Young, H[eber] C. Kimball O[rson] Hide G[eorge] A Smith, A[masa]. Limon [Lyman] J[ohn] Tailor [Taylor.]

High Preas A[lpheus] Cutler, R[eynolds] Cahoon I[saac] Morly John Smith. W[illiam]. W. Phelps N[ewel] K Whitney G[eorge] Miller W[illia]m Cla[y]ton L[ucien] Woodworth Joseph [C.] Kingsbury O[rson] Spencer[.] we clothed. and praid. all to gether. Twelve [apostles] and High Preas. W[illiam] W. Phelps being Mouth. the Lord was with us[.]

—Heber C. Kimball, Diary.

5 P.M. met the brethren in the [Nauvoo] Temple for prayers.

—William Clayton, Diary.

Sunday, December 7, 1845
Nauvoo Temple

[R]eturned to the [Nauvoo] Temple whare I [Heber C. Kimball] found my wife [Vilate].[135] Bishop [Newel K.] Whitney and wife went in with me[.] I arived at 10 found 6 or Eight present. O[rson] Spencer come in my room and read my procclamation to me and my wife.[136]

Present	B[righam] Young.	Mary Ann
	Heber C. Kimball.	Vilate Kimball
	Orson. Hide [Hyde].	Marinda Hide
	P[arley] P Pratt	Mary Ann Pratt
	John Tailor. [Taylor]	Leonora Tailor

135. This, writes Quinn (*Origins,* 515), is the "first Sunday prayer circle in the temple in which women participated, and the first time in months that Brigham Young allowed women to join in a prayer circle."

136. Probably the *Proclamation of the Twelve Apostles of the Church of Jesus Christ of Latter-day Saints To All the Kings of the World,* published in October in Liverpool, England.

G[eorge] A Smith.   Barshebe [Bathsheba] Smith
Willard Richards
High Preas present
John Smith   Clarrisa
A[lpheus] Cutler   Lois
R[eynolds] Cahoon   Thirza
N[ewel]. K. Whitney,   Elizebeth Ann
Cornelius [P.] Lott,   Permila
I[saac] Morl[e]y   Lucy
O[rson] Spencer   Catherine
W[illia]m Cla[y]ton   Agness Smith
George Miller   Mary Cathrine
Joseph Young,   Sister [Mercy] T[h]om[p]son
Levi Richards,   Mary Smith
Joseph Fielding
W[illiam] W Phelps,   Sally
Joseph Kingburay,
L[ucien] Woodworth,   Phebe
John Bernhisel

The following [above] Persons are members of the Holy Order of the
Holy Preasthood having Recieved it in the Life time of Joseph and
Hirum [Smith], the Prophets. Elder B[righam] Young. went and gave the
Brethren and Sisters present a view of the Seprate rooms. and the object
of them. then pute up the Veil and choe [showed] the Order of it. The
Brethren and sisters clothed half past one commenced our meeting at two
Oclock. Meeting by prair by Joseph Fielding, sung humn and Elder John
Tailor spoke a chort [short] time then H[eber]. C. Kimball spoke[.] Elder
B[righam] was sick and had to retire to his room and Lay down on his
couch, then Elder O[rson] Hide gave a chort [short] Exertation after he
closed, him [hymn] sung. then H[eber] C K[imball] N[ewel] K. [Whit-
ney] brock Bread. blessed by H[eber] C K[imball.] Elder B[righam]
Young come in [and] pertock [and it was] carrid round by N[ewel] K
[Whitney.] Wine. blest by Joseph Young. Carrid round by N[ewel] K.
[Whitney] singing while the wine going round then El[der] P[arley] P
Pratt rose and spoke on a simeler object before the pople[.] W[illiam] W
Phe[l]ps spoke[.] It was 3 Oclock when we partoock of sacrement[.] great
Solemnity rested on the Breth[ren] and sisters, great union in our meet-
ing. Seven present have not had thare Last Anointing. L[ucien] Wood-

worth and wife Sister [Mercy R.] T[h]om[p]son W[illia]m Cla[y]ton Joseph Kingsbury. John Benhisel. Sister Marinda Hide Agness Smith the wife of Don [Carlos] Smith.[137] John Smith our Patriarch spoke a chort [short] time then Elder B[righam] Young. said this quorum should meet heare Evry Sabath. and take of the Sacrament. the Br[ethren] and Sisters ware completly clothed [in priesthood robes]. Elder B[righam] Young gave us good council we offerd up the Signs Little after fore got through at five. G[eorge] A Smith mouth. When he got through all went home. in good spirrits.

—Heber C. Kimball, Diary.

....

In the [Nauvoo] Temple all day. All the first quorum with one or two exceptions were present both male and female. About 1 o'clock we clothed. Dressed in ceremonial robes and aprons. The meeting was opened by prayer by Joseph Fielding. After which Elders [John] Taylor, [Orson] Hyde, [William W.] Phelps, [Parley P.] Pratt and John Smith each expressed their feelings in regard to our present privilege of meeting in the Temple in spite of the combined opposition of men and devils. During the speaking, the Bishops having provided Bread and Wine, the bread was broke by Brother [Heber C.] Kimball and then blessed by him and handed round by Bishop [Newel K.] Whitney. Joseph Young then blessed the wine which was also passed around by Brother Whitney. President [Brigham] Young then addressed the company. He said the time would come when the Celestial law would be put in force and that law forbids any man taking the name of God in vain. But we have men in our midst who do not scruple to say by God, by Jesus Christ, God damn you &c. and the time will come when the law will be put in force on all such. He gave much good instruction and the spirit of God rested upon him. He stated "that a few of the quorum had met twice a week ever since Joseph and Hyrum [Smith] were killed and during the last excitement, every day and in the hottest part of it twice a day to offer up the signs and pray to our heavenly father to deliver his people and this is the cord which has bound

137. Of this list of those who had not yet received the second anointing, Quinn (*Origins,* 515-16) notes, "Orson and Catharine Spencer, Joseph Fielding, and Levi Richards (who were present) must therefore have received it at some previous but unrecorded date. The list also suggests that Orson Hyde (who received his second anointing during [Joseph] Smith's lifetime) did so with another woman (possibly deceased) rather than his first and legal wife Marinda, who was Joseph Smith's plural wife" (source citations omitted).

this people together. If this quorum and those who shall be admitted into it will be as diligent in prayer as a few has been I promise you in the name of Israels God that we shall accomplish the will of God and go out in due time from the gentiles with power and plenty and no power shall stay us." After the exhortation we offered up the signs and had prayers for the usual subject. Joseph Young being mouth. We were then dismissed until next Sunday at 11 o'clock.

—William Clayton, Diary.

....

[T]oday the *Holy order* [Quorum of the Anointed] partook of the sacrament for the first time in the *House of the Lord* in Nauvoo [Illinois].

—Franklin D. Richards, Diary, LDS Archives.

....

I [Brigham Young] met with the Twelve [apostles] and others in the [Nauvoo] Temple. We partook of the sacrament, exhorted each other and prayed.

—"Manuscript History of Brigham Young,"
in *History of the Church*, 7:538.

Monday, December 8, 1845
Nauvoo Temple

The Br[ethren] are now begining to come in fore prair and council. Present. Pr[esident] B[righam] Young, H[eber] C Kimball, O[rson] Hide [Hyde] P[arley] P P[ratt], G[eorge] A Smith John Tailor [Taylor], Cornelius Lott, L[ucien] Woodworth W[illiam] W Phelps, Orson Spencer W[illia]m Cla[y]ton Joseph Kingsbury R[eynolds] Cahoon Levi Richards George Miller[.] our meting small this Ev[e]ning[.] It is now 25 to 7. all the Brethren clothed, 15 present. conv[e]rsing about fammins in England and other parts. Georg[e] Miller was mouth. Got through at 7 Oclock, then desmised and went home.

—Heber C. Kimball, Diary.

....

At 5 went to the [Nauvoo] Temple and met the brethren for prayer, Geo[rge]. Miller being mouth.

—William Clayton, Diary.

Tuesday, December 9, 1845
Nauvoo Temple

Present this Eve[ning] of the Twelve [apostles] B[righam] Young.

H[eber] C Kimball, O[rson] Hide [Hyde] P[arley P.] Pratt. John Tailor [Taylor] A[masa] Limon [Lyman] G[eorge] A Smith. High Preas A[lpheus] Cutler L[ucien] Woodworth G[eorge] Miller W[illiam] Phelps J[ohn] Berhisal O[rson] Spencer R[eynolds] Cahoon I[saac] Morl[e]y. we offerd up the sign[s,] John Tailor [Taylor] being mouth. after we began to [w]rite to thos[e] [Catholic] Preas our proposels to sell our city[.] Elder B[righam] Young and H[eber] C. Kimball. washed our selvs in pure water. fore [four] time[s] and also G[eorge] A Smith Am[asa] Limon. and the first washed in the Temple of the Lord and also finished a Leter to the Catholicks. giving our propsels. to sell we had a good time before the Lord. We shall come to Morrow with our wives[.] that is all the Holy order to go through with our washings and Anointing again in the Temple of our God[.]

—Heber C. Kimball, Diary.

Evening, we wrote out propositions for the sale of our lands for the benefit of the Catholic deputation.

—"Manuscript History of Brigham Young," in *History of the Church,* 7:539.

Wednesday, December 10, 1845
Nauvoo Temple

This morning I [Brigham Young] came to the [Nauvoo] Temple, the weather was plesant but cold engaged in fixing the curtains at the East window. assisted by bro[ther]. [Heber C.] Kimball and wife [Vilate] & bro[ther]'s. [Parley P.] Pratt & [Newel K.] Whitney[.] ... In the afternoon I put up the vail and completed the celestial room, and in company with bro[ther]. H[eber]. C. K[imball]. washed and anointed bro[ther]. [Willard] Richards and 2 PM. to 8 ocl[oc]k P.M. found all things ready and 9½ O[clock] we entered the celestial room for prayer.

—Brigham Young, Diary.

Pres[iden]t. [Brigham] Young, labored constantly to complete the arrangements of the rooms, preparatory to the endowments—the brethren commenced their washings and anointings about 5 P.M.

—Willard Richards, Diary.

W[illiam]. W. Phelps has been appointed door keeper this day in place of E[lde]r George A. Smith who is engaged with matters of more importance[.]

At one Oclock Lucy [Mack] Smith the Mother of the Prophet. And Agness the wife of Don C[arlos] Smith. Elizebeth Ann Whitney took dinner with me [Heber C. Kimball][138] and wife being the first time that the Old Lady went in to the Attick[.] Mother [Lucy Mack] Smith ses that she Eat verry harty. Sister Marry [Fielding] the widow of Hirum [Smith] the Patriarch also Sister Mercy R[achel] T[h]om[p]son [Smith]. His[139] — Robert T[h]om[p]so[n's] widow, took dinner with us[.]

At half past 3 o clock President Brigham Young, H[eber]. C. Kimball, John Taylor, P[arley]. P. Pratt, George Miller, Alpheus Cutler, W[illia]m Clayton, John M. Bernhisel and Lucian Woodworth retired to the Bishops room and consecrated 16 bottles of Oil which had been perfumed by Bishop Whitney for the purpose of anointing. ...

At 3 o clock Sister Mary Ann Young and Vilate Kimball, Elizabeth Ann Whitney, commenced washing and anointing each other being the first in this holy Temple of the Lord. This was done in the preparation room in the North West corner of the Attic story. About the same time President Young put up the vail in its place which things finish and complete the Celestial Room preparatory to the endowment. The following are the names of those present. viz.

> Pres[iden]t. Brigham Young & Mary Ann
> Heber C. Kimball & Vilate
> Orson Hyde & Nancy Marinda
> Parley P. Pratt & Mary Ann Pratt
> John Taylor & Leonora A Taylor
> George A. Smith & Bathsheba Smith
> Willard Richards -----
> Amasa Lyman & Marian Loisa Lyman
> John E. Page & Mary Page
> > High Priests.
> John Smith & Clarissa Smith
> ^Mother Lucy Smith^
> Newel K. Whitney & Elizabeth Ann
> George Miller & Mary Catherine

138. This paragraph is in the handwriting of Heber C. Kimball.

139. Kimball was apparently going to write "His [i.e., Hyrum Smith's] widow," but decided instead to identify her as the widow of Robert B. Thompson.

W[illiam]. W. Phelps & Sally Phelps
John M. Bernhisel -----
Levi Richards -----
Alpheas Cutler & Lois Cutler
Reynolds Cahoon & Thirza Cahoon
William Clayton -----
Lucian Woodworth & Phebe Woodworth
Orson Spencer & Catherine C
Agnes M. Smith
Mercy R[achel]. Thompson
Mary Smith

At 25 minutes past 4 o clock President Young and Heber C. Kimball commenced washing E[lde]r Willard Richards.

[A]bout 5 o clock Isaac Morley and his wife Lucy Morley came in. And about half past 5, Joseph Fielding and Joseph C. Kingsbury, C[ornelius]. P. Lott[.] We continued washing and anointing those present till about 7½ o clock.

At 20 minutes to 8 o clock president Young announced that all things were now ready to commence and go through with the ordinances. He said that after we get properly organized and ready to go on without confusion, no person will be permitted to talk, nor walk about in the main rooms, neither would any person be expected to be in the Celestial room only those who were necessary to carry on the work. At the same hour he took the chair and appointed P[arley]. P. Pratt and John Taylor ^W[illiam]. W. Phelps acted as serpent^140 to assist him, in taking those through who were now prepared. Those who were first taken through all the ceremonies were Heber C. Kimball and Vilate Kimball George A. Smith and Bathsheba W Smith, Orson Hyde and Nancy Marinda Hyde, John Smith and Clarissa Smith. Newel K. Whitney and Elizabeth Ann Whitney. These went through all the ordinances untill they were passed through the vail at which time it was half past nine o clock. Pres[iden]t. Young then called all present into the Celestial room where we kneeled down and Amasa Lyman offered up prayers.

Some of the brethren & sisters then retired home and the rest continued washing and anointing and taking through the whole ordinance until half past 3 o clock in the morning. The names of those who then went

---

140. In the Nauvoo temple endowment drama, people portrayed characters from the biblical story of the Garden of Eden, including the serpent or tempter.

through are President Brigham Young & Mary Ann Young William W. Phelps & Sally Phelps Parly P. Pratt & Mary Ann Pratt Amasa Lyman & Mariah Loisa Lyman George Miller & Mary Catherine Miller, John Taylor & Leonora A Taylor Lucian Woodworth & Phebe Woodworth John E. Page & Mary Page Joseph C. Kingsbury[,] Mary Smith, widow of Hyrum[, and] Agness Smith, widow of Don Carloss.

Those that assisted were Newel K Whitney, George A. Smith, Orson Hyde, Heber C. Kimball and C[ornelius]. P. Lott and Elizabeth Ann Whitney.

After all was lead through those present offered up the signs of the Holy Priesthood and offered up prayers Elder Orson Hyde gave praise to the Most High for his goodness. H[eber]. C. Kimball presides as Eloheem, Orson Hyde as Jehovah and George A Smith as Michael[141] and N[ewel]. K. Whitney as the serpent[.]

—William Clayton, Diary, kept for Heber C. Kimball.

This day commenced the giving of endowments in the House of the Lord.

—Thomas Bullock, Diary, in *Thomas Bullock Nauvoo Journal,* edited by Greg R. Knight (Orem, Utah: Grandin Book, 1994).

A.M. at the office quite unwell. At 9 o clock president [Brigham] Young came and said he wanted me [William Clayton] up to the [Nauvoo] Temple and would not take no for an answer. I accordingly quit work and went up into the Attic story where several of the brethren had already assembled. The Pres[iden]t. appointed George A. Smith door keeper, and gave him the key. E[lde]r [Heber C.] Kimball requested me to write his private journal today. ... President Young remarked [to Catholic priests Hamilton and Tucker] that we wished to realise from the sale of our property sufficient to take all our poor with us in a comfortable manner.[142] [...?] President Young said he would like to add a note to our pro-

141. In the Nauvoo temple endowment drama, Eloheim, Jehovah, and Michael helped to create the earth. Mormons today understand these figures to be God the Father, his son Jesus Christ, and Adam.

142. Father Hilary Tucker, of Quincy, Illinois, and Father George Hamilton, of Springfield, Illinois, had been sent to Nauvoo by Chicago bishop William Quarter (1806-48) regarding the possible purchase of property in Nauvoo. This interest was apparently generated by Almon W. Babbitt, who went to St. Louis, Missouri, on a mission to try to sell church property. The Catholic bishop in St. Louis received the

posals before it goes for publication to this effect, that if they agree to our propositions we will lease them the Temple for a period of from five to thirty five years at a reasonable price, the rent to be paid in finishing the unfinished parts of the Temple, the wall around the Temple Block, and the Block West of the Temple, and keeping the Temple in repair.

The council agreed to the amendment which was accordingly added to the proposals and handed to Mr Tucker. [...?]

W[illiam]. W. Phelps has been appointed door keeper this day in place of E[lde]r George A Smith who is engaged with matters of more importance.

At half past 3 I went in to the Bishops Room with President B[righam]. Young, H[eber]. C. Kimball, John Taylor, P[arley]. P. Pratt, George Miller, Alpheus Cutler, John M. Bernhisel & Lucian Woodworth where we consecrated 16 bottles of oil for the anointing.

At 3 3/4 E[lde]r [Orson] Hyde came into E[lde]r Kimballs room and said the news had arrived that [Jacob B.] Backenstos was acquited.

At 3 o clock Sisters Mary Ann Young, Vilate Kimball and Elizabeth Ann Whitney commenced washing and anointing each other being the first in this Temple.

This was done in the preparation room in the North West corner of the Attic story. About the same time president Young put up the vail in its place which finishes and completes the Celestial room preparatory to the endowment.

Last evening President B[righam]. Young and H[eber]. C. Kimball washed themselves in pure water four times. Also George A. Smith, and Amasa Lyman being the first ones washed in this the Holy Temple of the Lord.

The following is a list of those present this afternoon. Pres[iden]t. B[righam]. Young & Mary Ann Young, Heber C. Kimball & Vilate Kimball, Orson Hyde & Nancy Marinda Hyde, Parley P. Pratt & Mary Ann Pratt, John Taylor & Leonora A. Taylor, George A. Smith & Bathsheba Smith, Willard Richards, Amasa Lyman & Mariah Loisa Lyman John E. Page and Mary Page. High Priests John Smith & Clarissa Smith, Mother Lucy [Mack] Smith, Newel K. Whitney & Elizabeth Ann Whitney, George Miller & Mary Catherine Miller, W[illiam]. W. Phelps & Sally

---

support of Quarter, who then dispatched Tucker and Hamilton. However, on January 7, 1846, Tucker notified the Saints that his church could not raise the money to purchase the property. See *History of the Church,* 7:565.

Phelps, John M. Bernhisel, Levi Richards, Alpheus Cutler & Lois Cutler, Reynolds Cahoon & Thirza Cahoon, William Clayton, Lucian Woodworth & Phebe Woodworth, Orson Spencer & Catherine C. Spencer, Agness M. Smith, Mercy R. Thompson, Mary Smith, [and] Isaac Morley & Lucy Morley[, who] came in about 5 o clock and in half an hour after Joseph Fielding, Joseph C. Kingsbury and C[ornelius]. P. Lott. At 25 minutes past 4 o clock president Young and E[lde]r H[eber]. C. Kimball commenced washing E[lde]r Willard Richards. They continued washing and anointing those present till about half past seven. At 20 minutes to 8 o clock president Young announced that all things were now ready to commence and go through with the ordinances. He said that after we get properly organized and ready to go on without confusion no person will be permitted [to] talk nor move about in the main rooms, neither will any person be expected to remain in the Celestial Room only those who were necessary to carry on the works. At the same hour he took the chair and apointed Parley P. Pratt & John Taylor to assist him in taking those through who were now prepared. Those who were first taken through all the ceremonies were Heber C. Kimball & Vilate Kimball, George A. Smith & Bathsheba W. Smith, Orson Hyde & Nancy Marinda Hyde, John Smith & Clarissa Smith, Newel K. Whitney & Elizabeth Ann Whitney. These went through all the ordinance work untill they were passed through the vail at which time it was half past nine o clock. President Young then called all present into the Celestial room where we kneeled down and Amasa Lyman offered up prayers. At this time I went home being very unwell and tired having been writing and keeping minutes all the day.

—William Clayton, Diary.

The Twelve [apostles] commenced the washing and anointing in the temple of the Lord.

—"Life of Norton Jacob," typescript, L. Tom Perry Special Collections, Harold B. Lee Library, Brigham Young University, Provo, Utah.

The work of the endowment begins today[.] a cold morning and some snow on the ground.
—Franklin D. Richards, Diary, LDS Archives.

Three p.m., Sisters Mary Ann Young, Vilate Kimball and Elizabeth Ann Whitney commenced administering the ordinances in the Temple.

203

We consecrated oil. ...

The main room of the attic story is eighty-eight feet two inches long and twenty-eight feet eight inches wide. It is arched over, and the arch is divided into six spaces by cross beams to support the roof. There are six small rooms on each side about fourteen feet square. The last one on the east end on each side is a little smaller.

The first room on the south side beginning on the east is occupied by myself [Brigham Young], the second by Elder [Heber C.] Kimball, the third by Elders Orson Hyde, Parley P. Pratt and Orson Pratt; the fourth by John Taylor, George A. Smith, Amasa Lyman and John E. Page; the fifth by Joseph Young and the Presidents of the Seventies; the sixth, a preparation room.

On the north side, the first east room is for Bishop [Newel K.] Whitney and the lesser priesthood, the second is for the high council, the third and fourth for President George Miller and the high priests' quorum, the fifth the elders' room, and the sixth the female preparation room.

Four-twenty-five p.m., Elder Heber C. Kimball and I [Brigham Young] commenced administering the ordinances of endowment.

Five o'clock, Isaac Morley and his wife Lucy, Joseph Fielding, Joseph C. Kingsbury and Cornelius P. Lott came in.

Nine-thirty p.m., we assembled for prayers. Amasa Lyman was mouth.

We continued officiating in the Temple during the night until three-thirty a.m. of the 11th.

The following administered to:
> Willard Richards;
> Heber C. Kimball and his wife, Vilate;
> George A. Smith and Bathsheba W.;
> John Smith and Clarissa;
> Newel K. Whitney and Elizabeth Ann;
> Brigham Young and Mary Ann;
> William W. Phelps and Sally;
> Parley P. Pratt and Mary Ann;
> Amasa Lyman and Mariah Louisa;
> George Miller and Mary Catharine;
> John Taylor and Leonora;
> Lucien Woodworth and Phebe;
> John E. Page and Mary;
> Joseph C. Kingsbury;

Mary Smith, widow of Hyrum [Smith];

Agnes Smith, widow of Don Carlos [Smith].

—"Manuscript History of Brigham Young,"
in *History of the Church,* 7:541–42.

Nauvoo temple endowments performed on this date for:

First Company: Heber C. Kimball, Vilate Kimball, George A. Smith, Bathsheba W. Smith, Orson Hyde, Marinda Nancy Hyde, John Smith, Clarissa Smith, Newel K. Whitney, and Elizabeth Ann Whitney.

Second Company: Brigham Young, Mary Ann Young, William W. Phelps, Sally Phelps, Parley P. Pratt, Mary Ann Pratt, Amasa Lyman, Maria L. Lyman, George Miller, Mary C. Miller, John Taylor, Leonora Taylor, Lucien Woodworth, Phoebe Woodworth, John E. Page, Mary Page, Joseph C. Kingsbury, Mary Smith, and Agnes Coolbrith Smith.

—Summary of information compiled by the Temple Index
Bureau, *Nauvoo Temple Endowment Register: 10 December
1845 to 8 February 1846.*

Thursday, December 11, 1845

Nauvoo Temple

This morning I [Brigham Young] came early to the [Nauvoo] Temple[,] went and took breakfast with bro[ther] Joseph Kingsbury[,] returned to the Temple [and] found several of the brethren there, ... spent some time acting as Eathloheim [Eloheim] [after] having ~~joined~~ been occupied with bro[ther] H[eber]. C. K[imball] until 3. O[clock]. PM. in anointing[.] [T]he brethren in the [Holy Order] met in council[143] and [I]

---

143. "This," writes Quinn (*Origins,* 516–17), "was the last meeting of the Anointed Quorum as Joseph Smith originally established it—a hand-picked group of men and women who comprised 1 percent of faithful adults at church headquarters." The next day, Quinn continues (*Origins,* 517), "at 10:15 a.m., the general membership of the LDS church began receiving the anointing and endowment ordinances in the Nauvoo temple, and the apostles continued the initiations until midnight. Every Sunday morning until he closed the Nauvoo temple in February 1846, Brigham Young conducted a prayer circle meeting to which all endowed persons were invited. Continuing the previous terminology, he told these newly endowed people that they were also members of the 'First Quorum' established by the martyred prophet. However, when the newly endowed numbered in the hundreds, it was no longer possible for every interested person to participate in the prayer circle. Within weeks thousands had been endowed, and the temple was too small to

laid before the brethren S[amuel]. Brannons letter[144] & other matters[.] staid in the Temple this night[.]

—Brigham Young, Diary.

I [William Clayton] will now give a description of the way the attic Story is finished. The main room is 88 feet 2 inches long and 28 feet 8 inches wide It is arched over, and the arch is divided into six spaces by cross beams to support the roof[.] There are 6 small rooms on each side the main room about 14 feet square each. The last one on the West end on each side is a little smaller. The first room on the South side beginning on the East end is President Brigham [Young']s Room the second E[lde]r H[eber]. C. Kimball, the third ~~George A Smith and others of the Twelve~~ ^P[arley]. P. Pratt and Orson Pratt^ the fourth John Taylor, ~~and others of the Twelve~~, ^Amasa Lyman, J[ohn]. E. Page & G[eorge] A. Smith^ the fifth Joseph Young and presidents of Seventies. The sixth is a preparation room for the male Members.

On the North side, the first from the East end is for Bishop Whitney & the lesser Priesthood; the second for the High Council. The third and fourth president George Miller and the High Priests quorum[,] The fifth the Elders Quorum and the sixth the female preparation Room.

The main room is divided into apartments for the ceremonies of the endowment. Beginning from the door at the West end is an alley about 5 feet wide extending to about 3 feet beyond the first Beam of the arch[.] on each side of the Alley is a small room partitioned of where they saints receive the first part of the ceremony or where the man is created and a help mate given to him. From these rooms too the third partition in the Arch is planted the garden, which is nicely decorated and set off with shrubs and trees in pots & Boxes to represent the Garden of Eden. In this apartment is also an alt[a]r. Here the man and woman are placed & commandments given to them in addition to what is given in the creation. Here also after the man & woman have eaten the forbidden fruit is given to them a charge at the Alter and the first and second tokens of the Aaronic Priesthood, They are then thrust out into a room which is dark being the one on the North side between the fourth and fifth division of the arch which represents the telestial kingdom or the world. Opposite to

accommodate a meeting of everyone who had joined the 'First Quorum.' After the Mormons left Nauvoo, the term became a nostalgic memory, especially for those initiated during Joseph Smith's administration."

144. See the entry of William Clayton below, under date.

this is another apartment of the same size representing the terrestrial kingdom and between these two is an alley about 4 feet wide. In the telestial kingdom, after the man has proved himself faithful he receives the first signs & tokens of the Melchizedek priesthood and an additional charge. Here also he vouches for the conduct of his companion. They are then left to prove themselves faithful, after which they are admitted into the terrestrial kingdom, where at the alter they receive an additional charge and the second token of the Melchizedek Priesthood and also the key word on the five points of fellowship.

There are words given with every token and the new name is given in the preparation room when they receive their washing and annointing.

After [they have] received all the tokens and words and signs they are led to the vail where they give each to Eloheem through the vail and are then admitted into the Celestial Room.

The Celestial room occupies the remainder of the main room being the space between two divisions of the Arch. This is adorned with a number of splendid mirrors, paintings and portraits. On the East wall are the following Portraits viz. in the centre Pres[ident]. B[righam]. Young and next to the left H[eber]. C. Kimball, Orson Hyde. To the right, Willard Richards John Taylor and George A. Smith.

On the East side of the first division of the Arch in the centre is the portrait of L[ucius]. N. Scovil,[145] next to the right is George A. Smith, next John Smith the Patriarch To the left is Barsheba [Bathsheba] Smith, and Mother Lucy [Mack] Smith.

On the West side of this partition in the centre is the portrait of[,] to the left[,] H[eber]. C. Kimball & Caroline Smith[146] To the right W[illia]m Cottier[147] John L. Smith.

---

145. According to art historian Jill Major, "Because of the scant time the first Nauvoo Temple was open for sacred ordinances, portraits of prominent Nauvoo citizens were borrowed to adorn the temple walls." Scoville's portrait may have been hung because of its availability, and also to recognize his work on the building committee that oversaw construction of the Nauvoo Masonic Lodge, and in preparing Joseph Smith's Red Brick Store for the introduction of the endowment. See Jill C. Major, "Artworks in the Celestial Room of the First Nauvoo Temple," *BYU Studies* 41 (2002), 2:47-69, for more on the temple portraits.

146. Caroline Amanda Grant Smith (1814-45) was the wife of apostle and patriarch William Smith and sister-in-law of Joseph Smith.

147. William Cottier (1820-?) was one of the Nauvoo temple's stone cutters. He received his endowment in the temple in December 1845 and later joined the followers of Sidney Rigdon.

On the East side of the second division in the centre stands a brass clock over which there is a splendid portrait of the late Hyrum Smith and next to the right C[harles]. C. Rich, George Miller & Clarissa Smith. To the left sister [Sarah] Rich, next Mary Catherine Miller and last Leonora A. Taylor.

There are also a number of maps. A large map of the world hangs on the North side wall, and three maps of the United States and a plot of the City of Nauvoo hangs on the West partition. On the South wall hangs another large map of the United States. besides a number of large mirrors and paintings.

In the centre and body of the Celestial Room are two splendid tables and four splendid sofas. Also a small table opposite the large Window on the East end of the room on which stands the Celestial and terrestrial Globes.

All the rooms are nicely carpeted and has a very splendid and comfortable appearance. There are a number of handsome chairs in it.

~~This morning~~ B[righam]. Young & wife, H[eber]. C. Kimball and G[eorge]. A. Smith, also sister Mary Smith, Mercy R. Thompson, W[illiam]. W. Phelps and his wife tarried in the Temple all night, We only obtained about an hour and a half sleep. In the morning sister Young and the other sisters went home. B[righam]. Young and myself went to Joseph C Kingsburys and eat breakfast. We there had an interview with Willard Snow who has just returned from his Mission to Boston. From thence we returned back to the Temple and found several of the brethren had come in with the expect[at]ions of receiving their anointings These following viz. Alpheus Cutler Reynolds Cahoon, Orson Spencer, Joseph Young, Isaac Morley, and Wm Clayton also Lucy Morley, Lois Cutler, Tirzah Cahoon, Catherine C. Spencer, Ruth Clayton, and Permelia Lott, each received their washings and anointings. We commenced a little before one o clock. George A. Smith and myself[148] washed the brethren and B[righam]. Young and Amasa Lyman anointed them assisted by George Miller. Sister Vilate Kimball and Elizabeth Ann Whitney attended to washing the females. At 2 o clock they also washed and anointed Mercy R. Thompson[.]

At 1 o clock E[lde]r Orson Pratt came up into the room while we were attending to washing and anointing. He has just returned from his mission to the East and brought with him $400 worth of six shooters.

See 4 pages back. The men were washed by G[eorge]. A. Smith &

---

148. Clayton probably means Heber C. Kimball.

John Taylor, and anointed by myself[149] and B[righam]. Young. The sisters were washed and anointed by sister Whitney Mary Ann Young and ~~Mary Smith~~ ——————— Elizabeth Ann Whitney.

About half past 1 o clock mother Lucy [Mack] Smith arrived. The weather is cold and some inclined to snow.

A Little before three Sister Elizebeth Ann Whitney and My wife[150] got through washing the sisters about half past 3 [and] the following were taken through all the ordinance & ceremony viz

     Alpheas Cutler & Lois Cutler
     Reynolds Cahoon & Tirzah Cahoon
     Isaac Morley & Lucy Morley
     Orson Spencer & Catherine C. Spencer
     William Clayton & Ruth Clayton
     Cornelius P. Lott & Permelia Lott

also mother Lucy [Mack] Smith and John Smith with her as proxy ^Also John M. Bernhisel^ Mercy R. Thompson with whom brother John Taylor acted as a proxy[.] President Young officiated as Eloheem P[arley]. P. Pratt as Jehovah and George A. Smith as Michael[.]

The first charge was given in the garden by President Young, the other two charges by H[eber]. C. Kimball, who also received most of them through the vail and Amasa Lyman received the remainder.

Immediately after all these were taken through, myself[151] and George A. Smith washed and anointed David Candland and John D. Lee. Sisters Elizabeth Ann Whitney and Mary Smith washed and anointed their wives whose names are Aggatha Ann Lee and Mary Ann Candland. They were assisted by Vilate Kimball. It was about 5 o clock PM, when they commenced washing and anointing these.

A little before six we commenced taking them through the ceremonies Heber C. Kimball acting as Eloheem George A. Smith as Jehovah Orson Hyde as Michael W[illiam]. W. Phelps as the serpent[.] We were also assisted by P[arley]. P. Pratt.

President [Young] having gone out some time ago returned while we were in the garden. The signs & tokens were all given by H[eber]. C. Kimball. He also received them through the vail. It was about half past seven when we got through Those last who were taken through were

149. Probably Heber C. Kimball.
150. Probably Kimball's wife, Vilate.
151. Probably Heber C. Kimball.

then instructed farther regarding the signs by E[lde]r Orson Hyde.

The President then called all those who were present into the Celestial room. We formed a circle, offered up the signs, and then offered up prayers for the sick; for our families and that the Lord would frustrate the plans of our enemies. E[lde]r John E. Page being mouth.

After we got through president Young called the following persons into Hebers Room viz. H[eber]. C. Kimball, P[arley]. P. Pratt, J[ohn]. Taylor, O[rson]. Hyde, John E. Page, George A. Smith, Amasa Lyman, Newel K. Whitney, George Miller and W[illia]m. Clayton. The President then stated that he had received a letter from Samuel Brannan saying that he had been at Washington and had learned that the Secretary of War and the heads of the government were laying plans and were determined to prevent our moving West, alleging that it is against the Law for an armed body of men to go from the United States to any other government. They say it will not do to let the Mormons go to California nor Oregon, neither will it do to let them tarry in the States and they must be exterminated from the face of the earth.[152]

We offered up the signs of the Holy priesthood and prayed that the Lord would defeat and frustrate all the plans of our enemies and inasmuch as they make plots and lay plans to exterminate this people and destroy the priesthood from off the earth that the curse of God may come upon them even all the evil which they design to bring upon this people. And that the Lord would preserve the lives of his servants and lead us out of this ungodly nation in peace.

After we got through there was a unanimous feeling that the Lord would answer our prayers and defeat our enemies. Pres[iden]t. Young said we should go away from here in peace in spite of our enemies.

It was now a little after 9 o'clock and we soon after retired to our homes. President Young and Amasa Lyman tarried in the Temple all the night.
—William Clayton, Diary, kept for Heber C. Kimball.
....

A.M. went to the [Nauvoo] Temple around 9 o clock. Pres[iden]t. [Brigham] Young and H[eber]. C. Kimball were going out to breakfast. They continued to work untill half past 3 o clock this morning. After I [William Clayton] left they took the following through President Brig-

---

152. Church leaders had asked for support in securing government contracts to construct blockhouses or to carry mail on the Oregon Trail.

ham Young & Mary Ann Young, William W. Phelps & Sally Phelps, Parley P. Pratt & Mary Ann Pratt, Amasa Lyman & Mariah Loisa Lyman, George Miller & Mary Catherine Miller, John Taylor & Leonora Taylor, Lucian Woodworth & Phebe Woodworth, John E. Page & Mary Page, Joseph C. Kingsbury, Mary Smith, widow of Hyrum Smith, Agness Smith, widow of Don Carlos.

I spent the forenoon writing the history of these proceedings in E[lde]r Kimballs Journal also gave a description of the upper room. At 12 Pres[iden]t. Young said I could go and fetch my wife [Ruth] if I had a mind to. I immediately went down and returned with her at 1 o clock. I then went into the preparation room and was washed by E[lde]r H[eber]. C. Kimball & George A. Smith, and then anointed a priest and a king unto the most High God by Pres[iden]t. Young and Amasa Lyman and pronounced clean from the blood of this generation.

Those who were anointed at the same time were Alpheus Cutler, Isaac Morley, Orson Spencer, Reynolds Cahoon, myself and Joseph Young. Amongst the females were Lucy Morley, Lois Cutler, Thirzah Cahoon, Catherine C. Spencer, Ruth Clayton and Permelia Lott. Brother [Cornelius P.] Lott was washed and anointed last evening. Sister Jane Young is sick and unable to attend. After washing and anointing we all passed through the ceremonies together with Mother [Lucy Mack] Smith, Mercy R. Thompson and brother Lott. It was about half past seven when we got through. Afterwards those present offered up the signs of the Holy Priesthood and had prayers John E. Page being mouth.

Pres[iden]t. Young then called the following persons into brother Kimballs room viz. H[eber]. C. Kimball, P[arley]. P. Pratt, O[rson]. Hyde, John Taylor, Amasa Lyman, George A. Smith John E. Page, N[ewel]. K. Whitney, George Miller and myself. The Pres[iden]t. stated that he had received a letter from brother Samuel Brannan stating that he had been at Washington [D.C.] and had learned th[at] the Post Master General and Secretary of War were making preparations to prevent our going West, alleging that it is against the Law for an armed body of men to go from the States to another government. They say the Mormons must not be suffered to remain in the State and neither will it do to let us go to California and there is no other way but to exterminate them and obliterate them from the face of the earth. We offered up the signs and asked our heavenly father to overrule them and inasmuch as the heads of this government are plotting the utter destruction of this people that he will curse them and let all the evil which they design to bring upon us come upon themselves.

Pres[iden]t. Young said we shall go out from this place in spite of them. All the brethren felt agreed that God will deliver us from the grasp of this ungodly and mobocratic nation.

At 9 o clock me and my wife went home thankful for the blessings and privileges of the day.

Before we had prayers however John D. Lee, Aggatha Ann Lee, David Candland & Mary Ann Candland were washed and anointed and taken through the vail.

—William Clayton, Diary.

The following are the Records of the washings and Anointings of the Seventies begining with the first Presidency (of the Seventies)

Thursday 1 o'clock, P.M. President Jos[eph]. Young was washed by George A. Smith and anointed by President Brigham Young & Amasa Lyman — And Jane Young his Wife was washed and anointed by Eliza[beth] A. Whitney.[153]

Male Department	Female Department
Names by whom washed	

A condensed Table form for Record Keeping

[See page 213 for remainder of entry]

—"General Record of the Seventies. Book B," John D. Lee,
principal scribe, photocopy in the editors' possession,
original in LDS Archives.

[A]t 5 PM ... myself [John D. Lee] and wife received our washing & anointing. we being [having been] previously notified by Pres[ident] B[righam] Young to go home[,] When I was first engaged in the Temple or rather at the close of the same, & [to] purify our hearts by fasting & prayer & clense our bodies by washing in clean water. After passing through the sacred ordinances of the House of the Lord Pres[ident] B[righam] Young then informed me that my services was needed all the while here in the Temple during the time of giving Endowments[.] I accordingly returned home about 10 at night with feelings of gladness &

---

153. The following column headers indicate an attempt to record and categorize the names of all persons receiving the preliminary stages of the endowment ceremony: the washing and anointing. As only men were washed and anointed on this date, Lee did not use these column headers but arranged the names as they appear on page 215.

No. Name	Members	by washed and by whom Anointed		Age	Month day year
	Pres Jos Young	George A Smith Pres B Young & A. Lyman		47	April 17 1844
2nd	Levi W Hancock	P. P. Pratt	H C Kimball	41	" " "
3rd	Henry Herriman	"	"		June 9th 1845
4th	Zerah Pulsipher	"	"	56	6th " "
5th	Albert P. Rockwood	"	"	34	9th " "
6th	Benjamin L. Clapp	"	"	31	Aug 19th " "
7th	Jedediah M Grant	"	"	29	Feb 21. " "

All except [illegible] was washed & anointed Fri 10 A.M. Dec 12th 1845.

| & Thurs P.M. | John D. Lee | Heber Kimball | Heber C Kimball | 33 | Sept 6th 45 |
| and | David Candland | G A Smith | " | | " " |

—"General Record of the Seventies. Book B," oversized portion, John D. Lee, principal scribe, photocopy in editors' possession, original in LDS Archives.

joyful acclamations of Praise to the Giver of All Good.

—John D. Lee, Diary, LDS Archives.

Elder Heber C. Kimball and I [Brigham Young] went to Joseph Kingsbury's and ate breakfast and returned to the [Nauvoo] Temple. ...

I officiated in the Temple with the brethren of the Twelve [apostles]. We administered the ordinances of endowment to:

Isaac Morley and his wife, Lucy;

Orson Spencer and Catharine C.;

Joseph Young;

Alpheus Cutler and Lois;

Reynolds Cahoon and Thirza;

William Clayton and Ruth;

Cornelius P. Lott and Permelia;

Mother Lucy [Mack] Smith and Mercy R[achel]. Thompson.

At eight p.m., we assembled for prayer. Elder John E. Page was mouth. After which I called the Twelve [apostles] and bishops together and informed them that I had received a letter from Brother Samuel Brannan, stating that he had been at Washington [D.C.] and had learned that the secretary of war and other members of the cabinet were laying plans and were determined to prevent our moving west; alleging that it is against the law for an armed body of men to go from the United States to any other government.

They say it will not do to let the Mormons go to California nor Oregon, neither will it do to let them tarry in the states, and they must be obliterated from the face of the earth.

We prayed that the Lord would defeat and frustrate all the plans of our enemies, and inasmuch as they lay plans to exterminate this people and destroy the priesthood from off the earth, that the curse of God may come upon them, and all the evil which they design to bring upon us, may befall themselves; and that the Lord would preserve the lives of his servants and lead us out of this ungodly nation in peace.

I said we should go out from this place in spite of them all, and the brethren all felt that God would deliver us from the grasp of this ungodly and mobocratic nation.

Brother Amasa Lyman and I tarried in the Temple all night.

—"Manuscript History of Brigham Young," in *History of the Church,* 7:543-44.

In the order of Endowment, a list is made out the day previous, of those who wish to take their endowments. Every person is required to wash himself clean, from head to foot. Also to prepare and bring a good supply of food, of the best quality, for themselves and those who labor in the house of the Lord. In the latter about twenty-five persons are required in the different departments to attend to the washing, anointing, blessing, ordaining, and sealing. From twenty-five to fifty persons are passed through in twenty-four hours.

I was among the first to receive my washings and anointings [on December 11, 1845], and even received my second anointing [on January 14, 1846], which made me an equal in the order of the Priesthood, with the right and authority to build up the kingdom in all the earth, and power to fill any vacancy that might occur. I have officiated in all the different branches, from the highest to the lowest. There were about forty men who attained to that order in the Priesthood, including the twelve Apostles and the first presidency, and to them was intrusted the keeping of the records. I was the head clerk; Franklin D. Richards was my assistant clerk. My office was in room number one, at President [Brigham] Young's apartments.

I kept a record of all the sealings, anointings, marriages and adoptions.

I was the second one adopted to Brigham Young. I should have been his first adopted son, being the first that proposed it to him, but always ready to give preference to those in authority, I placed A[lbert]. P. Rockwood's name first on the list. I also had my children adopted to me in the Temple. Brigham Young had his children adopted to himself, and we were the only ones, to my knowledge, that had our children so adopted at the Temple at Nauvoo [Illinois]. As time would not permit attending to all the people, the business was rushed through day and night.

—John D. Lee, *Mormonism Unveiled; or The Life and Confessions of the Late Mormon Bishop, John D. Lee* (St. Louis, Missouri: Bryan, Brand & Company, 1877), pp. 169-70.

....

Nauvoo temple endowments performed on this date:

First Company: Alpheus Cutler, Lois Cutler, Reynolds Cahoon, Thirza Cahoon, Isaac Morley, Lucy Morley, Orson Spencer, Catherine Spencer, William Clayton, Ruth Clayton, Cornelius P. Lott, Permelia Lott, Lucy Mack Smith, and Mercy R. Thompson.

Second Company: David Candland, Mary Ann Candland, John D. Lee, and Aggatha Ann Lee.

—Summary of information compiled by the Temple Index Bureau, *Nauvoo Temple Endowment Register: 10 December 1845 to 8 February 1846.*

ADAMS, HARRIET DENTON. Born January 31, 1787, in Hartsford, Connecticut. Married James Adams ca. 1809. Moved to Oswego, New York; then in 1821 to Springfield, Illinois. Baptized LDS in 1836. Sealed to husband May 28, 1843. Initiated into Anointed Quorum October 8, 1843. Died August 21, 1844, in Nauvoo, Illinois.

ADAMS, JAMES. Born January 24, 1783, in Limsbury Township, Connecticut. Married Harriet Denton ca. 1809. Moved to Oswego, New York; then in 1821 to Springfield, Illinois. Justice of the peace, 1823; probate judge, 1841 (hence "Judge" Adams). Baptized LDS in 1836; ordained a patriarch. Named Deputy Grand Master of second Masonic Grand Lodge of Illinois in 1840. Helped to establish Nauvoo's Masonic lodge in 1842. Member of original endowment company, May 4, 1842. Sealed to wife May 28, 1843. Married plural wife July 1843. Died August 11, 1843, in Nauvoo, Illinois.

ALLEN, JOSEPH STEWART. Born June 25, 1806. Married Lucy Diantha Morley September 2, 1835. May have been initiated into Anointed Quorum March–December 1845. Received Nauvoo temple endowment December 25, 1845. Sealed to first wife and married plural wife in Nauvoo temple February 4, 1846. Died April 25, 1889.

ALLEN, LUCY MORLEY. Born October 4, 1815. Daughter of Isaac and Lucy Morley. Married Joseph S. Allen September 2, 1835. May have been

217

initiated into Anointed Quorum March–December 1845. Received Nauvoo temple endowment December 25, 1845. Sealed to husband in Nauvoo temple February 4, 1846. Died October 19, 1908, at ninety-three years of age.

BABBIT, ALMON W. Born October 1, 1813, in Cheshire, Massachusetts. Married Julia Ann Johnson November 23, 1833. Baptized LDS ca. 1833. Participated in Zion's Camp, 1834. Ordained seventy February 28, 1835; later ordained high priest. Mission to Canada, 1837–38. President of Kirtland Stake, Ohio, 1841–43. Moved to Illinois 1842. Joined Council of Fifty by April 18, 1844. Initiated into Anointed Quorum May 12, 1844. Elected to Illinois state legislature 1844. Received Nauvoo temple endowment January 7, 1846. Sealed to wife, to three plural wives, and received second anointing January 24, 1846, in Nauvoo temple. Disfellowshipped 1839, 1841, 1843, and 1851. Migrated to Utah. Appointed secretary of Utah Territory 1852. Killed September 7, 1856.

BE[A]MAN, LOUISA. Born February 7, 1815, in Lavonia, New York. Sister of Mary Adeline Be[a]man, wife of Joseph Bates Noble. Joined LDS church by spring 1834. With other Saints, moved to Kirtland, Ohio; Far West, Missouri; and Nauvoo, Illinois. Sealed as plural wife to Joseph Smith April 5, 1841, by brother-in-law, Joseph Bates Noble. Initiated into Anointed Quorum January 26, 1845. Received Nauvoo temple endowment December 29, 1845. Resealed to Joseph Smith (deceased) and received second anointing in Nauvoo temple January 14, 1846. Migrated west. Died May 15, 1850, in Salt Lake City.

BERNHISEL, JOHN M. Born June 23, 1799, in Lloydsville, Pennsylvania. Studied medicine. Baptized LDS while practicing medicine in New York. Settled in Nauvoo, Illinois, in 1843; resided in Mansion House. Initiated into Anointed Quorum September 28, 1843. Joined Council of Fifty March 11, 1844. Married Julia Ann Van Orden, ca. 1845. Sealed to four wives and received second anointing in Nauvoo temple January 20, 1846. Sealed to three additional wives February 1846. Migrated to Utah, 1847–48. Utah representative to U.S. Congress, 1849–63. Died September 28, 1881, in Salt Lake City.

CAHOON, REYNOLDS. Born April 30, 1790, in Cambridge, New York. Veteran of War of 1812. Married Thirza Stiles December 11, 1810.

Baptized LDS November 1830 in Kirtland, Ohio. Ordained elder, then high priest, 1831. Mission to Ohio, Indiana, Illinois, and Missouri, 1831. Labored on Kirtland House of the Lord; appointed counselor to Kirtland bishop. Moved to Missouri, 1838; then to Iowa, 1839. Married plural wife 1842. Initiated into Anointed Quorum October 12, 1843. Received second anointing November 12, 1843, at which time his first wife was also sealed to him. Joined Council of Fifty March 11, 1844. Received Nauvoo temple endowment December 11, 1845. Sealed to wife, to plural wife, to new plural wife, and received second anointing in Nauvoo temple January 16, 1846. Migrated to Utah, 1848. Died April 29, 1861, in Salt Lake County.

CAHOON, THIRZA STILES. Born October 18, 1789. Married Reynolds Cahoon December 11, 1810. Baptized LDS October 1830 in Kirtland, Ohio. Moved to Missouri, 1838; then to Iowa, 1839. Initiated into Anointed Quorum October 29, 1843. Received second anointing November 12, 1843, at which time she was also sealed to her husband. Received Nauvoo temple endowment December 11, 1845. Resealed to husband and received second anointing in Nauvoo temple January 16, 1846. Migrated to Utah, 1848. Died November 20, 1867.

CLAYTON, RUTH MOON. Born June 13, 1817, in Penwortham, England. Sister of Margaret Moon. Married William Clayton October 9, 1836, in Eccleston Parish, England. Sealed to husband July 22, 1843. Initiated into Anointed Quorum March 29, 1845. Received Nauvoo temple endowment December 11, 1845. Resealed to husband and received second anointing in Nauvoo temple January 26, 1846. Died January 15, 1894, in Salt Lake City.

CLAYTON, WILLIAM. Born July 17, 1814, in Carnock Moss, England. Married Ruth Moon October 9, 1836, in Eccleston Parish, England. Joined LDS church 1837. Migrated to America 1840; settled in Nauvoo, Illinois, 1842. Secretary to Joseph Smith. Joined Nauvoo Masons April 16, 1842. Sealed to Margaret Moon, Ruth's sister, as plural wife April 27, 1843. Sealed to first wife July 22, 1843. Initiated into Anointed Quorum February 3, 1844. Joined Council of Fifty March 11, 1844. Sealed to three additional wives, two in 1844, one in 1845. Received Nauvoo temple endowment December 11, 1845. Resealed to wives and received second anointing in Nauvoo temple January 26, 1846. Migrated west. Died December 4, 1879, in Salt Lake City.

COOLBRITH, AGNES M. Born July 8, 1808, in Scarborough, Maine. Married Don Carlos Smith, brother of Joseph Smith, July 30, 1835. Husband died August 7, 1841. Sealed (probably for time only) as plural wife to Joseph Smith January 6, 1842 (may have been sealed for eternity to first husband at this time). Initiated into Anointed Quorum by February 3, 1844. Received Nauvoo temple endowment December 10, 1845. Sealed to Don Carlos Smith for eternity, to George A. Smith for time, and received second anointing in Nauvoo temple January 28, 1846. Did not join Saints west. Married William Pickett ca. spring 1847. Left for Utah 1851; relocated to California 1852. Mother of Ina Coolbrith, prominent California poet. Died December 26, 1876, in Oakland, California.

CUTLER, ALPHEUS. Born February 29, 1784, in Plainfield, New Hampshire. Married Lois Lathrop November 17, 1808. Veteran of War of 1812. Joined LDS church January 20, 1833. Ordained elder. Moved to Kirtland, Ohio. Ordained high priest, 1836. Moved to Missouri, then to Nauvoo, Illinois. Initiated into Anointed Quorum October 12, 1843. Received second anointing November 15, 1843, at which time his wife was also sealed to him. Joined Council of Fifty March 11, 1844. Received Nauvoo temple endowment December 11, 1845. Resealed to first wife, sealed to plural wife, and received second anointing in Nauvoo temple January 14, 1846. Sealed to five additional wives February 3, 1846. Left LDS church 1847-48. Settled in Iowa. Organized "The True Church of Jesus Christ" 1853. Died August 10, 1864, in Manti, Iowa.

CUTLER, LOIS LATHROP. Born September 24, 1788. Married Alpheus Cutler November 17, 1808. Joined LDS church, 1833. Moved to Missouri, then to Nauvoo, Illinois. Initiated into Anointed Quorum October 29, 1843. Received second anointing November 15, 1843, at which time she was also sealed to her husband. Received Nauvoo temple endowment December 11, 1845. Resealed to husband and received second anointing in Nauvoo temple January 14, 1846. Left LDS church 1847-48. Settled in Iowa. Died 1878 at about ninety years of age.

DECKER, HARRIET PAGE WHEELER. Born September 7, 1803, in Hillsboro, New Hampshire. Moved to New York. Married Isaac Decker, 1821. Mother of Lucy Ann Decker. Moved to Ohio and joined LDS church, 1833. Moved to Missouri and then to Illinois. Separated from first husband and sealed to Lorenzo Dow Young as plural wife March 9, 1843.

Initiated into Anointed Quorum January 30–March 20, 1845. Received Nauvoo temple endowment January 7, 1846. Resealed to husband and received second anointing in Nauvoo temple January 26, 1846. Member of original pioneer emigrant company to Great Salt Lake Valley, 1847. Died December 23, 1871.

DECKER, LUCY ANN. Born May 17, 1822, in Phelps, New York, to Lucy and Isaac Decker. Married William Seeley, 1833. Separated or divorced by 1841. Sealed as plural wife to Brigham Young June 15, 1842. Initiated into Anointed Quorum January 26, 1845. Received second anointing March 21, 1845. Received Nauvoo temple endowment by January 1846. Resealed to husband and received second anointing in Nauvoo temple January 14, 1846. Died January 24, 1890.

DURFEE, ELIZABETH DAVIS. Born March 11, 1791, in Riverhead, New York. Married Gilbert Godsmith April 13, 1811. Husband died December 24, 1811. Married Joseph Brackenbury ca. 1818–19. Joined LDS church April 10, 1831. Husband died January 7, 1832. Married Jabez Durfee March 3, 1834. Moved from Missouri to Illinois. Sealed as plural wife to Joseph Smith by June 1842 (she remained married to, and living with, her first husband). Initiated into Anointed Quorum October 1, 1843. Separated from husband by late 1845. Received Nauvoo temple endowment December 23, 1845. Resealed to Joseph Smith (for eternity) and sealed to Cornelius P. Lott (for time) in Nauvoo temple January 22, 1846. Left husband and LDS church late 1846. Moved to southern California; later to Kansas. Joined Reorganized Latter Day Saint church 1869. Died late 1876.

FIELDING, HANNAH GREENWOOD. Born September 4, 1808, in Bolton, England. Married Joseph Fielding June 11, 1838, in Preston, England. Migrated to America. Initiated into Anointed Quorum by February 3, 1844. May have received second anointing by December 7, 1845. Received Nauvoo temple endowment December 12, 1845. Sealed to husband and received second anointing in Nauvoo temple January 23, 1846. Migrated west. Died September 9, 1877, in Ogden, Utah.

FIELDING, JOSEPH. Born March 26, 1797, in Bedfordshire, England. Brother to Mary and Mercy Fielding. Joined LDS church, 1836. Married Hannah Greenwood June 11, 1838, in Preston, England. Migrated to

America. Presided over LDS British mission, 1838-40. Initiated into Anointed Quorum December 9, 1843. Joined Council of Fifty April 18, 1844. Sealed to plural wife by July 1845. May have received second anointing by December 7, 1845. Received Nauvoo temple endowment December 12, 1845. Sealed to first wife, resealed to second wife, and received second anointing in Nauvoo temple January 23, 1846. Migrated west. Died December 19, 1863, in Salt Lake City.

FROST, OLIVE GREY. Born July 24, 1816, in Bethel, Maine. Sister of Mary Ann Frost, plural wife of Parley P. Pratt. Joined LDS church October 1839. Traveled with sister and Pratt to England 1840-42. Arrived in Nauvoo, Illinois, April 1843. Sealed as plural wife to Joseph Smith ca. mid-1843. Suffered mental breakdown following death of Joseph Smith. Sealed (for time) to Brigham Young November 7, 1844. Initiated into Anointed Quorum January 26, 1845. Died October 6, 1845, in Nauvoo, Illinois.

GREENE, JOHN P. Born September 3, 1793, in Herkimer, New York. Married Rhoda Young February 11, 1813. Joined LDS church ca. 1833. Member of Kirtland high council 1836. Branch president in New York City 1839. Wife died January 8, 1841. Member of Nauvoo city council 1841. Married Mary Eliza Nelson December 6, 1841. Joined Nauvoo Masons April 29, 1842. Nauvoo city marshal 1843. Joined Council of Fifty March 1844. Initiated into Anointed Quorum May 11, 1844. Died September 10, 1844, in Nauvoo. Received second anointing in Nauvoo temple by proxy January 31, 1846.

HYDE, CHARLES W. Born July 16, 1814, in Livingstone, New York. Initiated into Anointed Quorum May 2, 1845. Received Nauvoo temple endowment January 8, 1846. Migrated to Salt Lake City. Died December 15, 1891, in Salt Lake City.

HYDE, MARINDA NANCY JOHNSON. Born June 28, 1815, in Pomfret, Vermont. Joined LDS church, 1832, in Ohio. Married Orson Hyde September 4, 1834. Relocated to Missouri, then to Nauvoo, Illinois. Sealed as plural wife to Joseph Smith ca. April 1842. Initiated into Anointed Quorum February 18, 1844. Received Nauvoo temple endowment December 10, 1845. Sealed to husband and may have received second anointing in Nauvoo temple January 11-12, 1846. Resealed to Joseph Smith. Migrated west. Settled in Iowa until 1852, then moved to Utah. Active in LDS Relief Society. Divorced husband 1870. Died March 24, 1886, in Spring City, Utah.

HYDE, ORSON. Born January 8, 1805, in Oxford, Connecticut. Affiliated with Methodists and Campbellite movement. Joined LDS church October 2, 1831. Ordained elder. Various church missions. Member of Kirtland high council. Member of Zion's Camp. Married Marinda Nancy Johnson September 4, 1834. Ordained as a member of the first Quorum of Twelve Apostles February 15, 1835. Disfellowshipped 1835. Church mission to England 1837–38. Voluntarily left LDS church 1838; reaffiliated, 1839. Church mission to Middle East, 1840–42. Relocated to Nauvoo, Illinois. Sealed to two plural wives ca. February–March 1843 and 20 July 1843. Initiated into Anointed Quorum December 2, 1843. Received second anointing without any of his wives January 25, 1844. Joined Council of Fifty March 13, 1844. Received Nauvoo temple endowment December 10, 1845. Sealed/resealed to wives and received second anointing in Nauvoo temple January 11-12, 1846. Migrated west. Sustained as president of Twelve December 27, 1847. Settled in Utah, 1852. Presided over church first in Nevada, then in Sanpete County, Utah. Divorced first wife, 1870. Seniority in Twelve readjusted April 10, 1875; did not succeed to presidency of LDS church after Brigham Young's death. Died November 28, 1878, in Spring City, Utah.

JACOBS, ZINA D. H. Born January 31, 1821, in Watertown, New York. Sister of Presendia Lathrop Huntington, plural wife of Joseph Smith and later of Heber C. Kimball. Joined LDS church April 1835. Moved to Kirtland, Ohio; Far West, Missouri; and Nauvoo, Illinois. Married Henry Jacobs March 1841. Sealed as plural wife to Joseph Smith October 27, 1841. Initiated into Anointed Quorum January 30, 1845. Resealed to Joseph Smith (for eternity) and Brigham Young (for time) in the Nauvoo temple February 2, 1846 (Henry Jacobs was witness to the ceremony). Migrated to Utah. Active in LDS female Relief Society; appointed general president of Relief Society April 1888. Died August 28, 1901, in Salt Lake City.

KIMBALL, HEBER C. Born June 14, 1801, in Sheldon, Vermont. Married Vilate Murray November 7, 1822. Father of Helen Mar Kimball, plural wife of Joseph Smith. Joined Masons by 1823. Joined LDS church

April 1832. Ordained elder. Member of Zion's Camp. Ordained as a member of the first Quorum of Twelve Apostles February 14, 1835. Moved to Kirtland, Ohio; Far West, Missouri; and Nauvoo, Illinois. Missions to England 1837-38, 1839-41. Member of original endowment company, May 4, 1842. Sealed to first plural wife ca. 1842. Received second anointing January 20, 1844, at which his first wife, Vilate Murray Kimball, was also sealed to him. Joined Council of Fifty March 11, 1844. Sealed to eleven plural wives August-December 1844 and five plural wives, 1845. Received Nauvoo temple endowment December 10, 1845. Sealed/resealed to wives, plus one new plural wife, and received second anointing in Nauvoo temple January 7-8, 1846. Sealed to eighteen additional plural wives January-February 1846. Sustained as first counselor to LDS church president December 27, 1847. Migrated to Utah; arrived July 24, 1847. Member of First Presidency, 1847-68. Died June 22, 1868, in Salt Lake City.

KIMBALL, HELEN MAR. Born August 25, 1828, to Heber C. and Vilate M. Kimball. Family joined LDS church April 1832. Moved to Kirtland, Ohio; Far West, Missouri; and Nauvoo, Illinois. Sealed as plural wife to Joseph Smith ca. May 1843. Initiated into Anointed Quorum January 26, 1845. Received Nauvoo temple endowment January 1, 1846. Married (for time) Horace Whitney February 3, 1846. Resealed to Joseph Smith and received second anointing in Nauvoo temple February 4, 1846. Migrated to Utah. Wrote pro-polygamy treatise, *Why We Practice Plural Marriage* (1884). Died November 15, 1896, in Salt Lake City.

KIMBALL, VILATE MURRAY. Born June 1, 1806. Married Heber C. Kimball November 7, 1822. Mother of Helen Mar Kimball, plural wife of Joseph Smith. Stepdaughter of Fanny Murray Young, plural wife of Joseph Smith. Joined LDS church April 1832. Moved to Kirtland, Ohio; Far West, Missouri; and Nauvoo, Illinois. Initiated into Anointed Quorum November 1, 1843. Received second anointing January 20, 1844, at which time she was also sealed to her husband. Received Nauvoo temple endowment December 10, 1845. Resealed to husband and received second anointing in Nauvoo temple January 7-8, 1846. Migrated to Utah. Died October 22, 1867.

KINGSBURY, JOSEPH C. Born May 2, 1812, in Enfield, Connecticut. Joined LDS church, 1832, in Kirtland, Ohio. Married Caroline Whitney (daughter of Newel K. and Elizabeth Ann Whitney) February 3, 1836. Wife died October 10, 1842. Sealed to deceased wife March 23, 1843. Married Sarah Ann Whitney (sister-in-law) civilly April 29, 1843. (Sarah Ann Whitney had previously been sealed as a plural wife to Joseph Smith.) Initiated into Anointed Quorum January 26, 1845. Sealed to Dorcas Adelia Moore, and resealed to first wife, March 4, 1845. Sealed to three plural wives 1845-46. Received Nauvoo temple endowment December 10, 1845. Resealed to first (deceased), second (living), and a plural wife January 26, 1846. Received second anointing with two wives January 28, 1846. Migrated to Utah, where he was an LDS bishop, superintendent of the church tithing office, and patriarch. Died October 15, 1898, in Salt Lake City.

KNIGHT, VINSON. Born March 14, 1804, in Chester, New York. Married Martha McBride March 14, 1826. Joined LDS church, 1834. Moved to Ohio, Missouri, and Nauvoo, Illinois. Ordained elder, 1836. Appointed Presiding Bishop, 1841. Member of Nauvoo city council, 1841. Joined Nauvoo Masons April 9, 1842. Initiated into Anointed Quorum and sealed to first wife and/or to plural wife before death on July 31, 1842, in Nauvoo.

LAW, JANE SILVERTHORN. Born April 2, 1815, in Canada. Married William Law ca. 1833. Joined LDS church, 1836. Relocated to Nauvoo, Illinois, 1839. Initiated into Anointed Quorum October 1, 1843. May or may not have been sealed to husband. Left LDS church 1844. Moved to Pennsylvania, then to Wisconsin. Died September 8, 1882, in Shullsburg, Wisconsin.

LAW, WILLIAM. Born September 8, 1809, in Tyrone County, northern Ireland. Migrated to America, 1818. Married Jane Silverthorn ca. 1833. Joined LDS church, 1836. Relocated to Nauvoo, Illinois, 1839. Set apart as second counselor to Joseph Smith January 24, 1841. Joined Nauvoo Masons April 25, 1842. Member of original endowment company, May 4, 1842. May or may not have been sealed to wife. Opposed plural marriage. Became disaffected from LDS church and was excommunicated April 18, 1844. Published the *Nauvoo Expositor* June 7, 1844. Moved to Pennsylvania, then to Wisconsin. Practiced medicine. Died January 19, 1892, in Shullsberg, Wisconsin.

LIGHTNER, MARY E. ROLLINS. Born April 9, 1818, in Lima, New York. Joined LDS church November 1830. Moved to Independence, Missouri; later to Nauvoo, Illinois. Married Adam Lightner August 11, 1835. Sealed as a plural wife to Joseph Smith by late February 1842, though still married to and living with first husband. Initiated into Anointed Quorum January 30, 1845. Resealed to Joseph Smith (for eternity) and (for time) to Brigham Young May 22, 1845. Received second anointing and resealed to Joseph Smith in Nauvoo temple January 15 and January 17, 1846, respectively. Continued to live with first husband. Migrated to Wisconsin. Eventually relocated to Utah. Active in LDS Relief Society. First husband died mid-1885. Died December 17, 1913, in Minersville, Utah.

LOTT, CORNELIUS P. Born September 27, 1898. Married Permelia Darrow April 27, 1823. Father of Melissa Lott, plural wife of Joseph Smith. Sealed to wife September 20, 1843. Initiated into Anointed Quorum December 9, 1843. Received second anointing February 4, 1844. Joined Council of Fifty April 18, 1844. Received Nauvoo temple endowment December 11, 1845. Resealed to wife, sealed to three plural wives (including Elizabeth Durfee, plural wife of Joseph Smith [deceased]), and received second anointing in Nauvoo temple, January 22, 1846. Sealed to three additional plural wives February 1846–March 1847. Died July 6, 1850, at ninety-five years of age.

LOTT, PERMELIA DARROW. Born December 15, 1804. Married Cornelius P. Lott April 27, 1823. Mother of Melissa Lott, plural wife of Joseph Smith. Sealed to husband September 20, 1843. Initiated into Anointed Quorum December 23, 1843. Received second anointing February 4, 1844. Received Nauvoo temple endowment December 11, 1845. Resealed to husband and received second anointing in Nauvoo temple, January 22, 1846. Died January 6, 1882.

LYMAN, AMASA. Born March 30, 1813, in Lyman, New Hampsire. Joined LDS church April 27, 1832. Ordained elder. Moved to Kirtland, Ohio. Ordained high priest, 1833. Member of Zion's Camp, 1834. Married Maria Louise Tanner June 10, 1835. Moved to Missouri, then to Nauvoo, Illinois. Joined Nauvoo Masons April 8, 1842. Ordained LDS apostle August 20, 1842. Appointed counselor to First Presidency ca. February 4, 1843. Initiated into Anointed Quorum September 28, 1843. Church mission to Indiana, 1843–44. Joined Council of Fifty April 18,

1844. Joined Quorum of Twelve Apostles August 12, 1844. Sealed to three plural wives September–November 1844. Received second anointing April 18, 1845, at which time his first wife, Mary Louisa Tanner Lyman, was also sealed to him. Sealed to fourth plural wife July 1845. Received Nauvoo temple endowment December 10, 1845. Resealed to wives and received second anointing in Nauvoo temple January 13, 1846. Sealed to three additional plural wives January 16 (two) and 28, 1846. Migrated west. Presided over church in southern California 1851–57. Presided over church in England 1860-62. Presided over church in Fillmore, Utah, 1863. Relieved of apostleship October 6, 1867; excommunicated May 12, 1870. Died February 4, 1877, in Fillmore.

LYMAN, MARY LOUISA TANNER. Born November 28, 1818. Married Amasa Lyman June 10, 1835. Initiated into Anointed Quorum December 22, 1844. Received second anointing April 18, 1845, at which time she was also sealed to her husband. Received Nauvoo temple endowment December 10, 1845. Resealed to husband and received second anointing in Nauvoo temple January 13, 1846. Died May 3, 1906.

MARKS, ROSANNAH ROBINSON. Born ca. 1792 in Rutland, Vermont. Married William Marks May 2, 1813. Baptized LDS prior to April 1835 in Portage, New York. Initiated into Anointed Quorum October 1, 1843. Received second anointing October 22, 1843, at which time she was also sealed to her husband. Did not subsequently receive Nauvoo temple endowment, Nauvoo temple marriage sealing, or Nauvoo temple second anointing ordinance. Died October 18, 1863.

MARKS, WILLIAM. Born November 15, 1792, in Rutland, Vermont. Married Rosannah Robinson May 2, 1813. Baptized LDS prior to April 1835 in Portage, New York. Ordained elder prior to June 3, 1836. Member Kirtland (Ohio) high council 1837. Appointed president of Far West Stake, Missouri, 1838. Appointed president of Nauvoo, Illinois, stake October 5, 1839. Joined Nauvoo Masons April 20, 1842. Member of original endowment company, May 4, 1842. Received second anointing October 22, 1843, at which time his wife was also sealed to him. Did not subsequently receive Nauvoo temple endowment, sealing, or second anointing. Joined Council of Fifty March 19, 1844. Concerned about Twelve's succession to the presidency of the church following Joseph Smith's death. Rejected as Nauvoo stake president October 7, 1844. Moved to Fulton

City, Illinois, 1845. Counselor to James J. Strang, 1846–50. Helped found the Reorganized Church of Jesus Christ of Latter Day Saints, 1860. Appointed counselor to Joseph Smith III April 1863. Died May 22, 1872, in Plano, Illinois.

MILLER, GEORGE. Born November 25, 1794, near Standardville, Virginia. Joined the Masons, 1819. Married Mary Fry June 25, 1822. Moved to Illinois by 1834. Baptized LDS August 12, 1839, by John Taylor. Moved to Iowa fall 1839; moved to Nauvoo, Illinois, November 1840. Ordained bishop February 1841. Mission to Kentucky 1841–42. Worshipful Master of Nauvoo's Masonic lodge. Member of original endowment company May 4, 1842. Mission to Wisconsin pineries 1842–43. Joined Council of Fifty March 11, 1844. Appointed trustee-in-trust for the church August 9, 1844. Received second anointing August 15, 1844, at which time his wife was also sealed to him. Sustained as "second bishop" of LDS church October 7, 1844. Received Nauvoo temple endowment December 10, 1845. Sealed to wife and received second anointing in Nauvoo temple January 13, 1846. Sealed to two plural wives January 25, 1846. Left Nauvoo February 1846. Rejected Brigham Young as church president ca. January 1847. Disfellowshipped from LDS church October 20, 1848; excommunicated December 3, 1848. Affiliated first with Lyman Wight, then with James J. Strang. Died 1856 in Meringo, Illinois.

MILLER, MARY FRY. Born January 29, 1801. Married George Miller June 25, 1822. Baptized LDS 1839. Moved to Iowa 1839; then to Nauvoo, Illinois, 1840. Initiated into Anointed Quorum by February 3, 1844. Received second anointing August 15, 1844, at which time she was also sealed to her husband. Received Nauvoo temple endowment December 10, 1845. Sealed to husband and received second anointing in Nauvoo temple January 13, 1846.

MOON, MARGARET. Born January 14, 1820. Sister of Ruth Moon Clayton. Sealed as a plural wife to William Clayton April 27, 1843. Initiated into Anointed Quorum March 29, 1845. Sealed to husband and received second anointing in Nauvoo temple January 26, 1846.

MORLEY, ISAAC. Born March 11, 1786, in Montague, Massachusetts. Veteran of War of 1812. Married Lucy Gunn June 20, 1812. Father of Lucy Morley Allen. Baptized LDS November 15, 1830. Set apart as first counselor to Presiding Bishop June 3, 1831; released May 27, 1840. Moved to Missouri, 1831. Moved to Hancock County, Illinois, 1839. Appointed president of Lima Stake, Illinois, October 1840. Initiated into Anointed Quorum December 23, 1843. Sealed to two plural wives, first by December 19, 1843, then on January 14, 1844. Received second anointing February 26, 1844, at which time his wife Lucy was also sealed to him. Moved to Nauvoo 1845. Joined by Council of Fifty March 1, 1845. Received Nauvoo temple endowment December 11, 1845. Sealed to wife and received second anointing in Nauvoo temple January 14, 1846. Sealed to five additional plural wives January 22 (four) and 27, 1846. Migrated to Utah; settled Sanpete Valley 1849. Member of the Utah territorial legislature 1851-55. Died June 24, 1865, in Fairview, Utah.

MORLEY, LUCY GUNN. Born January 24, 1786, in Montague, Massachusetts. Married Isaac Morley June 20, 1812. Mother of Lucy Morley Allen. Baptized LDS, 1830. Moved to Missouri, then to Illinois. Initiated into Anointed Quorum December 23, 1843. Received second anointing February 26, 1844, at which time she was also sealed to her husband. Moved to Nauvoo, 1845. Received Nauvoo temple endowment December 11, 1845. Sealed to husband and received second anointing in Nauvoo temple January 14, 1846. Died January 3, 1848, in Florence, Nebraska.

MURRAY, FANNY YOUNG. Born November 8, 1787, in Hopkinton, Massachusetts. Married Robert Carr May 5, 1806. Separated by 1815. Married Roswell Murray (father of Vilate Murray Kimball, wife of Heber C. Kimball) February 2, 1832. Joined LDS church, 1832. Moved to Kirtland, Ohio; Missouri; and eventually to Nauvoo, Illinois. Husband died fall 1839. Sealed as plural wife to Joseph Smith November 2, 1843. Initiated into Anointed Quorum December 23, 1843. Received Nauvoo temple endowment January 7, 1846. Migrated to Utah. Died June 11, 1859, in Salt Lake City.

NOBLE, JOSEPH BATES. Born January 14, 1810, in Egremont, Massachusetts. Baptized LDS, 1832. Married Mary Adeline Be[a]man September 11, 1834. Member of Zion's Camp 1834. Performed first plural marriage sealing ceremony for Joseph Smith and Louisa Be[a]man, his sister-in-law, April 5, 1841. Sealed to two plural wives April 5 and June 28, 1843. Initiated into Anointed Quorum March 20, 1845. Sealed to wives (except one) and received second anointing in Nauvoo temple January 23, 1846. Migrated to Utah 1847. Appointed counselor to bishop in Salt Lake City; later called to stake high council. Died August 17, 1900, in Bear Lake, Idaho, at ninety years of age.

NOBLE, MARY BE[A]MAN. Born October 19, 1810, in Livonia, Massachusetts. Sister of Louisa Be[a]man, plural wife of Joseph Smith. Married Joseph Bates Noble September 11, 1834. Initiated into Anointed Quorum March 20, 1845. Sealed to husband and received second anointing in Nauvoo temple January 23, 1846. Migrated to Utah. Died February 16, 1851, in Salt Lake City.

PAGE, JOHN E. Born February 25, 1799, in Trenton Township, New York. Married Betsey Thompson July 1, 1831. Joined LDS church August 18, 1833. Wife died October 1, 1833. Married Lorain Stevens December 26, 1833. Moved to Kirtland, Ohio, fall 1835. Wife died fall 1838. Moved to Missouri, 1838. Ordained member of Quorum of Twelve Apostles December 19, 1838. Married Mary Judd ca. January 1839. Moved to Illinois, 1839. Joined Nauvoo Masons April 21, 1842. Presided over church in Pittsburgh, 1842-43. May have been sealed to wife and/or sealed to plural wives before June 27, 1844. Initiated into Anointed Quorum January 26, 1845. Joined Council of Fifty March 1, 1845. Received Nauvoo temple endowment December 10, 1845. Supported James J. Strang. Disfellowshipped from LDS church February 9, 1846; excommunicated June 26, 1846. Moved to Wisconsin. Affiliated with Hedrickites. Died October 14, 1867, in De Kalb County, Illinois.

PAGE, MARY JUDD. Born November 26, 1818, in Bastard Township, Leeds County, Ontario, Canada. Joined LDS church. Married John E. Page ca. January 1839. Moved to Missouri and Illinois. May have been sealed to husband before June 27, 1844. Initiated into Anointed Quorum January 26, 1845. Received Nauvoo temple endowment December 10, 1845. Moved with husband to Wisconsin. Died March 6, 1907.

PHELPS, SALLY WATERMAN. Born July 24, 1797, in Franklin, New York. Married William W. Phelps April 28, 1815. Baptized LDS 1831. Moved with husband to Missouri, Ohio, and Illinois. Initiated into Anointed Quorum December 23, 1843. Received second anointing February 2, 1844, at which time she was also sealed to her husband. Received Nauvoo temple endowment December 10, 1845. Resealed to husband and received second anointing in Nauvoo temple January 15, 1846.

PHELPS, WILLIAM W. Born February 17, 1792, in Hanover, New Jersey. Married Sally Waterman April 28, 1815. Newspaper editor. Baptized LDS 1831. Moved to Missouri 1831. Church editor and publisher. Relocated to Ohio 1835-36, then returned to Missouri. Excommunicated March 10, 1838. Refellowshipped July 1840. Moved to Nauvoo, Illinois, 1841. Clerk and confidant to Joseph Smith 1841-44. Initiated into Anointed Quorum December 9, 1843. Received second anointing February 2, 1844, at which time his wife was also sealed to him. Joined Council of Fifty March 11, 1844. Received Nauvoo temple endowment December 10, 1845. Resealed to wife and received second anointing in Nauvoo temple January 15, 1846. Sealed to two plural wives February 2, 1846. Excommunicated and rebaptized December 1847. Moved to Utah 1849. Died March 6, 1872, in Salt Lake City.

PRATT, MARY ANN FROST. Born January 14, 1809, in Bethel, Maine. Sister of Olive Grey Frost, plural wife of Joseph Smith. Joined LDS church August 1836. Married Parley P. Pratt May 9, 1837. Traveled with husband and sister to England 1840-42. Arrived in Nauvoo, Illinois, April 1843. Sealed to husband June 23, 1843. Sealing cancelled by Joseph Smith. Sealed (possibly for time only) to husband July 24, 1843. Initiated into Anointed Quorum December 22, 1844. Received Nauvoo temple endowment December 10, 1845. Resealed to husband and received second anointing January 10-12, 1846, in Nauvoo temple. Sealed to Joseph Smith February 7, 1846, in Nauvoo temple. Migrated to Utah. Divorced husband 1853. Died August 24, 1891, in Pleasant Grove, Utah.

PRATT, ORSON. Born September 19, 1811, in Hartford, New York. Brother of Parley P. Pratt. Joined LDS church September 19, 1830. Moved to Ohio. Undertook several church missions. Ordained member of first Quorum of Twelve Apostles April 26, 1835. Married Sarah M. Bates July 4, 1836. Mission to England, 1839-41. Settled in Nauvoo, Illinois. Excommunicated August 20, 1842. Excommunication ruled illegal/invalid by Joseph Smith; rebaptized and restored to former standing January 20, 1843. Initiated into Anointed Quorum December 23, 1843. Received second anointing without wife January 26, 1844. Joined Council of Fifty March 11, 1844. Sealed to plural wife ca. fall 1844. Sealed to first wife November 22, 1844. Sealed to second plural wife December 1844; to third plural wife 1845. Received Nauvoo temple endowment December 12, 1845. Sealed/resealed to wives and received second anointing January 8 and 13, 1846, in Nauvoo temple. Sealed to fourth plural wife January 17, 1846. Migrated to Utah 1847. Several more church missions. Named Church Historian 1874. Seniority in Twelve readjusted April 10, 1875; did not succeed to presidency of LDS church after Brigham Young's death. Revised LDS scriptures. Died October 3, 1881, in Salt Lake City.

PRATT, PARLEY P. Born April 12, 1807, in Burlington, New York. Brother of Orson Pratt. Married Thankful Halsey September 9, 1827. Joined LDS church September 1830. Moved to Kirtland, Ohio. Mission to Missouri. Member of Zion's Camp, 1834. Ordained member of first Quorum of Twelve Apostles February 21, 1835. Wife died March 25, 1837. Married Mary Ann Frost May 9, 1837. Various church missions including to England 1839-40/40-43. Returned to Nauvoo, Illinois. Sealed to wife June 23, 1843. Sealing cancelled by Joseph Smith. Sealed to deceased first wife (Thankful), sealed (possibly for time only) to living first wife (Mary Ann), and sealed to first plural wife (Elizabeth Brotherton) July 24, 1843. Initiated into Anointed Quorum December 2, 1843. Received second anointing without wives January 21, 1844. Joined Council of Fifty March 11, 1844. Sealed to three additional plural wives September-November 1844; to fifth plural wife October 15, 1845. Mission to New York. Received Nauvoo temple endowment December 10, 1845. Sealed to wives and received second anointing January 10-12, 1846, in Nauvoo temple. Sealed to sixth plural wife February 8, 1846. Migrated to Salt Lake Valley 1847. Mission to Pacific Islands and South America 1851-52. Divorced first wife, Mary Ann Frost Pratt, 1853. Mission to California 1854-55. Killed May 13, 1857, near Van Buren, Arkansas.

PRATT, SARAH BATES. Born February 5, 1817, in Henderson, New York. Joined LDS church in 1835. Married Orson Pratt July 4, 1836. Moved to Nauvoo, Illinois. Sealed to husband November 22, 1844. Initiated into Anointed Quorum December 12, 1844. Received Nauvoo temple endowment December 12, 1845. Resealed to husband and received second anointing January 8 and 13, 1846, in Nauvoo temple. Migrated to Utah. Became disaffected from LDS church, separated from husband, and was excommunicated October 4, 1874. Died December 25, 1888, in Salt Lake City.

RICHARDS, JENNETTA RICHARDS. Born August 21, 1817, in Walker-fold, England. Married Willard Richards September 24, 1838. Moved to Nauvoo, Illinois. Sealed to husband May 29, 1843. Initiated into Anointed Quorum November 1, 1843. Received second anointing January 27, 1844. Died July 9, 1845, in Nauvoo, Illinois. Posthumously resealed to husband January 22, 1846, in Nauvoo temple.

RICHARDS, LEVI. Born April 14, 1799, in Hopkinton, Massachusetts. Brother of Rhoda and Willard Richards. Joined LDS church December 31, 1836. Moved to Missouri. Mission to England 1840–43. Moved to Nauvoo, Illinois. Physician to Joseph Smith. Initiated into Anointed Quorum December 9, 1843. Married Sarah Griffin December 25, 1843. Joined Council of Fifty March 11, 1844. May have received second anointing by December 7, 1845. Sealed to wife, sealed to plural wife, and received second anointing January 27, 1846, in Nauvoo temple. Located to Salt Lake City 1853. Died June 18, 1876, in Salt Lake City.

RICHARDS, RHODA. Born August 8, 1784, in Framingham, Massachusetts. Sister of Levi and Willard Richards. Joined LDS church June 2, 1837. Moved to Nauvoo, Illinois. Sealed as plural wife to Joseph Smith June 12, 1843. Resealed to Joseph Smith (for eternity) and sealed to Brigham Young (for time) early 1845. May have been initiated into Anointed Quorum sometime between March and December 1845. Received Nauvoo temple endowment January 10, 1846. Resealed to husbands and received second anointing January 31, 1846, in Nauvoo temple. Migrated to Utah. Died January 17, 1879, in Salt Lake City, at ninety-four years of age.

RICHARDS, WILLARD. Born June 24, 1804, in Hopkinton, Massachusetts. Brother of Levi and Rhoda Richards, the latter a plural wife of Joseph Smith and Brigham Young. Joined LDS church December 31, 1836. Mission to England 1837-41. Married Jennetta Richards September 24, 1838. Ordained member of Quorum of Twelve Apostles April 14, 1840. Moved to Nauvoo, Illinois, 1841. Joined Nauvoo Masons April 7, 1842. Member of original endowment company May 4, 1842. Sealed to two plural wives January 18, 1843. Sealed to first wife May 29, 1843. Sealed to third plural wife June 12, 1843. Church Historian and Recorder. Received second anointing January 27, 1844. Joined Council of Fifty March 11, 1844. Sealed to two additional plural wives December 22-23, 1845. Received Nauvoo temple endowment January 10, 1846. Sealed/resealed to wives and received second anointing January 22-24, 1846, in Nauvoo temple. Sealed to four additional plural wives January-February 1846. Migrated to Utah 1847. Sustained as second counselor to LDS church president December 27, 1847. Died March 11, 1854, in Salt Lake City.

RIGDON, SIDNEY. Born February 19, 1793, in Saint Clair Township, Pennsylvania. Married Phoebe Brook March 1819. Baptist minister. Joined Disciples of Christ 1830. Joined LDS church November 1830. Confidant to Joseph Smith. Set apart as first counselor to LDS church president March 18, 1833. Various church missions. Imprisoned in Liberty Jail 1838-39. Moved to Illinois 1839. Nauvoo postmaster. Joined Nauvoo Masons March 15, 1842. Quarreled over plural marriage with Joseph Smith, who wanted to drop him as counselor, but church members voted to sustain him. Joined Council of Fifty March 19, 1844. Initiated into Anointed Quorum May 11, 1844. Wanted to be named guardian to church after Joseph Smith's death. Excommunicated September 8, 1844. Moved to Pennsylvania, founded new church 1845. Moved to New York 1850. Died July 14, 1876, in Friendship, New York.

SESSIONS, SYLVIA PORTER. Born July 31, 1818, in Andover Surplus, Maine. Daughter of Patty Bartlett Sessions, plural wife of Joseph Smith. Family joined LDS church mid-1834. Married Windsor P. Lyon April 21, 1838. Moved to Nauvoo, Illinois, 1840. Sealed as plural wife to Joseph Smith February 8, 1842 (but remained married to, and continued to live with, first husband). First husband excommunicated from LDS church 1842 (rebaptized 1846). May have borne a child by Joseph Smith. Resealed to Joseph Smith (for eternity) and sealed to Heber C. Kimball (for time) September 19, 1844. Continued to live with first husband. Initiated into Anointed Quorum January 30-March 20, 1845. May have received second anointing with Heber C. Kimball April 26, 1845. Received Nauvoo temple endowment December 16, 1845. Resealed to husbands January 26, 1846, in Nauvoo temple. First husband died mid-January 1849. Married Ezekiel Clark, a non-Mormon, ca. 1850. Migrated to Utah (with husband) 1854. Died April 13, 1882, in Bountiful, Utah.

SMITH, BATHSHEBA W. BIGLER. Born May 3, 1822, near Shinnston, West Virginia. Joined LDS church. Married George A. Smith July 25, 1841. Initiated into Anointed Quorum December 23, 1843. Sealed to husband January 20, 1844. Received second anointing January 31, 1844.

Received Nauvoo temple endowment December 10, 1845. Resealed to husband and received second anointing January 13, 1846, in Nauvoo temple. Migrated to Utah. Died September 20, 1910, in Salt Lake City.

SMITH, CLARISSA LYMAN. Born June 27, 1790. Married John Smith September 11, 1815. Mother of George A. Smith. Joined LDS church 1832. Moved to Ohio 1833. Initiated into Anointed Quorum October 8, 1843. Received second anointing February 26, 1844, at which time she was also sealed to her husband. Received Nauvoo temple endowment December 10, 1845. Resealed to husband and received second anointing January 15, 1846, in Nauvoo temple. Migrated to Utah. Died February 14, 1854, in Salt Lake City.

SMITH, EMMA HALE. Born July 10, 1804, in Harmony, Pennsylvania. Married Joseph Smith January 18, 1827. Joined LDS church. Moved with husband to Kirtland, Ohio; Missouri; and Nauvoo, Illinois. Named president of Nauvoo all-female Relief Society 1842. Sealed to husband May 28, 1843. Initiated into Anointed Quorum and received second anointing September 28, 1843. Husband killed June 27, 1844. Did not affiliate with LDS church under Brigham Young. Married Louis Bidamon December 23, 1847. Died April 30, 1879, in Nauvoo.

SMITH, GEORGE A. Born June 26, 1817, in Potsdam, New York, to John and Clarissa Smith. Cousin of Joseph Smith. Joined LDS church September 10, 1832. Moved to Ohio 1833. Member Zion's Camp 1834. Moved to Missouri 1838. Ordained member of Quorum of Twelve Apostles April 26, 1839. Mission to England 1839-41. Married Bathsheba Bigler July 25, 1841. Initiated into Anointed Quorum December 2, 1843. Sealed to wife January 20, 1844. Received second anointing January 31, 1844. Joined Council of Fifty March 11, 1844. Sealed to plural wife November 29, 1844. Sealed to four additional plural wives 1845. Received Nauvoo temple endowment December 10, 1845. Resealed to wives and received second anointing January 13, 1846, in Nauvoo temple. Sealed to two additional plural wives January-February 1846. Migrated to Utah 1847. Resided in Iowa 1847-49. Helped to settle southern Utah 1850-52. Church Historian and Recorder 1854. Sustained as first counselor to LDS church president October 7, 1868. Traveled to Jerusalem 1872-73. Died September 1, 1875, in Salt Lake City.

SMITH, HYRUM. Born February 9, 1800, in Tunbridge, Vermont, to Joseph and Lucy Mack Smith. Brother of Joseph, Samuel H., and William Smith. Joined Masons. Married Jerusha Barden November 2, 1826. Joined LDS church 1830. Member of Zion's Camp 1834. Sustained as assistant counselor to First Presidency September 3, 1837. Wife died October 14, 1837. Sustained as second counselor to LDS church president November 7, 1837. Married Mary Fielding December 24, 1837. Moved to Nauvoo, Illinois, 1839. Ordained Patriarch to the Church September 1840, and assistant president January 24, 1841. Senior Warden and Worshipful Master, pro. tem., of Nauvoo's Masonic lodge. Member of original endowment company May 5, 1842. Sealed to deceased wife and to living wife May 29, 1843. Sealed to two plural wives (including Mary Fielding's sister Mercy Rachel Fielding Thompson) ca. August 1843. Received second anointing October 8, 1843. Killed (with brother Joseph) June 27, 1844, in Carthage jail, Carthage, Illinois.

SMITH, JOHN. Born July 16, 1781, in Derryfield, New Hampshire. Married Clarissa Lyman September 11, 1815. Father of George A. Smith. Joined LDS church 1832. Sustained as assistant counselor to the First Presidency September 3, 1837. Presided over branches of church in Missouri, Iowa, and Illinois. Sealed to plural wife August 13, 1843. Initiated into Anointed Quorum September 28, 1843. Received second anointing February 26, 1844, at which time first wife was also sealed to him. Joined Council of Fifty April 18, 1844. Received Nauvoo temple endowment December 10, 1845. Resealed to wives and received second anointing January 15, 1846, in Nauvoo temple. Migrated to Utah 1847; president of Salt Lake Stake 1847-48. Ordained as Patriarch to the Church January 1, 1849. Died May 23, 1854, in Salt Lake City.

SMITH, JOSEPH. Born December 23, 1805, in Sharon, Vermont, to Joseph and Lucy Mack Smith. Brother of Hyrum, Samuel H., and William Smith. Married Emma Hale January 18, 1827. Founded Church of Christ (later Church of the Latter Day Saints; Church of Jesus Christ of Latter-day Saints) and sustained as first elder April 6, 1830. Sustained as president of the high priesthood of LDS church January 25, 1832. Moved to Kirtland, Ohio; Missouri; and Nauvoo, Illinois. Sealed to first plural wife April 5, 1841. Sealed to some thirty-plus other plural wives before death. Member of original endowment company, May 5, 1842. Mayor of Nauvoo. Sealed to first wife (Emma) May 28, 1843. Received second anointing September 28, 1843. Candidate for U.S. president 1844. Killed (with brother Hyrum) June 27, 1844, in Carthage jail, Carthage, Illinois.

SMITH, LUCY MACK. Born July 8, 1775, in Gilsum, New Hampshire. Married Joseph Smith January 24, 1796. Mother of Hyrum, Joseph, Samuel H., and William Smith. Joined LDS church 1830. Resided in New York, Ohio, Missouri, and Illinois. Initiated into Anointed Quorum October 8, 1843. Received second anointing November 12, 1843. Received Nauvoo temple endowment December 11, 1845. Did not migrate west. Died May 14, 1856, near Nauvoo, Illinois.

SMITH, MARY FIELDING. Born July 21, 1801, in Honiden, England. Sister of Joseph and Mary Fielding. Married Hyrum Smith December 24, 1837. Sealed to husband May 29, 1843. Initiated into Anointed Quorum October 1, 1843. Received second anointing October 8, 1843. Received Nauvoo temple endowment December 10, 1845. Resealed to husband and received second anointing January 15 and 30, 1846, in Nauvoo temple. Died September 21, 1852, in Salt Lake City.

SMITH, SAMUEL H. Born March 13, 1808, in Tunbridge, Vermont, to Joseph and Lucy Mack Smith. Brother of Hyrum, Joseph, and William Smith. Joined LDS church, 1830. Married Mary Bailey August 13, 1834. Moved to Ohio, Missouri, Illinois. Various church missions. Wife died January 25, 1841. Married Levire Clark April 29, 1841. Joined Nauvoo Masons April 9, 1842. Initiated into Anointed Quorum December 17, 1843. Died July 30, 1844, in Nauvoo, Illinois.

SMITH, WILLIAM B. Born March 13, 1811, in Royalton, Vermont, to Joseph and Lucy Mack Smith. Brother of Hyrum, Joseph, and Samuel H. Smith. Joined LDS church, 1830. Married Caroline Amanda Grant February 14, 1833. Resided in New York, Ohio, Missouri, and Illinois. Ordained member of first Quorum of Twelve Apostles February 15, 1835. Dropped from and restored to Twelve, 1839. Joined Nauvoo Masons April 25, 1842. Polygamist in fall 1843. Joined Council of Fifty April 25, 1844. Initiated into Anointed Quorum May 12, 1844. Ordained presiding patriarch May 24, 1845. Sealed to additional plural wives 1845. Dropped from Twelve, then excommunicated October 12, 1845. Campaigned against Brigham Young, aligned with competing churches. Served in Civil War. Rebaptized LDS but withdrew. Joined Reorganized Church of Jesus Christ of Latter Day Saints 1878. Died November 13, 1894, in Osterdock, Iowa.

SNOW, ELIZA ROXCY. Born January 21, 1804, in Becket, Massachusetts. Moved to Ohio 1806. Became known for her poetry. Affiliated with Campbellite movement. Joined LDS church April 5, 1835. Moved to Kirtland, Ohio, then to Missouri, and eventually to Nauvoo, Illinois. Joined LDS female Relief Society. Sealed as plural wife to Joseph Smith June 29, 1842. Sealed (for time) to Brigham Young October 3, 1844. Initiated into Anointed Quorum January 26, 1845. Received Nauvoo temple endowment December 17, 1845. Resealed to Joseph Smith (for eternity) and to Brigham Young (for time) and received second anointing February 3 and 6, 1846, in Nauvoo temple. Migrated west, moved into Lion House, presided over Relief Society. Traveled to Palestine 1872. Died December 5, 1887, in Salt Lake City.

SPENCER, CATHERINE CURTIS. Born March 21, 1811, in Canaan Center, New York. Married Orson Spencer April 13, 1830. Joined LDS church 1841. Initiated into Anointed Quorum December 23, 1843. May have received second anointing by December 7, 1845. Received Nauvoo temple endowment December 11, 1845. Sealed to husband and received second anointing January 15, 1846, in Nauvoo temple. Died March 12, 1846, near Keosauqua, Iowa.

SPENCER, ORSON. Born March 14, 1802, in West Stockbridge, Massachusetts. Married Catherine Curtis April 13, 1830. Joined LDS church 1841. Initiated into Anointed Quorum December 2, 1843. Joined Council of Fifty March 19, 1844. Nauvoo mayor 1845. May have received second anointing by December 7, 1845. Received Nauvoo temple endowment December 11, 1845. Sealed to wife, sealed to plural wife, and received second anointing January 15, 1846, in Nauvoo temple. Mission to England 1847-49. Moved to Salt Lake City. Died October 15, 1855, in St. Louis, Missouri.

TAYLOR, JOHN. Born November 1, 1808, in Milnthorpe, England. Joined Methodist church ca. 1823. Moved to Canada 1828-29. Married Leonora Cannon January 28, 1833. Joined LDS church May 9, 1836. Moved to Missouri in fall 1838. Ordained a member of the Quorum of Twelve Apostles December 19, 1838. Church mission to England 1839-41. Settled in Nauvoo, Illinois, July 1841. Joined Nauvoo Masons April 22, 1842. Editor of *Times and Seasons* 1842-46. Initiated into Anointed Quorum September 28, 1843. Sealed to two plural wives December 12, 1843, and

February 25, 1844. Received second anointing January 30, 1844, at which time first wife (Leonora) was also sealed to him. Joined Council of Fifty March 11, 1844. Wounded during attack on Joseph and Hyrum Smith in Carthage jail. Received Nauvoo temple endowment December 10, 1845. Resealed to wives, as well as to a third plural wife, and received second anointing January 7 and 15, 1846, in Nauvoo temple. Sealed to six additional plural wives January 1846. Left Nauvoo 1846. Church mission to England 1846-47. Migrated to Utah 1847. Church mission to France 1850-52. Church mission to eastern U.S. 1854-57. Various civil positions in Utah. Sustained as president of Quorum of Twelve Apostles October 6, 1877. Sustained as president of LDS church October 10, 1880. Died July 25, 1887, in Kaysville, Utah.

TAYLOR, LEONORA CANNON. Born October 5, 1796, in Peel, Isle of Man, England. Married John Taylor January 28, 1833. Joined LDS church May 1836. Initiated into Anointed Quorum November 1, 1843. Received second anointing January 30, 1844, at which time also sealed to her husband. Received Nauvoo temple endowment December 10, 1845. Resealed to husband and received second anointing January 7 and 15, 1846, in Nauvoo temple. Died December 9, 1868, in Salt Lake City.

THOMPSON, MERCY R. FIELDING. Born June 15, 1807, in Honiden, England. Sister of Joseph and Mary Fielding. Married Robert B. Thompson June 4, 1837. Husband died August 27, 1841. Sealed to deceased husband May 29, 1843. Sealed as plural wife to brother-in-law Hyrum Smith ca. August 11, 1843. Initiated into Anointed Quorum November 1, 1843. Received Nauvoo temple endowment December 11, 1845. Sealed to John Taylor for time, resealed to Robert B. Thompson for eternity, and received second anointing January 23, 1846, in Nauvoo temple. Died September 15, 1893, in Salt Lake City.

WHITNEY, ELIZABETH ANN SMITH. Born December 26, 1800, in Derby, Connecticut. Married Newel K. Whitney October 20, 1822. Mother of Sarah Ann Whitney, plural wife of Joseph Smith. Affiliated with Campbellite movement in Ohio. Joined LDS church November 1830. Relocated to Nauvoo, Illinois, 1839. Sealed to husband August 21, 1842. Counselor to Emma Smith in Female Relief Society presidency. Initiated into Anointed Quorum October 8, 1843. Received second anointing October 27, 1843. Received Nauvoo temple endowment December 10,

1845. Resealed to husband and received second anointing January 7 and 12, 1846, in Nauvoo temple. Migrated west. Died February 15, 1882.

WHITNEY, NEWEL K. Born February 5, 1795, in Marlborough, Vermont. Married Elizabeth Ann Smith October 20, 1822. Father of Sarah Ann Whitney, plural wife of Joseph Smith. Affiliated with Campbellite movement in Ohio. Joined LDS church November 1830. First bishop of LDS church in Kirtland, Ohio. Relocated to Nauvoo, Illinois, 1839. Joined the Masons in Ohio. Member of the original endowment company May 4, 1842. Sealed to wife August 21, 1842. Received second anointing October 27, 1843. Joined Council of Fifty March 11, 1844. Named trustee-in-trust August 9, 1844. Sealed to plural wife September 10, 1844. Sustained as "first bishop" of LDS church October 7, 1844. Received Nauvoo temple endowment December 10, 1845. Resealed to wife and received second anointing January 7 and 12, 1846, in Nauvoo temple. Sustained as Presiding Bishop of LDS church April 6, 1847. Migrated west. Died September 23, 1850, in Salt Lake City.

WHITNEY, SARAH ANN. Born March 22, 1825, in Kirtland, Ohio, to Newel K. and Elizabeth Ann Whitney. Affiliated with Campbellite movement in Ohio. Family joined LDS church November 1830. Relocated to Nauvoo, Illinois, 1839. Sealed as plural wife to Joseph Smith July 27, 1842. Married civilly to Joseph C. Kingsbury April 29, 1843. Initiated into Anointed Quorum January 26, 1845. Sealed (for time) to Heber C. Kimball March 17, 1845. Received second anointing May 27, 1845. Received Nauvoo temple endowment January 1, 1846. Resealed to Heber C. Kimball (for time) and to Joseph Smith (for eternity), and received second anointing, January 12, 1846, in Nauvoo temple. Migrated west. Husband died 1868. Died September 4, 1873, in Salt Lake City.

WIGHT, LYMAN. Born May 9, 1796, in Fairfield, New York. Veteran of War of 1812. Married Harriet Benton January 5, 1823. Affiliated with Campbellite movement. Joined LDS church November 14, 1830. Church missions to Missouri and Ohio. Moved to Missouri late 1833. Recruited for Zion's Camp 1834. Jailed in Liberty Jail, 1838-39, escaped, moved to Iowa. Ordained member of Quorum of Twelve Apostles April 8, 1841. Relocated to Nauvoo, Illinois, fall 1841. Joined Nauvoo Masons April 25, 1842. Various church missions; returned to Nauvoo June 1843. Mission to Wisconsin to purchase timber for Nauvoo construction 1843. Advocated

Texas as gathering place. Joined Council of Fifty April 18, 1844. Initiated into Anointed Quorum May 14, 1844, at which time was also possibly sealed to first wife and to three plural wives. Moved to Texas. Excommunicated December 3, 1848, for rejecting Brigham Young's leadership of LDS church. Died March 31, 1858, in Dexter, Texas.

WOODRUFF, PHOEBE CARTER. Born March 8, 1807, in Scarborough, Maine. Married Wilford Woodruff April 13, 1837. Settled in Nauvoo, Illinois. Sealed to husband November 11, 1843. Initiated into Anointed Quorum December 23, 1843. Received second anointing January 28, 1844. Migrated to Utah. Died November 10, 1885, in Salt Lake City.

WOODRUFF, WILFORD. Born March 1, 1807, in Avon (Farmington), Connecticut. Joined LDS church December 31, 1833. Member of Zion's Camp 1834. Church missions to Arkansas, Tennessee, and Kentucky 1834-36. Married Phoebe Carter April 13, 1837. Church mission to Fox Islands 1837. Ordained member of Quorum of Twelve Apostles April 26, 1839. Church mission to England 1839-41. Settled in Nauvoo, Illinois, October 1841. Joined Nauvoo Masons April 26, 1842. Sealed to wife November 11, 1843. Initiated into Anointed Quorum December 2, 1843. Received second anointing January 28, 1844. Joined Council of Fifty March 13, 1844. Mission to eastern U.S. 1844; returned to Nauvoo August 1844. Sealed to three plural wives 1846. Migrated to Utah 1847. Appointed Assistant Church Historian 1856. Various civil positions and church missions. Sustained as president of Quorum of Twelve Apostles October 10, 1880. Sustained as president of LDS church April 7, 1889. Issued manifesto outlawing plural marriage 1890. Died September 2, 1898, in San Francisco, California, at age ninety-one.

WOODWORTH, LUCIEN. Born April 3, 1799. Married Phoebe Watrous ca. 1825. Father of Flora Ann Woodworth, plural wife of Joseph Smith. Joined LDS church, settled in Nauvoo, Illinois. Initiated into Anointed Quorum September 28, 1843. Joined Council of Fifty March 11, 1844. Received Nauvoo temple endowment December 10, 1845. Sealed to wife and received second anointing January 17, 1846, in Nauvoo temple. Sealed to four plural wives January 1846. Died November 20, 1867.

WOODWORTH, PHOEBE WATROUS. Born October 1, 1805. Married Lucien Woodworth ca. 1825. Mother of Flora Ann Woodworth, plural wife of Joseph Smith. Joined LDS church, settled in Nauvoo, Illinois. Ini-

241

tiated into Anointed Quorum October 29, 1843. Received Nauvoo temple endowment December 10, 1845. Sealed to husband and received second anointing January 17, 1846, in Nauvoo temple. Died August 10, 1864.

YOUNG, BRIGHAM. Born June 1, 1801, in Whittingham, Vermont. Brother of Joseph Young. Joined Methodist church ca. 1822. Married Miriam Works October 8, 1824. Joined LDS church April 9, 1832. Wife died September 8, 1832. Church missions to Canada. Moved to Kirtland, Ohio, 1833. Married Mary Ann Angell February 10, 1834. Member of Zion's Camp 1834. Ordained member of first Quorum of Twelve Apostles February 14, 1835. Various church missions. Relocated to Missouri 1838; expelled from Missouri 1839. Church mission to England 1839-41. Named president of Quorum of Twelve Apostles January 19, 1841. Arrived in Nauvoo, Illinois, July 1, 1841. Joined Nauvoo Masons April 7, 1842. Member of original endowment company, May 4, 1842. Sealed to four plural wives June 14, 1842; November 2, 1843 (two); and May 8, 1844. Sealed to deceased wife and to living first wife May 29, 1843. Received second anointing November 22, 1843. Joined Council of Fifty March 11, 1844. Called for Twelve Apostles to lead the church after Joseph Smith's death, August 8, 1844. Sealed to five additional plural wives 1845. Received Nauvoo temple endowment December 10, 1845. Resealed to wives and received second anointing January 7 and 12, 1846, in Nauvoo temple. Sealed to nineteen additional plural wives January/February 1846. Guided Mormon exodus to Great Salt Lake Valley 1846-47. Sustained as president of LDS church December 27, 1847. Utah territorial governor. Died August 29, 1877, in Salt Lake City.

YOUNG, JANE BICKNELL. Born August 14, 1814, in Utica, New York. Married Joseph Young February 18, 1834, in Kirtland, Ohio. Moved to Missouri and Illinois. Initiated into Anointed Quorum February 3, 1844. Received second anointing January 12, 1845, at which time she was also sealed to her husband. Received Nauvoo temple endowment December 12, 1845. Resealed to husband and received second anointing January 16, 1846, in Nauvoo temple. Moved to Iowa 1846-50. Arrived in Utah September 1850. Died January 15, 1913, in Tacoma, Washington, at ninety-eight years of age.

YOUNG, JOSEPH. Born April 7, 1797, in Hopkinton, Massachusetts.

Brother of Brigham Young. Member of Methodist church. Joined LDS church April 6, 1832. Various church missions. Married Jane Bicknell February 18, 1834. Ordained one of first seven presidents of seventy February 28, 1835. Witnessed Haun's Mill massacre October 30, 1838. Located to Nauvoo, Illinois, 1840. Initiated into Anointed Quorum February 3, 1844. Received second anointing January 12, 1845, at which time wife was sealed to him. Joined Council of Fifty March 1, 1845. Received Nauvoo temple endowment December 12, 1845. Resealed to wife and received second anointing January 16, 1846, in Nauvoo temple. Moved to Iowa, 1846-50. Arrived in Utah September 1850. Church mission to England 1870. Died July 16, 1881, in Salt Lake City.

YOUNG, MARY ANN ANGELL. Born June 8, 1808, in North Providence, Rhode Island. Married Brigham Young February 10, 1834. Moved to Ohio and Missouri, resettled in Nauvoo, Illinois. Sealed to husband May 29, 1843. Initiated into Anointed Quorum November 1, 1843. Received second anointing November 22, 1843. Received Nauvoo temple endowment December 10, 1845. Resealed to husband and received second anointing January 7 and 12, 1846, in Nauvoo temple. Migrated to Utah. Died June 27, 1882, in Salt Lake City.

SOURCES

Todd Compton, *In Sacred Loneliness: The Plural Wives of Joseph Smith* (Salt Lake City: Signature Books, 1997); *Deseret News 2003 Church Almanac* (Salt Lake City: Deseret News, 2002); Ehat, "Introduction of Temple Ordinances"; "Mormon Biographical Registers," *Joseph Fielding Smith Institute for LDS History* at smithinstitute.byu.edu/register; D. Michael Quinn, *The Mormon Hierarchy: Origins of Power* (Salt Lake City: Signature Books and Smith Research Associates, 1994); and George D. Smith, "Nauvoo Roots of Mormon Polygamy, 1840-46: A Preliminary Demographic Report," *Dialogue: A Journal of Mormon Thought* 27 (Spring 1994).

INDEX

Aaronic priesthood, xx, xxi, xxiiin29, 2, 4, 5, 6

Abbif, Hiram, 3, 3-4n12

Adam, xxi, 46

Adams, Augusta, xxxv

Adams, George J., 80, 80n45, 112, 112n31, 192

Adams, Harriet Denton, xxvii, xxxiv, xxxix, 19-20n6, 29, 29n22, 217

Adams, James, xix, xxi, xxiv, xxvii, xxxiv, xxxix, 4, 4n13, 5, 6, 7, 17, 18, 19, 19-20n6, 20, 21, 22, 92n2, 217

Adams County, Illinois, 96n12, 146n71, 149

adoption, xxxvii, 215

adultery, 10n20, 28n19

Aikens, Mary, xxxiv, xlii

Aldrich, Mark, 100n16

Ale, Baurak, 26

Ale, Beurach, see Ale, Baurak

Alleghany, Pennsylvania, 133

Allen, Ethan, 40n40

Allen, Joseph Stewart, xxxix, 217

Allen, Lucy Morley, xxxix, 217-18, 228, 229

Alley, Sarah B., xli

Alstead, New Hampshire, 136n62

Alton, Illinois, 193n134

Ancient of Days, 6

Andover Surplus, Maine, 234

Angell, Mary Ann, see Young, Mary Ann

animals, 135, 142. See also livestock

anointing, 27, 45, 46, 47, 56n11, 62n18, 94n6, 99n14, 103, 105, 205-206n143, 208. See also washing and anointing

anointing, second, see second anointing

Anti-Mormon Committee, 151n78

anti-Mormons, 178

apostasy, xxi

"Appeal to the Green Mountain Boys," 36n34

Arizona, 135n59

Arkansas, 241

Arlington House, 157

Arsenal, 128

arson, 175

authority, ordinance of, xxi

Avon (Farmington), Connecticut, 241

Babbit, Almon W., xxxix, 76, 135, 136, 146, 149, 154, 160, 161, 189, 190, 201-202n142, 218

Backenstos, Jacob, 133, 133n56, 142, 144, 146, 146n71, 147, 148, 149, 149n77,

245

Nauvoo temple, xi, xxxiii, xxxix, xl, xli, 3,
5, 6, 9n16, 9-10n17, 42, 53, 83, 84n50,
85, 87, 88, 95, 103, 104, 111, 112, 115-
16n36, 125n45, 129, 130, 130n49,
132, 136n63, 140n65, 141, 142, 143,
145, 147, 153, 158n80, 159n85, 164-
65n93, 177n110, 183, 184n120, 185,
185n122, 188, 193, 194, 196, 197, 198,
200, 200n140, 201, 201n141, 202, 205,
205-206n143, 207n145, 207n147,
210, 214, 215, 217, 218, 219, 220, 221,
222, 223, 225, 226, 227, 228, 229,
230-31, 232, 233, 234, 235, 236, 237,
238, 239, 240, 241, 242, 243; completion of, xix-xx; construction of, xvii,
xxiv, xxxviii, 88n56; decorations in,
208; dedication of, xvi, 189; description and dimensions of rooms, 186-
87, 189, 189n128, 190, 204, 206-208;
furnishings in, 183; layout of, xviii;
rooms in, 182, 182n117; temple committee, 130-31n50, 189, 190
Nelson, Mary Eliza, 222
Nephi, Utah, 177n110
Nevada, 149n76, 223
New Hampshire, 137, 226
New House, 25
New Jersey, 14n22
New Testament, xiv
New York, xiv, 40n40, 75n35, 83n48,
128, 143, 144n69, 145, 168n94,
172n101, 176n108, 218, 220, 232,
234, 237
New York City, 145n70, 222
New York Store, 178
Noble, Joseph Bates, xxxi, xxxv, xli, 94n6,
98, 99, 218, 229-30
Noble, Mary Adeline Beaman, xxxi, xli,
94n6, 230
Noon, Sarah Peak, xxxiv, xl
North Providence, Rhode Island, 243

Oakland, California, 220
Oaks, Dallin H., 172n101
Oath of Vengeance/Retribution, 121n42

obedience, 20n7
Ogden, Utah, 221
Ohio, xiv, xvii, 135, 136, 219, 220, 225,
230, 231, 235, 237, 238, 239, 240, 243
oil, 122, 199; consecrated, 204; lamp,
130n49; olive, 120n41
Old Testament, ix, xvi
Oneida Native American, 96n10
ordinance work, xxxii
ordinances, ix, x, xi, xiii, xv, xvi, xvii,
xviii, xx, xxix, xxx, xxxvi, 2, 7,
9-10n17, 15n27, 19, 20, 20n7, 26n16,
28n19, 38, 40n42, 42, 47, 53n7, 54n8,
57n12, 67n27, 72, 91, 105n23,
120n41, 200, 203, 204, 205-206n143,
207n145, 212
ordinations, 191, 243; administration of,
xxiiin29
Oregon, 78n40, 133n56, 142, 144, 210,
214
Oregon expedition, 139
Oregon Trail, 210n152
Orton, Roger, 191, 191n132
Osterdock, Iowa, 237
Oswego, New York, 217
Ottawa, Illinois, 168n94
Ottawa, Ontario, Canada, 142
Oxford, Connecticut, 223

Pacific Islands, 232
Pack, John, 128, 128n47, 136, 137
Page, John E., xxxv, xli, 78n40, 93, 94,
100, 107, 109, 110, 112, 113, 114, 115,
119, 122, 127, 144, 159, 174, 187, 190,
199, 201, 202, 204, 205, 206, 210, 211,
214, 230
Page, Mary Judd, xli, 94, 199, 201, 202,
204, 205, 211, 230
Palestine, 238
Palmyra, Missouri, 162n89
Partridge, Caroline Ely, xli
Partridge, Eliza Maria, xxviin42, xxxiv,
19-20n6
Partridge, Emily Dow, xxviin42, xxxiv,
19-20n6